Communities

PROGRAM AUTHORS

Dr. Candy Dawson Boyd
Professor, School of Education
Director of Reading Programs
St. Mary's College
Moraga, California

Dr. Geneva Gay
Professor of Education
University of Washington
Seattle, Washington

Rita Geiger
**Director of Social Studies and
    Foreign Languages**
Norman Public Schools
Norman, Oklahoma

Dr. James B. Kracht
**Associate Dean for Undergraduate
    Programs and Teacher Education**
College of Education
Texas A&M University
College Station, Texas

Dr. Valerie Ooka Pang
Professor of Teacher Education
San Diego State University
San Diego, California

Dr. C. Frederick Risinger
**Director, Professional Development
    and Social Studies Education**
Indiana University
Bloomington, Indiana

Sara Miranda Sanchez
**Elementary and Early Childhood
    Curriculum Coordinator**
Albuquerque Public Schools
Albuquerque, New Mexico

CONTRIBUTING AUTHORS

Dr. Carol Berkin
Professor of History
Baruch College and the Graduate
    Center
The City University of New York
New York, New York

Lee A. Chase
Staff Development Specialist
Chesterfield County Public Schools
Chesterfield County, Virginia

Dr. Jim Cummins
Professor of Curriculum
Ontario Institute for Studies in
    Education
University of Toronto
Toronto, Canada

Dr. Allen D. Glenn
Professor and Dean Emeritus
Curriculum and Instruction
College of Education
University of Washington
Seattle, Washington

Dr. Carole L. Hahn
Professor, Educational Studies
Emory University
Atlanta, Georgia

Dr. M. Gail Hickey
Professor of Education
Indiana University-Purdue
    University
Fort Wayne, Indiana

Dr. Bonnie Meszaros
Associate Director
Center for Economic Education and
    Entrepreneurship
University of Delaware
Newark, Delaware

Editorial Offices: Glenview, Illinois • Parsippany, New Jersey • New York, New York
Sales Offices: Parsippany, New Jersey • Duluth, Georgia • Glenview, Illinois •
Coppell, Texas • Ontario, California

www.sfsocialstudies.com

CONTENT CONSULTANTS

Catherine Deans-Barrett
World History Specialist
Northbrook, Illinois

Dr. Michael Frassetto
Studies in Religions
Independent Scholar
Chicago, Illinois

Dr. Gerald Greenfield
Hispanic-Latino Studies
History Department
University of Wisconsin, Parkside
Kenosha, Wisconsin

Dr. Frederick Hoxie
Native American Studies
University of Illinois
Champaign, Illinois

Dr. Cheryl Johnson-Odim
Dean of Liberal Arts and Sciences and
    Professor of History
African American
    History Specialist
Columbia College
Chicago, Illinois

Dr. Michael Khodarkovsky
Eastern European Studies
University of Chicago
Chicago, Illinois

Robert Moffet
U.S. History Specialist
Northbrook, Illinois

Dr. Ralph Nichols
East Asian History
University of Chicago
Chicago, Illinois

CLASSROOM REVIEWERS

Diana Vicknair Ard
Woodlake Elementary School
St. Tammany Parish
Mandeville, Louisiana

Dr. Charlotte R. Bennett
St. John School
Newburgh, Indiana

Sharon Berenson
Freehold Learning Center
Freehold, New Jersey

Betsy Blandford
Pocahontas Elementary School
Powhatan, Virginia

Gloria Cantatore
Public School #5
West New York, New Jersey

LuAnn Curran
Westgate Elementary School
St. Petersburg, Florida

Louis De Angelo
Office of Catholic Education
Archdiocese of Philadelphia
Philadelphia, Pennsylvania

Dr. Trish Dolasinski
Paradise Valley School District
Arrowhead Elementary School
Glendale, Arizona

Dr. John R. Doyle
Director of Social Studies Curriculum
Miami-Dade County Schools
Miami, Florida

Dr. Roceal Duke
District of Columbia Public Schools
Washington, D.C.

Peggy Flanagan
Roosevelt Elementary School
Community Consolidated School
    District #64
Park Ridge, Illinois

Mary Flynn
Arrowhead Elementary School
Glendale, Arizona

Sue Gendron
Spring Branch ISD
Houston, Texas

Su Hickenbottom
Totem Falls Elementary School
Snohomish School District
Snohomish, Washington

Sally Hunter
Highland Park Elementary School
Austin ISD
Austin, Texas

Allan Jones
North Branch Public Schools
North Branch, Minnesota

Brandy Bowers Kerbow
Bettye Haun Elementary School
Plano ISD
Plano, Texas

Sandra López
PSJA Service Center
San Juan, Texas

Martha Sutton Maple
Shreve Island School
Shreveport, Louisiana

Lyn Metzger
Carpenter Elementary School
Community Consolidated School
    District #64
Park Ridge, Illinois

Marsha Munsey
Riverbend Elementary School
West Monroe, Louisiana

Christine Nixon
Warrington Elementary School
Escambia County School District
Pensacola, Florida

Liz Salinas
Supervisor
Edgewood ISD
San Antonio, Texas

Beverly Scaling
Desert Hills Elementary
Las Cruces, New Mexico

Madeleine Schmitt
St. Louis Public Schools
St. Louis, Missouri

Barbara Schwartz
Central Square Intermediate School
Central Square, New York

Ronald Snapp
North Lawrence Community Schools
Bedford, Indiana

Lesley Ann Stahl
West Side Catholic Consolidated
    School
Evansville, Indiana

Carolyn Moss Woodall
Loudoun County of Virginia Public
    Schools
Leesburg, Virginia

Suzanne Zaremba
J. B. Fisher Model School
Richmond Public Schools
Richmond, Virginia

Contents

Unit 1
Our Community

iii

Unit 2 People in Communities

Unit 3 Where Are Communities?

v

Unit 4 History of Communities

Unit 5 Communities at Work

Unit 6 Community Government

Reference Guide

★ BIOGRAPHY ★

Maps

Skills

Reading Social Studies

Map and Globe Skills

Thinking Skills

Research and Writing Skills

Chart and Graph Skills

Fact File

Citizen Heroes

Issues and Viewpoints

Then and Now

Here and There

Literature and Social Studies

Map Adventure

Graphic Organizers

Charts, Graphs, Tables, Time Lines

Let the Discovery Begin

About 220 miles up, the International Space Station orbits Earth every 90 minutes. This sky-high community covers an area as large as two football fields. As in any community, people there work together. Scientists and astronauts from 16 countries, including the United States, are designing and building the space station. This picture shows what the space station will look like when it is completed.

You may live in a similar community one day. For now, turn the pages and make discoveries about other communities!

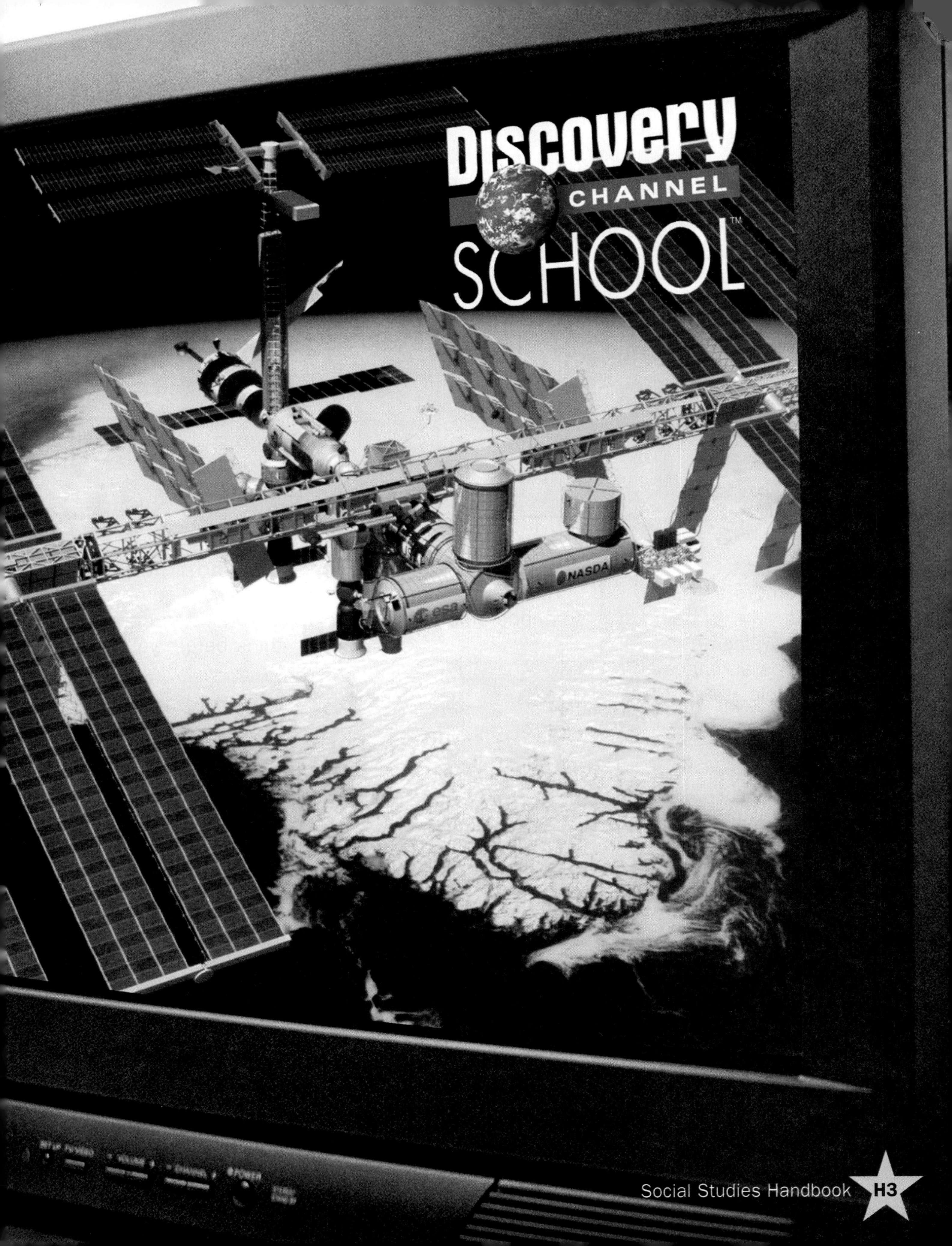
Discovery
CHANNEL
SCHOOL™
NASDA
esa

Building Citizenship Skills

There are six ways to show good citizenship: respect, caring, responsibility, fairness, courage, and honesty. In your textbook, you will learn about people who used these ways to help their community, state, and country.

Respect
Treat others as you would want to be treated. Welcome differences among people.

Caring
Think about what someone else needs.

Responsibility
Do what you are supposed to do, and think before you act.

Fairness
Take turns and follow the rules. Listen to what others have to say.

Courage
Do what is right even when the task is hard.

Honesty
Tell the truth, and do what you say you will do.

★ Citizenship in Action ★

Good citizens make careful decisions. They learn to solve problems. How will these children act like good citizens? Here are the steps they will follow.

Problem Solving

The children need to have their classroom plants and animals taken care of during winter vacation.

1 **Identify the problem.**

2 **Gather information.**

3 **List and consider options.**

4 **Consider advantages and disadvantages.**

5 **Choose and try a solution.**

6 **Decide if the solution worked.**

Decision Making

The students are deciding what talent they want to show in the third grade talent show. Before making a decision, each student should follow these steps.

1 **Tell what decision you need to make.**

2 **Gather information.**

3 **List your options.**

4 **Tell what might happen with each choice.**

5 **Make a decision.**

Building Geography Skills

Five Things to Think About

Geography is the study of Earth. People who study Earth sometimes look at it in five different ways. These ways are called the five themes of geography. Each theme is another way of thinking about a point on our planet. Look at the examples of Chicago below.

Location

Chicago is located in the state of Illinois. It is near the Indiana border.

Place

Chicago is a major shipping port. It is also an important center for air and rail transportation.

Movement

A train system rises over Chicago's downtown streets. This moves people around without stopping automobile traffic.

Places and People Change Each Other

People built up areas of the Lake Michigan shore to create special places such as this fountain.

Region

Chicago is in the midwest region of the United States. It is warm in the summers and cold in the winters. Many trees bloom from spring to fall.

How Does the Earth Look?

This is a photo of part of Earth as it looks from space. However, a complete view of Earth is best seen on a globe.

Which continent do you live on?

What Is a Globe?

This is a globe. A globe is a kind of map. It is a model, a small copy, of Earth in its actual round shape. You can turn a globe and see all of Earth's water and land.

Large areas of land are called continents.

Large bodies of salt water are called oceans.

What Is a Map?

A flat map is a drawing of a place. Maps show us where Earth's land and water are. A map can be a drawing of part of the earth.

This is a flat map of North America, one of Earth's seven continents. It also shows three of Earth's four oceans.

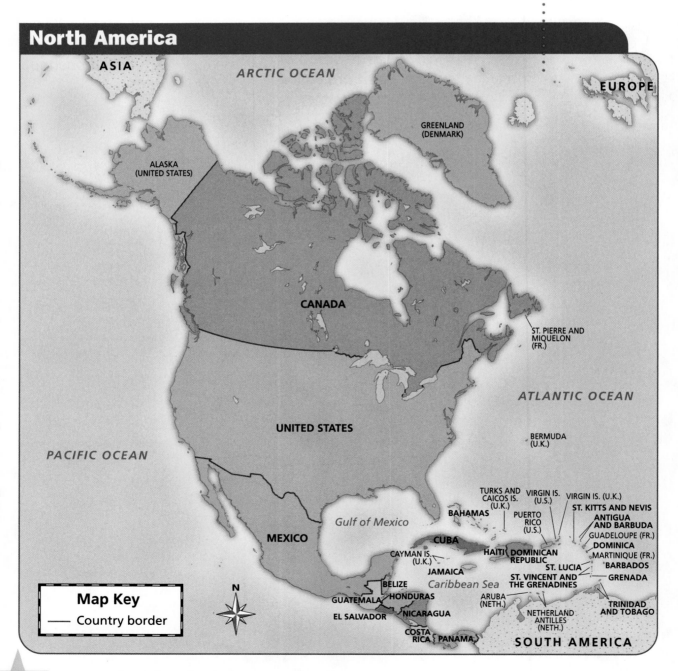

North America

Map Key
— Country border

Map Features

Maps have many features that help us read and use them.

Maps have titles. What is the title of this map? Many maps have symbols that stand for something else. A symbol could be a shape or a spot of color. How many symbols are used on this map? A key, or legend, is the box in which all symbols on a map are explained. What does a circled black star mean on this map?

A border is a line that divides a state or country from another. How many states border South Dakota?

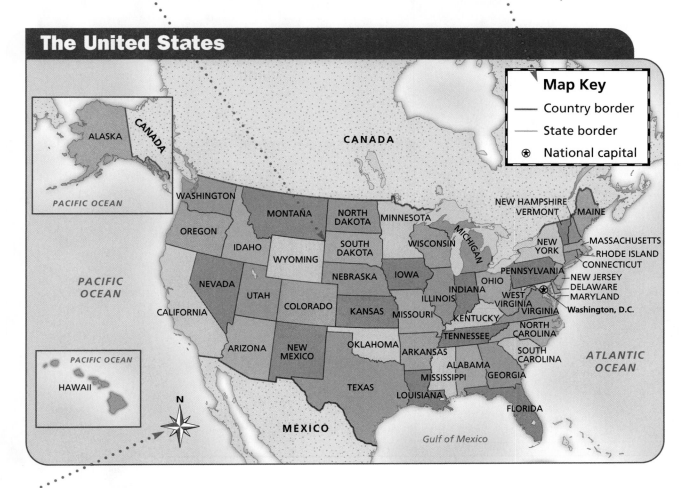

A compass rose is a decorative pointer that shows which way on a map north, south, east, and west are. On the compass roses in this textbook, north is straight up and is marked with an "N." East is to the right, south is straight down, and west is to the left. In which direction would you travel to get from New York to Florida? In which direction is California from Utah?

Landforms and Water

This map shows many landforms. Landforms are different types of land on Earth's surface. Mountains, hills, and plains are all examples of landforms. A plain is a large area of flat land.

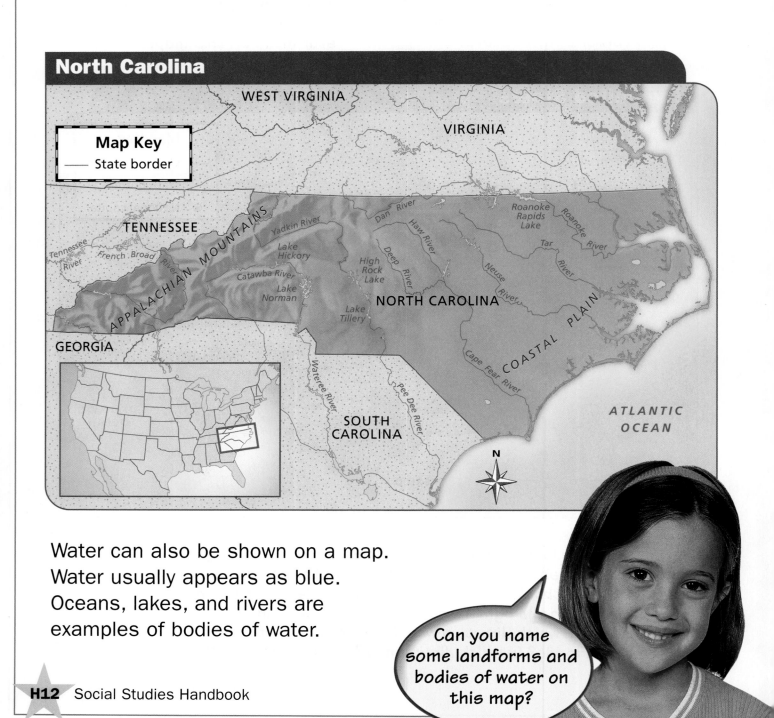

North Carolina

Map Key
— State border

Water can also be shown on a map. Water usually appears as blue. Oceans, lakes, and rivers are examples of bodies of water.

Can you name some landforms and bodies of water on this map?

Read a City Map

A city map shows the streets, buildings, and natural features of a city. Natural features are things like rivers or lakes or mountains. What natural features do you see on this map of Austin, Texas? Name one street that you see.

A city map lets you pick out a route. A route is a way to go from one place to another. Trace a route from the state capitol to the Ney Museum.

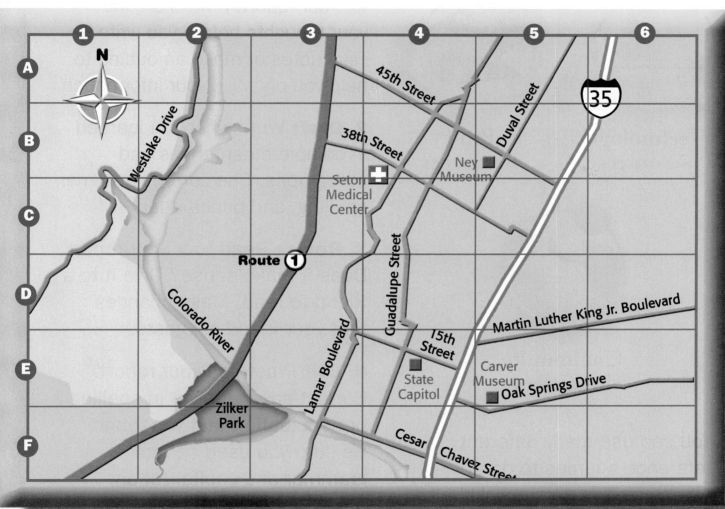

This map has a grid. A grid is a pattern of lines that form squares. The squares have numbers and letters. You can use a grid to find places on a map. Point to the state capitol. Name the square's letter and number. What is found in square B-5?

Building Research Skills
Gather and Report Information

When you need to find information for a report or a project, you can use three main reference resources:

Technology Resources

Print Resources

Community Resources

You can use many different reference sources to do research. This section will help you decide which resources are the best ones to use. After you finish your research, you will need to share what you learned with others. One way to share is to write a report. Follow these five steps when you write:

1. Prewrite Decide on the topic for your report. Always organize your thoughts before you write. Take notes or make an outline to help you organize your information.

2. Draft Write what you learned in complete sentences and paragraphs. Use correct grammar, spelling, and punctuation.

3. Revise Read over your report. Does it make sense? Give it to a friend to read. Make changes that your friend suggests.

4. Edit Proofread your report. Correct any mistakes in spelling or punctuation that you found. Be sure you used correct grammar and capitalization.

5. Publish Write a final copy of your report. Make it as neat as you can.

Technology Resources

There are many kinds of technology resources for you to use when you are looking for information. You can use the Internet, CD-ROMs, software, television programs, and radio programs.

The Internet is a system of computers that can store information so that people all over the world can find it. The World Wide Web, which is part of the Internet, has many different kinds of information.

Other technology resources can also help you find the information that you are looking for. There are CD-ROMs of maps, encyclopedias, and dictionaries. Television channels offer programs on history, science, the arts, and geography. Radio programs may give you information about a particular event that happened in history.

Use Print Resources

There are many reference tools that you can use to find information that is in print. A reference tool is any source of information.

Books are reference tools. Libraries often have reference shelves with books such as atlases, almanacs, and encyclopedias. To find information in reference tools, you should look in three places—the table of contents, the glossary, and the index.

How to Use Your Social Studies Book

The **table of contents** tells you what is actually in your Social Studies book. The table of contents tells you what the chapters and lessons are in this book. It might tell you about any special people that are included in the book. The table of contents is the first place to look in a reference book. This social studies book is a reference book.

Go to the table of contents in this book. How many units and chapters are in this book? What do you think your favorite unit or chapter will be?

The glossary is another important part of a reference book. The **glossary** gives you the definitions of the important words used in the book. Go to the glossary of this book. It is on page R26. Look up the word *community.* What is the definition of this important word?

The index is also a very important part of a reference book. The **index** lists the topics that are covered in the book and the page number that you can find the topics on. The table of contents gives you the big idea of the book. The index gives you all the details. Go to page R34 and you will find the index. Find the entry for El Paso. Go to that page in the book. What did you learn about El Paso?

Encyclopedia An encyclopedia is a collection of articles, listed in alphabetical order, on many topics. When you need information quickly, an encyclopedia is a good choice.

Dictionary A dictionary is a collection of words, their spellings, their meanings, and their pronunciations. Words in a dictionary are arranged in alphabetical order. If you come across a word that you don't understand, you can look it up in a dictionary.

Atlas An atlas is a collection of maps. Some atlases have one kind of map. Others have many maps showing different things, such as elevation, crops, population, natural resources, languages spoken, and historical developments.

Almanac An almanac is a book that has lots of information about many different things. It has different sections for different topics and often shows information in charts, tables, and lists. Almanacs are usually updated every year, so almanacs have the latest statistics on populations, sports records, and other interesting topics.

Nonfiction Books A nonfiction book is a book that was researched and written on a particular topic. Nonfiction books may contain information useful for your research.

Use Community Resources

Besides technology and print resources, the people of your community are good sources of information. You can learn about the history and geography of your community by listening to a person who has lived there a long time.

Perhaps you've heard about a person in your community whose grandparent did something important for the community. You might want to meet with that person and learn more about those times. People who are doing important jobs in your community now are good sources of information too.

Interviews One way to find out what the people in your community know is to interview them. This means asking them questions about the topic you are studying.

Using a Survey Another way to gather information in your community is to do a survey.

A survey is a list of questions that you ask people and their recorded answers. This gives you an idea of what the people in your community know, think, or feel about a subject. You can either use yes/no questions or short-answer questions. To record the things you find out, you will want to make a tally sheet with a column for each question.

Writing for Information Another way to get information from people or organizations is to e-mail or write a letter. Use the following steps:

- Plan what you want to say before you write.

- Be neat and careful about spelling and punctuation.

- Tell who you are and why you are writing.

- Thank the person you write to.

Our Community

UNIT 1

What makes every community special?

My Best Friend Moved to Chicago

My best friend moved to Chicago
Where the wind blows all day
Where she shops on busy streets
And she walks to a park to play.

But I still live in El Paso
Where cactus and hillsides I see
And the only sounds I hear at night
Are coyotes, my dogs, and me.

Though my friend loves her city apartment
And is as happy as can be,
I feel good in my house here in Texas
For El Paso's a great home for me.

Greetings from

Chicago

Welcome to My Community

Our Communities

▶ Levittown, New York, is on Long Island, which is one of the biggest islands off the coast of the United States.

▶ Many things have changed in Bridgewater, Virginia, over the past 100 years. In the 1890s, there was a law against cows running around town with bells around their necks.

▶ El Paso, Texas, has a neighbor city called Juarez. It is across the river in Mexico.

4

▶ In 1871 most of the buildings in Chicago burned down. The Water Tower is one of the few buildings that did not burn.

▶ Each fall and spring, the sky over Astoria, Oregon, is full of ducks flying between their winter and summer homes.

Community Life

Target Skill

Main Idea and Details

- To find the **topic** of a paragraph, ask *who* or *what* the paragraph is about.

- To find the **main idea** in a paragraph, read the paragraph. Then ask yourself, "What one important idea do all the sentences tell about?"

- To find **supporting details** in a paragraph, read the paragraph. Then ask yourself, "Which sentences give information that supports the main idea?"

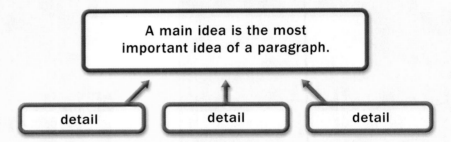

Supporting details are small pieces of information that tell about the main idea.

Read the following paragraph. The title states the topic. The main idea has been highlighted in blue. The supporting details have been highlighted in yellow.

Island Communities

Island communities are different from other communities. To get to an island, people come by boat or plane. People must also bring in their supplies by boat or plane. Sometimes bad weather keeps boats and planes from going out to an island. Then the island community is cut off from the rest of the world.

Life on Monhegan Island

Monhegan Island, Maine, is a small community that exists on its own without the help of others. The only way to get there is by ferry or other boat. No cars are allowed on Monhegan.

The island is quiet, except for the calls of birds and the crash of ocean waves. Artists and writers live there. They like the quiet and the beauty of nature.

In winter the island changes. Sometimes there are terrible storms. Then the ferry cannot run. The people of Monhegan must work together to make sure that everyone has food and heat. Because the island is cut off from the rest of the world, the people of Monhegan care deeply for one another. They also care deeply for their beautiful island home.

Use the reading skill of main idea and details to answer these questions.

❶ What is the main idea of the article?

❷ Name one detail from the first paragraph that tells more about the main idea.

❸ Name one detail from the second paragraph that tells more about the main idea.

Chapter 1

What Are Communities?

Lesson 1

El Paso, Texas

People live in communities.

1

Lesson 2

Astoria, Oregon

The United States has many kinds of communities.

2

Lesson 3

Timbuktu, Mali

The world has many kinds of communities.

3

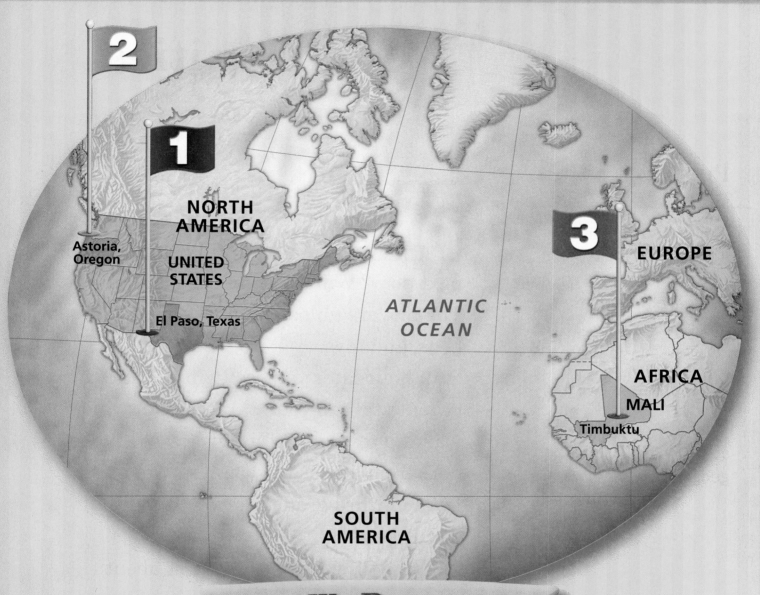

NORTH AMERICA

Astoria, Oregon

UNITED STATES

El Paso, Texas

ATLANTIC OCEAN

EUROPE

AFRICA

MALI

Timbuktu

SOUTH AMERICA

Why We Remember

People in a community share many needs and interests. They help each other and work together. The whole community helps to shape the people who live in it. People remember how a community was long ago as they make plans for the community's future. You are part of your community's future.

El Paso, Texas

Communities

Preview

Focus on the Main Idea
A community is a place where people live, work, and have fun together.

PLACES
El Paso, Texas

VOCABULARY
community
geography

You Are There
You've been watching as movers unload the moving van. Who will be moving in next door? Will there be any children? The movers unload two bicycles, bunk beds, and toys.

An hour later you see twins! While their parents talk to your parents, the twins walk up to you. "Hi!" they say. "We moved here from across the country. We're going to be in third grade. Do you think we'll like it here?"

What will you tell them first about your community?

Main Idea and Details As you read, look for details that help tell more about what a community is.

Carlos's Community

My name is Carlos. I live in a community called **El Paso, Texas.** A **community** is a place where people live, work, and have fun together. Many people live and work in El Paso.

My community is in a special place. Everything around my community is part of its geography. **Geography** is the study of Earth and how people live on it. The land around a place is also part of its geography.

El Paso is Spanish for "the pass." El Paso lies in a pass between two sets of mountains. El Paso is also on the border of Mexico, the country to the south of the United States.

If you come to El Paso, I can take you around my community. There are so many fun things to do and see. I think I'd take you to Rim Road first. There you can see into Mexico for miles.

Let me tell you about where I live.

REVIEW What is special about where El Paso is located?

🎯 **Main Idea and Details**

What Is a Community?

I live in El Paso with my parents, my brother, and my grandmother. We live in a neighborhood where everyone gets together for celebrations.

In my community, people help each other and care about one another. Everyone works together. People have jobs and businesses here. We have rules too. The rules help everyone live safely in our community.

Every day I go to school to learn from my teachers. I see the letter carrier deliver the mail. The police officer helps my little brother cross the street safely. My grandmother goes to the doctor. My mom and dad like to visit with the people at the stores where they shop. Who lives and works in your community?

REVIEW What are some things that people do in a community? **Main Idea and Details**

These people make my community a special place to live.

Mills Street fronting San Jacinto Plaza.
El Paso, Texas

History of El Paso

I am very proud of my community. El Paso is over 400 years old. The history of El Paso is different from many places in the United States. El Paso was first settled by Native Americans and then by the Spanish. Many of the buildings in El Paso are from these early days. Some of our special celebrations come from our Spanish history.

The Rio Grande is a river that separates El Paso from the community of Juarez, Mexico. My family can go to Juarez by crossing a bridge that goes over the river. I like to go to Juarez. There are many places to eat and shop.

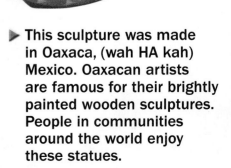

▶ This sculpture was made in Oaxaca, (wah HA kah) Mexico. Oaxacan artists are famous for their brightly painted wooden sculptures. People in communities around the world enjoy these statues.

REVIEW What groups of people settled in El Paso during its history?

⟳ **Main Idea and Details**

13

Where I Live by Carlos

City	El Paso
State	Texas
Country	U.S.A.
Continent	North America
Planet	Earth

Life in El Paso

El Paso is a part of other places. It is in the state of Texas, which is just one of the states of the United States of America. It is on the continent of North America, which is part of the planet Earth.

14

My family is an important part of the community of El Paso. My parents work in the community. They go to meetings where they help to make decisions about the future of El Paso. They vote for people who want to help the community. They help others who are in need of help.

El Paso is a special place to live, work, and have fun. What is special about where you live?

REVIEW What important things does Carlos's family do to be part of their community? ◎ **Main Idea and Details**

Summarize the Lesson

- A community is a place where people live, work, and have fun together.
- The land around a community is part of its geography.
- People make communities special places to live.
- Each community has its own history.
- Communities are small parts of the world in which we live.

LESSON 1 REVIEW

Check Facts and Main Ideas

1. ◎ **Main Idea and Details** On a separate sheet of paper, draw a diagram like the one shown below. Fill in the main idea.

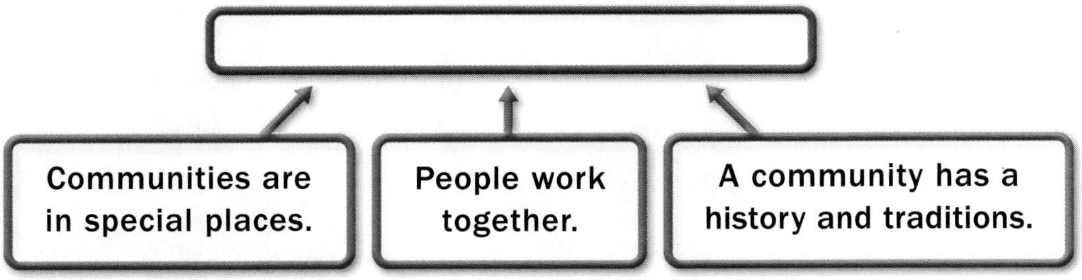

```
┌─────────────────────────────────────────┐
│                                         │
└─────────────────────────────────────────┘
        ↑              ↑              ↑
```

| Communities are in special places. | People work together. | A community has a history and traditions. |

2. Tell about the geography of El Paso.

3. Tell about the history of El Paso.

4. Name the state and country where El Paso is located.

5. **Critical Thinking:** *Draw Conclusions* Why do you think people came to live in El Paso?

Link to 🔗 **Art**

Make a Poster Draw a poster to announce a special celebration that your community has every year. Include the time of year you celebrate and some of the activities that you do during the celebration.

Caring in a Community

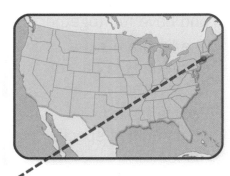

Cheshire, Connecticut

▶ **Lauren started Trios in Cheshire, Connecticut.**

Lauren, of Cheshire, Connecticut, has always been involved in projects that helped people in her community. She started a program called Trios. *Trios* is a word that means "threes." Trios brings together people from different age groups. They get together to learn from each other. Each group has one child, one teenager, and one senior citizen.

16

★ Caring

Respect
Responsibility
Fairness
Honesty
Courage

The groups go out and spend the day together at different places. Some places they have visited include a petting zoo, a pumpkin patch, and a children's science museum.

Everyone gets a lot out of the groups. The seniors tell stories to the children. The teenagers feel like big brothers or sisters to the younger children. The children have new, older friends to look up to and play with. As Lauren says, "You find out you have connections with everyone, no matter how different you seem."

Caring in Action

Link to Current Events As a class, find out about programs in your community that help people. Who started them? How do these programs show that people care for one another?

17

Astoria, Oregon
Denver, Colorado
Wilmington, North Carolina

Preview

Focus on the Main Idea
There are many kinds of communities in the United States.

PLACES
Astoria, Oregon
Wilmington,
    North Carolina
Denver, Colorado

VOCABULARY
location

United States Communities

You Are There You may have heard the song a hundred times. "Oh, beautiful for spacious skies, for amber waves of grain." You can close your eyes and see those "purple mountain majesties."

Wow! Our country is not only beautiful, it's big! It stretches from "sea to shining sea." Which part of "America, the Beautiful" reminds you of your community?

 Main Idea and Details
As you read, find details that tell about the communities.

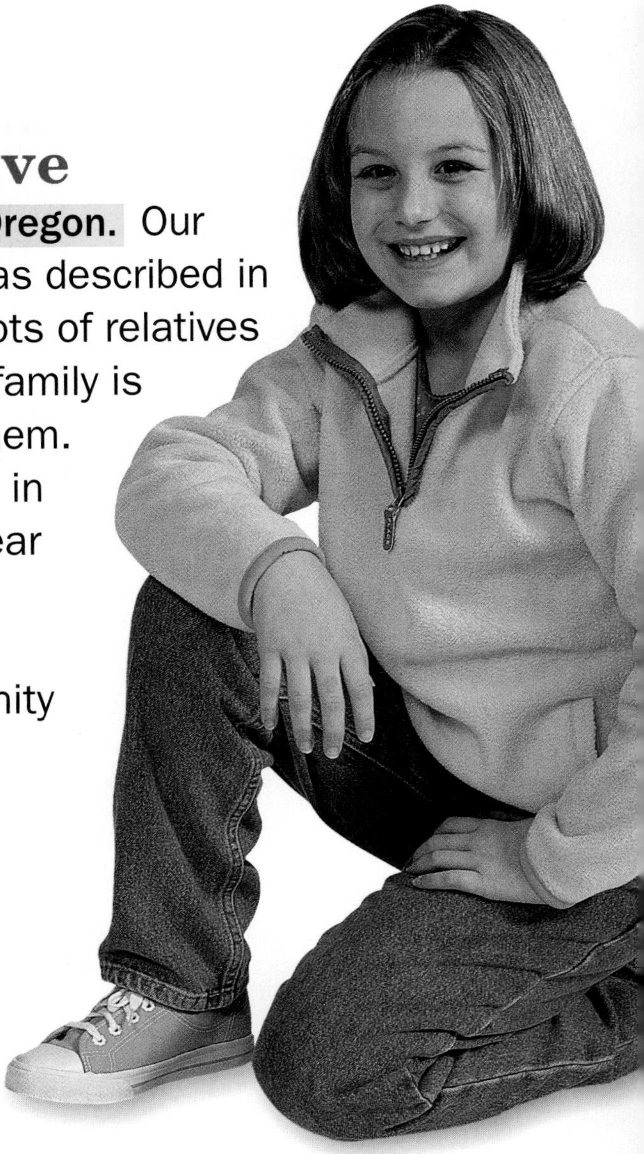

Where We Live

Hi, I'm Anna. I live in **Astoria, Oregon.** Our community is near one of the seas described in "America, the Beautiful." I have lots of relatives who live all over the country. My family is planning a trip to visit some of them. Some of my relatives live in small towns. Others live near cities. And some of my relatives live in a city. What kind of community do you live in?

Communities are located in special places. **Location** is where something can be found. The location of a place is part of its geography. Before good roads were built, communities were often started near lakes, rivers, or oceans. People and supplies, or goods, moved on boats. Farming communities were located in areas with rich soil. Where is your community located? Why?

REVIEW Why were many communities located near lakes, rivers, or oceans?

🎯 **Main Idea and Details**

19

Where Is Astoria?

Can you find Astoria on the map? This community is located where the Columbia River meets the Pacific Ocean.

The community of Astoria is almost 200 years old. Many people whose parents or grandparents came from Norway, Denmark, Finland, Sweden, and Iceland live in Astoria. Most of these countries are in a part of Europe called Scandinavia. The community has a special celebration in June. It is called the "Scandinavian Midsummer Festival."

People here like to fish, swim, boat, and even ride the waves in the Pacific Ocean. Astoria has many historical museums to visit. Is your community like Astoria?

REVIEW How do people in Astoria enjoy the ocean? ↻ **Main Idea and Details**

▶ **This is the town seal of Astoria, Oregon.**

Pacific Ocean

Astoria, Oregon

Columbia River

Where Is Wilmington?

Anna's grandparents live in **Wilmington, North Carolina.** Did you find Wilmington on the map? Their community is located between the Cape Fear River and the Atlantic Ocean. The lighthouse on the map shows the location of their community.

Wilmington was settled first by Native Americans, then by the English. There are lots of buildings in their community that show its history. The city of Wilmington is more than 250 years old.

Wilmington has some really great places to visit. You can see the birds and flowers at Airlie Gardens. You can go to Bald Head Island to swim or to Fort Fisher to explore. Fort Fisher is a sand fort! Is your community like Wilmington?

REVIEW What is special about Wilmington, North Carolina? ⊙ **Main Idea and Details**

Atlantic Ocean

Wilmington, North Carolina
Cape Fear

21

Denver, Colorado

Where Is Denver?

When I drove with my family to visit my grandparents, we stopped in Denver to see my cousins. We had a wonderful time hiking in the mountains. We found lots of beautiful rocks.

Remember those "purple mountain majesties" from "America, the Beautiful"? The song may have been talking about **Denver, Colorado.** Find Denver on the map. Denver is located at the foot of the Rocky Mountains near the middle of the United States. It is located where Cherry Creek and the South Platte River meet. Denver lies between the Atlantic and Pacific oceans.

Denver first began as a Native American Arapaho settlement. The Arapaho lived in this area for many years before fur traders arrived. Later, gold brought miners and prospectors to the Denver area.

REVIEW What is special about Denver, Colorado? **⊙ Main Idea and Details**

Summarize the Lesson

- People in the United States live in different kinds of communities.
- Communities are located in special places.
- Astoria, Wilmington, and Denver are communities in different regions of the United States.

LESSON 2 REVIEW

Check Facts and Main Ideas

1. **⊙ Main Idea and Details** On a separate sheet of paper, draw a diagram like the one shown. Fill in the main idea that tells about these communities.

```
        ┌──────────────────────────────────────┐
        │                                      │
        └──────────────────────────────────────┘
           ↑               ↑               ↑
┌────────────────┐ ┌────────────────┐ ┌────────────────────┐
│ Astoria is near│ │ Wilmington is  │ │ Denver is near the │
│ the Pacific    │ │ near the       │ │ middle of the      │
│ Ocean.         │ │ Atlantic Ocean.│ │ United States.     │
└────────────────┘ └────────────────┘ └────────────────────┘
```

2. Why were the early communities often located near rivers or oceans?

3. Tell about the geography of the communities of Astoria, Wilmington, and Denver.

4. Tell about the settlers in Astoria, Wilmington, and Denver.

5. **Critical Thinking: *Compare and Contrast*** Compare and contrast the fun things people do in the communities of Astoria, Oregon; Wilmington, North Carolina; and Denver, Colorado.

Link to 🔗 Geography

Making Maps Use a map of the United States to trace your state. Place a dot on the state for the community where you live. Explain your map to a friend.

Meet Sonia Manzano

Writer and Actress

New York City is the largest city in the United States. It is divided up into smaller parts called boroughs. One borough is the Bronx. Sonia Manzano grew up in the Bronx and now works in a very famous community. She works on *Sesame Street!*

For more information, go online to *Meet the People* at **www.sfsocialstudies.com**.

Sonia loved to sing, dance, and act. She went to school to study the arts. When she finished college, she decided to find a job that used these talents and helped children. Sonia became Maria on *Sesame Street*. Have you ever seen Maria on television?

Sonia has worked as Maria for almost 30 years. She is an important part of the New York City community. Her work helps change and improve the lives of children in New York and around the world. Did Sonia help you learn to read and count?

Sesame Street *has been called "the longest street in the world" because the show is produced in 19 different countries.*

BIOFACT

Sonia Manzano considers herself lucky that she can reach so many children with her work. She wants children to see that all kinds of families are important in our world. She wants everyone to know that all kinds of families need to work together to help their community.

Learn from Biographies

How did Sonia Manzano's decision to play Maria on *Sesame Street* help change and improve the lives of children?

World Communities

Preview

Focus on the Main Idea
Communities around the world are alike and different.

PLACES
Timbuktu, Mali
Sahara

VOCABULARY
culture

You Are There You have to close your eyes to keep out the stinging Sahara sand. You hear voices around you speaking French and Bambara. You're standing in a West African country rich in history that goes back hundreds of years. You're standing in the center of a city that is sometimes called "The City of Mysteries." What mysteries await your visit?

Main Idea and Details As you read, look for details that show how communities everywhere are alike in some ways and different in other ways.

26

Timbuktu Long Ago

You learned about some communities in the United States. There are communities all over the world. You might like to read about a community on the other side of the world. The name of the "City of Mysteries" is **Timbuktu** (tim BUHK too). It is in the West African country of **Mali.** From 1400 to about 1600, Timbuktu was a very wealthy city in a desert. During that time four to six centuries ago, you would see long lines of camels carrying blocks of salt and other goods strapped to their backs. The salt was traded for gold. Merchants from other parts of Africa would come to Timbuktu to do business.

During those years, many thousands of people lived in Timbuktu. The city was also a center of learning and religion. In the 1500s, there was a huge university in the city.

▶ These people in Timbuktu are wearing the clothes people usually wear in Mali.

REVIEW In what ways was Timbuktu an important city in the years between 1400 and 1600?

◉ **Main Idea and Details**

▶ A caravan of camels took weeks to cross the **Sahara** to reach Timbuktu.

Life in Timbuktu Today

▶ The kora is a common musical instrument in Mali.

Fewer people now live in Timbuktu than in earlier times. Parts of their culture are quite different from the culture in the United States. A **culture** is the way a group of people lives. Culture includes a group's language, music, religion, food, clothing, holidays, and beliefs.

Many people in Mali speak Bambara. However, the main language in Mali is French. Homes are different from those in the United States. They are made of mud bricks. The way people travel is also very different. There are few good roads. People walk or take buses. Some people still ride camels.

How is life there similar to and different from the way that you live?

▶ *Griots,* or storytellers, tell the history of Mali. Storytelling was important long ago. Malians had no written language then.

This building is a place for religious worship.

28

The weather in Timbuktu may also be different from where you live. Mali is located in a desert region. Very little rain falls here. The sun shines brightly almost every day.

Just as in the past, religion is very important to the people of Timbuktu. Three mosques (places of worship) were built in the city. Two of these are the Great Mosque and the Sankore Mosque. The third is Sidi Yahai.

REVIEW What details tell about the geography of Mali?
⦿ **Main Idea and Details**

LESSON 3 REVIEW

Check Facts and Main Ideas

1. ⦿ **Main Idea and Details** On a separate sheet of paper, draw a diagram like the one shown. Fill in some details about the culture of Timbuktu.

> **The culture of Timbuktu is made of many parts.**

> **The people speak French and Bambara.**

2. Tell about what makes up the culture of a community.

3. How is the community of Timbuktu today different from the way it was between 1400 and 1600? How is it the same?

4. When was Timbuktu a very wealthy city?

5. **Critical Thinking:** *Compare and Contrast* How is the community of Timbuktu today like your community? How is it different?

Link to ⦿⦿ Writing

Write sentences Make a list of how Timbuktu is the same and different today than it was from its past. Write three sentences about Timbuktu.

GEOGRAPHY OF THE WORLD

Africa is a large continent. It has 53 countries and is home to close to 700 million people. Most African people live in the countryside, but many people now are moving to towns and cities. Africa has mountains, rain forests, and the largest desert in the world, the Sahara.

Children are very important in Africa. Children are the future of the continent.

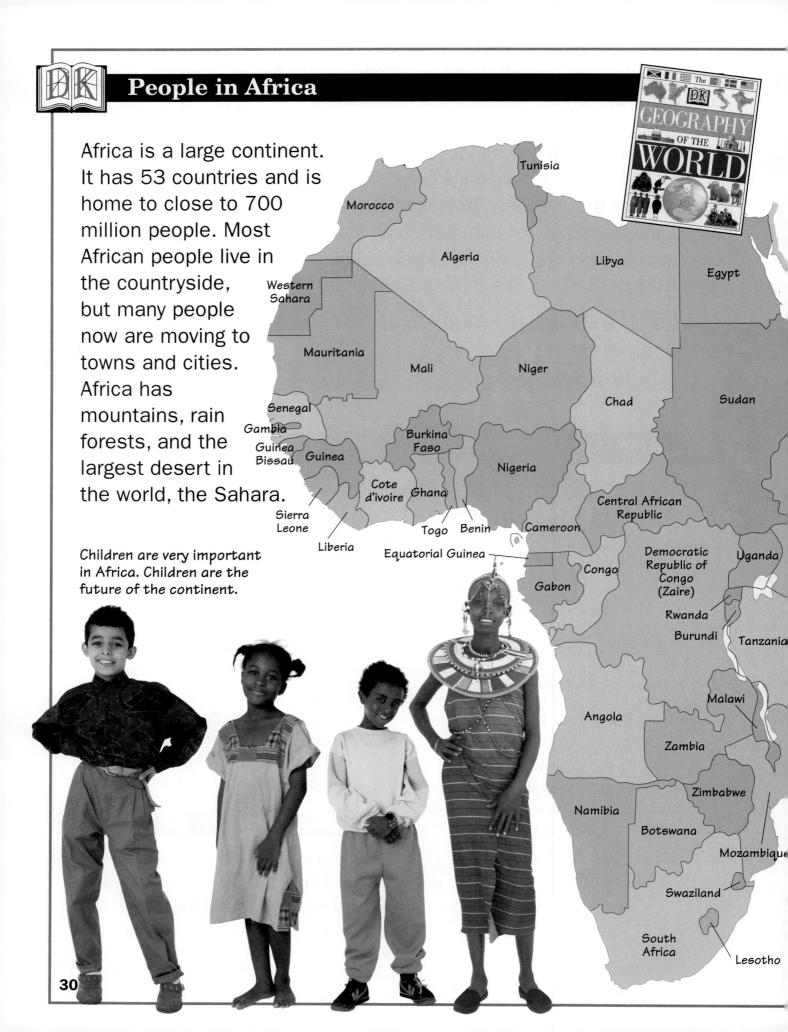

Tunisia

Morocco

Algeria

Libya

Egypt

Western Sahara

Mauritania

Mali

Niger

Chad

Sudan

Senegal

Gambia

Burkina Faso

Guinea Bissau

Guinea

Cote d'ivoire

Ghana

Nigeria

Sierra Leone

Togo   Benin

Cameroon

Central African Republic

Liberia

Equatorial Guinea

Congo

Democratic Republic of Congo (Zaire)

Uganda

Gabon

Rwanda

Burundi

Tanzania

Angola

Malawi

Zambia

Zimbabwe

Namibia

Botswana

Mozambique

Swaziland

South Africa

Lesotho

Some African people are herders, like this person tending goats in western Africa. He dresses the same way people did long ago. His clothing protects him from the hot sun and blowing sand.

Cities in Africa are growing. This is Johannesburg, in the country of South Africa.

Eritrea

Djibouti

Ethiopia

Somalia

Kenya

These men live in Tunisia, which is in the northern part of Africa.

In some countries in Africa, most people live in cities. The chart below shows the percentage of population that lives in cities.

Percentage of Urban Population in Some African Countries, 2000	
Algeria	59%
Burkina Faso	19%
Lesotho	28%
Libya	88%
Niger	21%
South Africa	50%
Tunisia	66%

Madagascar

31

Use Map Scales

Mali was a kingdom in Africa long before Mali became a country. When Mali was a kingdom, people in Africa often bought and sold salt and gold. These people, called traders, traveled long distances on many routes. Many of them passed through the city of Timbuktu in Mali.

What? Look at the map below that shows the Mali kingdom about 600 years ago. This map

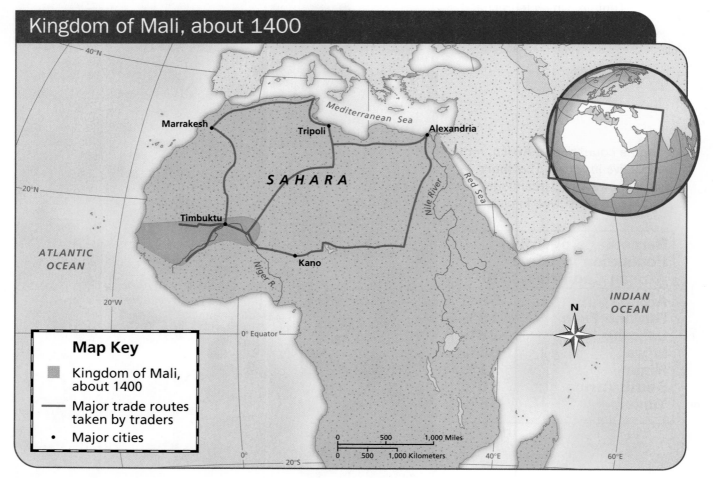

Kingdom of Mali, about 1400

Map Key

Kingdom of Mali, about 1400

Major trade routes taken by traders

Major cities

has a scale at the bottom. A map scale is a short measurement that allows a person using a map to measure very long distances, such as miles or kilometers.

Why? A map scale helps you figure out the actual distance in miles or kilometers between two places, such as communities.

How? To use a map scale to measure miles, put a ruler just below the line connecting the 0 with the 1,000-mile mark. How long in inches is the line? How many miles does that measurement stand for?

One inch on this map equals 1,000 miles on Earth. One-half inch would then equal one-half of the distance, or 500 miles. Now measure the distance between the cities of Kano and Alexandria. Place your ruler on the dot for Kano. Make sure your ruler also touches the dot for Alexandria. Count the number of inches between the two communities.

There are about two inches. Since each inch stands for 1,000 miles, you know that the actual distance between the cities is about 1,000 miles plus 1,000 miles, or a total of about 2,000 miles.

Think and Apply

1 What is a map scale? How is it useful?

2 Look at the map. Measure the distance in inches between Marrekesh and Timbuktu. How many miles does that equal?

3 About how many miles is it from Tripoli to Timbuktu?

For more information, go online to the *Atlas* at **www.sfsocialstudies.com**.

Chapter Summary

 Main Idea and Details

On a separate sheet of paper, fill in some details that make up a culture.

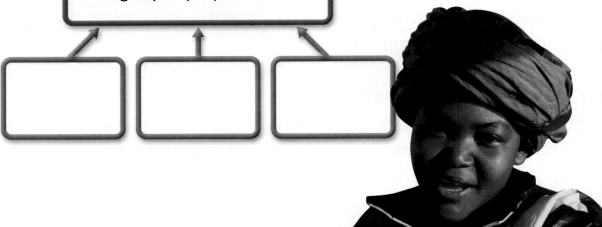

A culture is the way a group of people lives.

Vocabulary

Match each word with the correct definition or description.

1. community (p. 11)
2. geography (p. 11)
3. location (p. 19)
4. culture (p. 28)

a. the place something can be found

b. a place where people live, work, and have fun together

c. the way a group of people lives

d. the study of Earth and the way people live on it

Facts and Main Ideas

1. How are all communities alike?

2. Name one reason communities were often located on rivers or oceans before good roads were built.

3. **Main Idea** What are three things that people do together in a community?

4. **Main Idea** Are communities across the United States mostly of one kind or of many different kinds?

5. **Main Idea** Tell about the community of Timbuktu in the 1400s and 1500s.

6. **Critical Thinking:** *Compare and Contrast* How are communities around the world like each other and different from each other?

Write About It

1. **Write a description** of Timbuktu as it was 500 years ago. Tell about the climate, the ways goods were carried around, and what made the community famous.

2. **Write an advertisement** for your community. Be sure to tell about three things people do together in a community.

3. **Write a fact sheet** about the culture of your community. Include the five parts of a culture.

Apply Skills

Study the map on page 32. Look at the map scale. Then answer the questions. You will need a ruler.

1. What is the purpose of a scale?

2. What distance does 1 inch represent?

3. About how far is it from Tripoli to Alexandria?

Internet Activity

To get help with vocabulary, people, and terms, select the dictionary or encyclopedia from *Social Studies Library* at **www.sfsocialstudies.com**.

35

Lesson 1

Bridgewater, Virginia

Rural communities are in the countryside.

1

Lesson 2

Levittown, New York

Suburban communities are near cities.

2

Lesson 3

Chicago, Illinois

Urban communities are in cities.

3

CANADA

3

1

2

Chicago,
Illinois

Levittown,
New York

Bridgewater,
Virginia

UNITED STATES

ATLANTIC
OCEAN

MEXICO

Why We Remember

Some communities are small. Others are large.
Communities are alike in some ways and
different in other ways. When you compare
communities, you can understand more
about the people who live in them. What
kind of community do you live in?

Bridgewater, Virginia

Preview

Focus on the Main Idea
Rural communities are in the countryside and can be surrounded by farms and open land.

PLACES
Bridgewater, Virginia

VOCABULARY
rural community

A Rural Community

You Are There Every day you've been watching more and more tents go up at Harrison Park. You can't wait to see what's going in each one. The smells coming from the food tents give clues to what's cooking. Then the workers begin to build the rides. The Ferris wheel takes shape as they add each car to the circle.

The famous Lawn Party is the best part of the summer. People from all over Bridgewater come to have fun and be with friends.

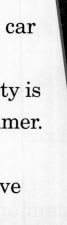

Main Idea and Details As you read, look for details that tell about a rural community.

Amy's Rural Community

I'm Amy, and I live on a farm in **Bridgewater, Virginia.** It's a rural community. A **rural community** is in the countryside where the towns are small and far apart. Usually, rural communities are surrounded by open lands and fields.

First, I'll tell you about the geography of my community. Bridgewater is located on the North River. It is in Rockingham County in the Shenandoah Valley in the state of Virginia.

On my family's farm, we grow apples, corn, and many other crops.

Bridgewater became the name of the town in 1835. Today about 5,000 people live in Bridgewater. Many of these people work in nearby Harrisonburg or other communities.

REVIEW What usually surrounds a rural community?
◎ **Main Idea and Details**

August

by Michael Lewis

Many people in rural communities live and work on farms. Here is part of a poem about how a farmer feels about August weather.

···

...Farmers do not mind the heat;
They know it ripens corn
    and wheat.
They love to see the sun
    rise red,
Remembering what their
    fathers said:
"An August month that's
    dry and warm
Will never
    do the harvest harm."

Community Life

Bridgewater is a small rural community, but there are plenty of things to do here! The 4-H Club meets once a month to talk about farm and community issues. Scouting also keeps Amy and her friends busy.

If you like sports, Bridgewater is the place for you. The 9- and 10-year-old All-Star team from the Bridgewater Little League won the Virginia state championship for the year 2000. Now that was exciting!

Bridgewater is a great place to live and go to school. Amy has lots of friends, and it seems everyone in town knows each other. In times of trouble, the whole town helps out.

REVIEW What are some things people do together in a rural community?

⊙ **Main Idea and Details**

Summarize the Lesson

- A rural community is in the countryside where the towns are small and far apart.
- Bridgewater is a rural community located in the state of Virginia.
- Bridgewater has many activities and things to do.

LESSON 1 REVIEW

Check Facts and Main Ideas

1. ⊙ **Main Idea and Details** On a separate sheet of paper, fill in some of the details that tell about life in a rural community.

> Rural communities are in the countryside.

2. What is a rural community?

3. Describe the different ways that people in Bridgewater have fun.

4. Describe the location of Bridgewater.

5. **Critical Thinking:** *Observe* How do you think that Bridgewater might have gotten its name?

Link to ⦿⦿ **Reading**

Poems Read the poem on p.40. Write a poem about your favorite season. Read it to the class.

Long Island

Levittown, New York

Preview

Focus on the Main Idea
Suburban communities have grown and changed over the years.

PLACES
Levittown, New York

VOCABULARY
suburban community

A Suburban Community

You Are There

Traffic along Hempstead Turnpike is so heavy. This street has everything! There are all kinds of stores and restaurants along it. But it seems as if everyone is going to Nassau Mall today. Finally, you get into Nassau Mall. There are shops where you can get school supplies, CDs, and clothes. There are a food court and movie theaters. Where will you go first?

Main Idea and Details As you read, look for the details that tell about how this suburban community grew.

Steve's Suburban Community

I'm Steve and I live in a suburban community called **Levittown, New York.** A **suburban community** is a community that is located near a large city. Usually, suburbs surround the large city. My parents and many other people who live in the suburbs work in the city. Many people work here too.

Levittown is located on Long Island, in the state of New York. It is just a train ride from the largest city in the United States, New York City.

Levittown is close to great parks and ocean beaches. One of my favorite places is Eisenhower Park, where I can hear free concerts in the summer. I also love to go to Jones Beach State Park on the Atlantic Ocean.

REVIEW Where are suburban communities located? **Main Idea and Details**

I live in a house like the houses in these pictures.

43

From Farm to Town

The houses of Levittown were built on land that was once a potato farm.

▶ Very few people lived here in 1945. There were farms and open land.

▶ Look how this area has changed! Now there are grassy lawns instead of fields. Houses and sidewalks cover the land. In what other ways has this area changed?

How Levittown Grew

People form communities because they want to be safe and comfortable. Abraham Levitt decided to build a community to meet these needs. He began building homes on a potato farm that he bought in 1947. William was one of his sons. The Levitt family planned and built a whole suburban community. In 1949 the first homes were ready for sale. In all, 17,000 homes were built. The community included schools, parks, stores, and places of worship.

The community was first called Island Trees. Later the name was changed to Levittown, after the Levitt family.

Many people moved from New York City to live in Levittown. Many other suburban communities across the United States were built. New highways helped suburban communities grow. People could get to work and home again easily.

REVIEW How did Levittown grow?
🎯 Main Idea and Details

Summarize the Lesson

- A suburb is a community located near a city.
- Many people who live in the suburbs work in the city.
- People form communities to meet their needs for feeling safe and comfortable.

LESSON 2 REVIEW

Check Facts and Main Ideas

1. 🎯 **Main Idea and Details** On a separate sheet of paper, draw a diagram like the one shown. Fill in the main idea about suburban communities.

```
┌──────────────────────────────────┐
│                                  │
└──────────────────────────────────┘
    ↑           ↑            ↑
```

| They are near a large city. | Many people work in the city. | Highways helped them grow. |

2. What steps did Levitt take to change a farm into a suburb?

3. What did Levitt include in his community plan?

4. What are some needs that lead people to form communities?

5. **Critical Thinking:** *Observe* Tell how transportation is important to your community.

Link to Language Arts

Make Up a Name Levittown used to be called Island Trees. What is the name of your community? Do you think it is a good name? Write and tell why. Do you think it is a bad name? Write and tell about a name you think would be better.

45

Read Together

Biography

Meet
William Levitt

1907–1994 • Builder

William Levitt was working with his father, Abraham Levitt. Abraham and his two sons learned everything they could about construction. They formed a company called Levitt & Sons.

▶ William Levitt, Abraham's oldest son, was in the Navy in 1943. When he got out, he and millions of other people who had been soldiers and sailors needed a place to live.

For more information, go online to *Meet the People* at **www.sfsocialstudies.com**.

Levitt & Sons built homes as quickly as possible. Each worker did the same job on every house. The houses were built in parts and then put together. These houses were cheap enough so that the soldiers and sailors returning from World War II could afford to buy them.

William Levitt created a new type of community. Small and large families lived there. Neighbors became close friends. Everyone had a TV and a washing machine.

William Levitt's company found a way to build homes with only 26 key steps. They could complete as many as 30 houses a day!

BIOFACT

▶ These pictures show a house and a neighborhood being built.

Learn from Biographies

After William Levitt built Levittown, suburbs like it seemed to sprout up all across the United States. Is there a suburb like Levittown near where you live?

Chicago, Illinois

Preview

Focus on the Main Idea
Urban communities are in cities where many people live and work.

PLACES
Chicago, Illinois
Tokyo, Japan

VOCABULARY
urban community
city
population
transportation

An Urban Community

You Are There As you walk in, you see Sue waiting for you. She's huge! Sue is the biggest, most complete dinosaur fossil ever found! If you like mummies, you'll find them here, too.

Planets, sea creatures, dinosaurs, coal mines—you can see them all in one city. It would take you days to visit all the museums here!

Lots of people live here. Do you know the real name of the place that some people call the "Windy City"?

 Main Idea and Details As you read, look for details that tell all about the city of Chicago, Illinois.

Chicago, An Urban Community

I'm Beth. I live in an urban community in the city of **Chicago, Illinois**. An **urban community** is a community that is in a city. A **city** has the largest **population,** or number of people, in an area.

Chicago is located on the western shore of Lake Michigan, at the mouth of the Chicago River. Chicago is in the state of Illinois, in the midwest part of the United States. More than three million people live in the city.

In 1779 Jean Baptiste Pointe Du Sable, a French-African fur trader, settled near the mouth of a river and a great lake. Many years later, a town grew in the area. In 1837 that town was called Chicago.

REVIEW Where is Chicago, Illinois, located?

Main Idea and Details

▶ Du Sable was the first person who was not a Native American to settle in Chicago.

© 1986 USPS

Jean Baptiste Pointe Du Sable
22
Black Heritage USA

49

The "El," or elevated train, travels above the streets.

Working in Chicago

People in Chicago work in many places. Chicago has large department stores, banks, and office buildings. The Sears Tower, which is the tallest office building in the United States, is in Chicago.

With so many people trying to get to work, they need ways to get around. Different forms of transportation move people from place to place. **Transportation** means carrying people or things from place to place. Many people use buses or the "El" to get around town. The "El" is the elevated, or raised, train system that runs through Chicago. The name of downtown Chicago, the Loop, came from the way the trains loop around that area.

REVIEW Why are the trains important to Chicago? ↻ **Main Idea and Details**

MAP ADVENTURE

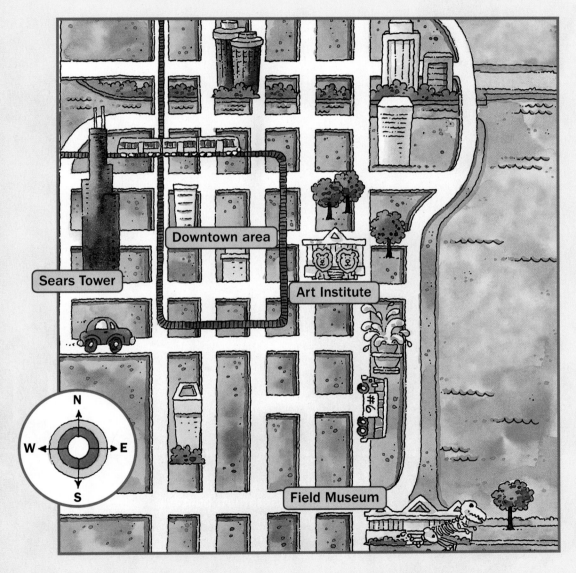

In Chicago you can visit many exciting places. Today, let's go to two museums here in town. Start at the Sears Tower.

- First, let's go south and east to visit the home of Sue, the *tyrannosaurus*. Can you find Sue's home on the map? What is this museum called?

- Now let's go to the home of famous works of art. From the Field Museum, what direction do we need to go to get to the Art Institute? Can you get there by train?

Buckingham Fountain was given to Chicago in 1927 by Kate Buckingham in honor of her brother. The fountain was sculpted by Marcel Francois Loyau. It is one of the largest fountains in the world. Every 60 seconds, 133 jets shoot about 14,000 gallons of water into the sky, reaching 150 feet high.

Community Life

Beth and her family love Chicago. They like to watch the boats sailing on Lake Michigan in the summer. They go to the beach and have great picnics. Beth's parents like to go to theaters.

The Adler Planetarium was the first planetarium built in the Western Hemisphere. Max Adler founded this museum in 1930.

Chicago has many museums. You could visit the Art Institute, but be careful of the lions that guard the doors!

REVIEW What are some things you can do in Chicago? ⊙ **Main Idea and Details**

Summarize the Lesson

- Urban communities are in cities with large populations.
- People use different types of transportation to get around in a city.
- Cities may have many museums, parks, and theaters.

LESSON 3 REVIEW

Check Facts and Main Ideas

1. ⊙ **Main Idea and Details** On a separate sheet of paper, draw a diagram like the one shown. Fill in some details about life in an urban community.

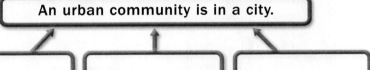

An urban community is in a city.

2. How is an urban community different from a rural community? How is it similar?

3. Name three fun things to do in Chicago.

4. Name one way that people in Chicago get around that is not found in rural communities.

5. **Critical Thinking: *Compare and Contrast*** How is a city similar to and different from its suburbs?

Link to ⊶ Mathematics

Use an Almanac to find out the populations of Houston, Texas; Chicago, Illinois; and Indianapolis, Indiana. Use the math symbols > (greater than), and < (less than) to compare these populations.

Another Big City

Tokyo, Japan

Chicago is a large city, but it's not the largest city in the United States or in the world. Tokyo, Japan, is on the other side of the world from Chicago. Tokyo is the largest city in Japan. In fact, there are more people living in Tokyo than in any other city in the world! Like cities everywhere, Tokyo sometimes is noisy and crowded. People travel to and through Tokyo on subways, buses, trains, and in cars.

▶ Tokyo has skyscrapers and traditional wooden buildings.

Tokyo, like Chicago and many other big cities, has several museums. People can see fine art at the Tokyo National Museum and the Metropolitan Art Museum. They can also visit a science museum and a zoo. There are concert halls and theaters in Tokyo.

▶ At the theater, audiences can watch traditional Japanese plays.

▶ The city also has many parks with beautiful Japanese gardens.

Classify

What? When you **classify**, you place things that have similar features together in a group. You can classify, or group, objects, ideas, living things, and even communities. This chart shows how to classify some objects.

Objects		Classify into Groups	
Car, bicycle, truck		Things that have wheels	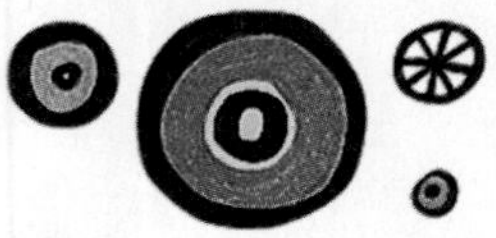
Cat, dog, table, chair		Things that have four legs	
Grass, flower, tree		Things that grow on the earth	

Why? Classifying can help you better understand the things you put into groups. One reason people classify communities is so that they can learn how similar communities solve problems.

How? To classify things, you find features of one group that make it different from other groups. For example, cities have larger populations than the suburbs or rural communities in their regions. Rural communities and suburbs have smaller populations. This feature of population helps you decide if a community fits into the city group.

A feature of rural communities is that they are in the countryside. A feature of suburbs is that they are near cities. You can list communities and their features in a chart.

Features of a Community	Classify into Groups
• In the countryside • Small population	Rural community
• Near a city • Medium-sized population	Suburban community
• In a city • Large population	Urban community

Use the information in this paragraph to classify these communities in Travis County, Texas.

Austin has a population of more than 500,000. It is the largest community in the county. Next to Austin is Rollingwood, a much smaller community. Many people who live in Rollingwood work in Austin. In the countryside, over 10 miles from Austin, is the community of Bee Cave. Its population is fewer than 700.

❶ Which community is a city? What feature helped you decide?

❷ Which community is a suburb? What feature helped you decide?

❸ Which community is a rural community? What feature helped you decide?

Chapter Summary

 Main Idea and Details

On a separate sheet of paper, fill in the details about the three types of communities.

There are different types of communities.

Vocabulary

Match each word with the correct definition or description.

1. rural community (p. 39)
2. suburban community (p. 43)
3. city (p. 49)
4. population (p. 49)
5. transportation (p. 50)
6. urban community (p. 49)

a. an urban community with the largest population in an area

b. the number of people living in a place

c. a community in the countryside

d. the moving of goods or people

e. a community in a city

f. a community near a city

Facts and Main Ideas

1. What usually surrounds a rural community?

2. What kind of community has the largest population in an area?

3. **Main Idea** Describe the size and location of a rural community.

4. **Main Idea** How have suburban communities changed over the years?

5. **Main Idea** Describe how a rural area can grow and change, forming a suburb.

6. **Critical Thinking:** *Classify* Is your community a rural community, a suburb, or a city?

Write About It

1 **Write a thank you note** to friends after your visit to their home in Bridgewater, Virginia. Tell them how Bridgewater is like your community and how it is different.

2 **Write an advertisement** for a new suburb. Give two examples of how your new community meets people's need for safety and comfort.

3 **Write a Top Five List.** Choose one type of community (rural community, a suburb, or an urban community). Tell five ways that people meet their need for recreation.

Internet Activity

To get help with vocabulary, people, and terms, select dictionary or encyclopedia from *Social Studies Library* at **www.scottforesman.com**.

Apply Skills

Read the newspaper story below. Use the information to classify each community.

HAYWARD COUNTY TRIBUNE

School Roundup

Washington School is the oldest school in Franklin, the largest community in Hayward County.

Students at Joyce School in Newberry, just outside Franklin, planted three new trees. Just ten years ago Newberry was farmland.

Third graders from the farming community of Johnston enjoyed their bus trip to the Hayward County History Museum in Franklin.

1 Classify Franklin as a rural community, suburb, or city.

2 Classify Newberry as a rural community, suburb, or city.

3 Classify Johnston as a rural community, suburb, or city.

America, the Beautiful

Words by Katharine Lee Bates
Music by Samuel A. Ward

Some of the words in this song tell about parts of our country. Think about a picture you might paint about one of the places in the song.

1. O beau - ti - ful for spa - cious skies, For am - ber waves of grain,
2. O beau - ti - ful for pa - triot dream That sees be - yond the years

For pur - ple moun - tain maj - es - ties A - bove the fruit - ed plain!
Thine al - a - bas - ter cit - ies gleam, Un - dimmed by hu - man tears!

A - mer - i - ca! A - mer - i - ca! God shed His grace on thee,

And crown thy good with broth - er-hood From sea to shin - ing sea!

Review

Main Ideas and Vocabulary

TEST PREP

Read the passage. Then answer the questions.

Communities are all over the world. Communities are alike in some ways because they are all places where people live, work, and have fun together.

Communities are different in some ways. Communities might be located near oceans or rivers. In these places, people may use ships for transportation. Some communities are located in deserts or mountains. People there use other forms of transportation.

Another difference is <u>population</u>. Cities have the largest populations of any communities in their areas. Suburban and rural communities have smaller populations.

Culture also varies from community to community. The way people live in Timbuktu is different from the way people live in Chicago.

1 According to the passage, how can river communities transport goods and people?

  A by camel   **C** by train

  B by ship   **D** by truck

2 In the passage the word *population* means

  A an urban community

  B the number of people living in a place

  C a city

  D the way a group of people lives

3 What is the main idea of the passage?

  A Cities have large populations.

  B Transportation is an important need.

  C Communities are both alike and different.

  D There are many kinds of cultures in the United States.

Vocabulary

Write sentences that describe your community. Use three or more of the vocabulary words below.

community (p. 11)

geography (p. 11)

location (p. 19)

culture (p. 28)

suburb (p. 43)

population (p. 49)

transportation (p. 50)

Apply Skills

Use a Map Scale on a Globe Look at a globe. Find the distance from your community to the North Pole. Measure the distance in inches between the two places. Describe how to use this number and the globe's map scale to find the distance to the North Pole.

Read on Your Own

Look for books like these in the library.

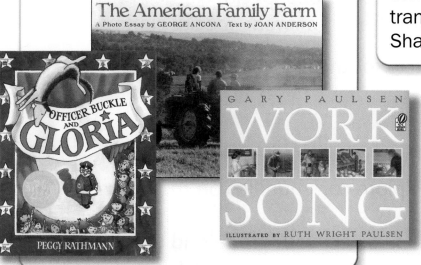

Write and Share

Be a News Reporter Give a news report. Tell two ways people in your community meet a need for transportation and recreation. Share your report with the class.

Discovery CHANNEL SCHOOL

UNIT 1 Project

Working in My Community

People work hard to make a community a good place to live. They work at many different jobs. With a partner, plan a TV interview of one of these people.

1 Choose one kind of worker in your community. Find out what that worker does.

2 Write questions to ask the person during an interview.

3 Decide whether to be the TV reporter or worker. The worker can tell about special clothes or equipment needed for the job or wear special clothes.

4 Perform your interview for the class.

Internet Activity

Explore communities on the Internet.
Go to www.sfsocialstudies.com/activities and select your grade and unit.

People in Communities

How do people help your
community grow?

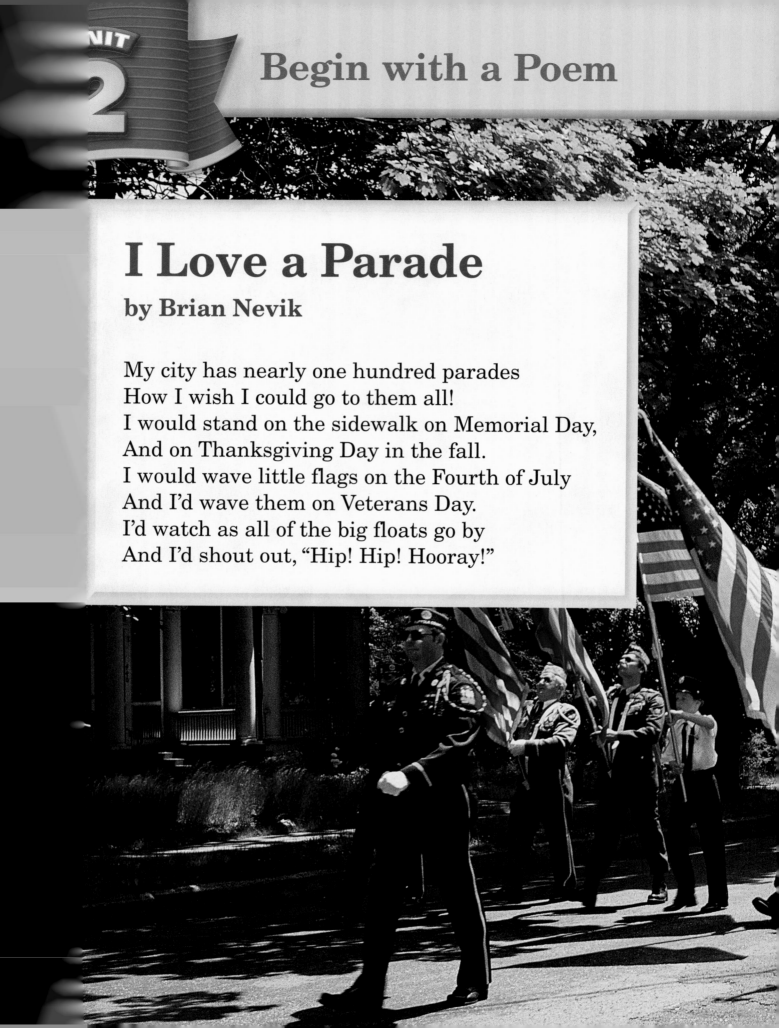

UNIT 2

I Love a Parade

by Brian Nevik

My city has nearly one hundred parades
How I wish I could go to them all!
I would stand on the sidewalk on Memorial Day,
And on Thanksgiving Day in the fall.
I would wave little flags on the Fourth of July
And I'd wave them on Veterans Day.
I'd watch as all of the big floats go by
And I'd shout out, "Hip! Hip! Hooray!"

Community Celebrations

▶ The first St. Patrick's Day celebration in the United States was held in Boston in 1737. Every year, about one-half million people come to watch the parade in Boston.

▶ Plymouth, Massachusetts, is known as "America's Hometown." Visiting nearby Plimoth (Plymouth) Plantation is a great way to celebrate Thanksgiving.

▶ Before it was part of the United States, New Orleans belonged to France, then Spain, and then France. Every year in New Orleans people wear costumes and have parades during a festival called Mardi Gras.

▶ Cinco de Mayo means "Fifth of May." Many people in Mexican American communities in the United States celebrate this holiday. There are parades, music, dancing, and special foods.

▶ For old-fashioned fun, some people in Kansas attend the state fair each summer. There they can see rodeo events, play sports, watch a parade, and enjoy food.

Reading Social Studies

Kinds of Celebrations

Target Skill

Compare and Contrast

Knowing how to compare and contrast information will help you understand some kinds of writing. We compare when we say how things are alike. We contrast when we say how things are different. Look at the diagram below.

Compare/Alike	**Contrast/Different**
Communities are made up of people.	Some communities are large, but others are small.

- Writers use words to signal likenesses and differences. The most common clue word for likenesses is *like*.

- Clue words such as *yet, but,* and *however* signal differences.

Read the paragraph. Likenesses and differences have been highlighted.

In Unit 1 you read about some kinds of communities. All communities are made up of people who live, work, and have fun together. Some communities are large, but others are small.

Celebrations

Today was Cindy's eighth birthday party. She wanted it to be like her parents' yearly New Year's Eve party, yet she knew it would be different. Only adults had come to her parents' party, but mostly children were coming to her party.

There would be cake and party hats, just like the New Year's Eve party. However, the cake would be different. Her cake said "Happy Birthday," not "Happy New Year."

One difference made Cindy a little sad. She wanted to stay up late with her friends. At her parents' party, she had stayed up very late. Her party, however, had to end early.

She was glad about some of the differences, though. Her friends would sing "Happy Birthday" and bring her presents.

Use the reading skill of compare and contrast to answer these questions.

1 Which clue words are in the passage?

2 How were the two parties alike?

3 Contrast those things that make Cindy happy with those that make her sad.

Chapter 3

People Move From Place to Place

Lesson 1

Ft. Wayne, Indiana

People move to new communities.

1

Lesson 2

Boston, Massachusetts

People learn new customs.

2

Lesson 3

New York City, New York

Where do people move from?

3

Lesson 4

Pittsburgh, Pennsylvania

People begin a new life in the United States.

4

CANADA

1

4

3

2

Boston

Fort Wayne

Pittsburgh

New York City

UNITED STATES

ATLANTIC OCEAN

PACIFIC OCEAN

MEXICO

Gulf of Mexico

Why We Remember

People come to the United States from all over the world. They leave communities behind, but they bring their memories and their cultures with them. They blend their cultures into the new communities that they join. Each community has its own special culture. Each community is special in its own way.

Fort Wayne, Indiana

Moving to a New Community

Preview

Focus on the Main Idea
People in a community may come from different places.

PLACES
Fort Wayne, Indiana

VOCABULARY
opportunity

You Are There You know some of the things that will happen today. Your parents will take you to your new school. Someone will bring you to the classroom. Then what?

Will the other children look at you when you enter the room? Where will you sit? What will you do during lunchtime?

You like your new home, but you miss your old friends. "Why did we have to move, anyway?" you ask yourself.

Ben

Compare and Contrast
Target Skill As you read, look for what is the same and what is different about the places people come from.

We Come from All Over!

Hi! I'm Tom. My family moved to Boston because of my father's job. I was worried about going to a new school, but I felt better when I got to my new classroom. A map on the wall had a sticker near my old town, **Fort Wayne, Indiana.**

Mrs. Wilson, the teacher, told the other students to write their names on stickers. Then they put their stickers on places where they had lived.

There were stickers all over the map. Boston had the most stickers. Many students had never lived anyplace else. Mrs. Wilson smiled and said, "Some of us have come from far away to live in our community."

REVIEW In what way are the students alike, and in what way are they different?

Compare and Contrast

I like my new school.

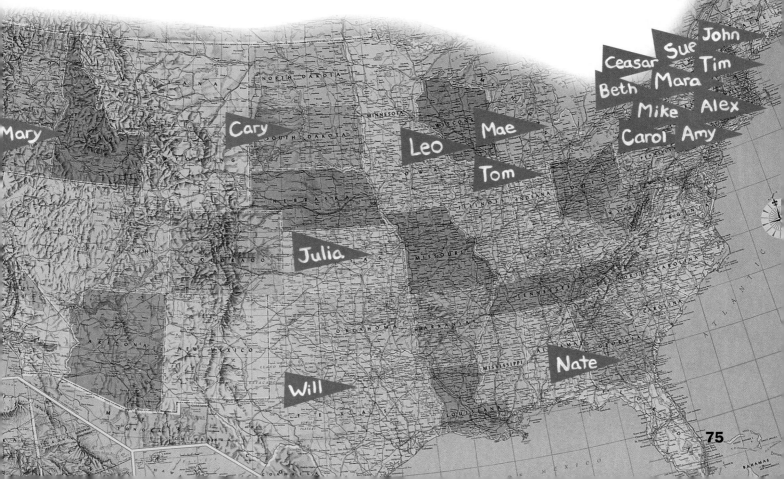

Why People Move

You just read that Tom's family moved to Boston because of his father's job. Many people move to a new city or country for a better job or a new opportunity. An **opportunity** is a chance for something better to happen. People move to find a better life for themselves or their children.

Some people move to the United States because they are seeking freedom. They want to be free to help choose the government or to follow a religion. They hope that in the United States they will be able to make more choices that will make their children's future better.

Throughout its history, people have come to the United States for many of these same reasons. They formed new communites here because they needed to feel safer than they had felt before. They set up systems of laws.

I moved here because of my father's job.

My parents wanted a place with better weather.

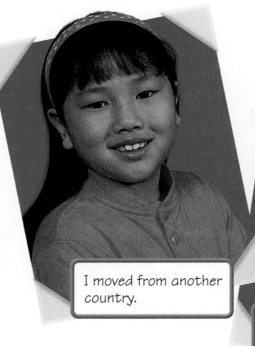

I moved from another country.

I moved here to a house in a different neighborhood.

The laws would protect everyone. Forming new communities gave people the chance to better their lives.

When people join a new community, they become a part of it. They might get jobs, go to school, and make friends there. They also have to follow the community's laws and respect other people. When everyone obeys the laws, they make their community a safe place in which to live.

REVIEW What is the same about the reasons why people move? What is different? ⊙ **Compare and Contrast**

Summarize the Lesson

- People move within the United States and from other countries.

- Some people move because they are seeking a better life.

- People have formed communities because they wanted to feel safe.

- Laws help make a community a good place to live.

LESSON 1 REVIEW

Check Facts and Main Ideas

1. ⊙ **Compare and Contrast** On a separate sheet of paper, fill in the diagram to compare and contrast reasons why people might move within the United States to reasons why people might move here from another country.

Compare/Alike	Contrast/Different

2. List reasons why people move to a new community.

3. Why have people formed new communities?

4. Why is it important for everyone to follow the laws of a community?

5. **Critical Thinking:** *Draw Conclusions* What are some of the things that you can do to keep your community a good place to live?

Link to ⛓ Art

Draw an Advertising Poster Suppose that you want to tell people why they should move into your community. Draw a poster that shows some of the good things that your community has to offer.

Boston,
Massachusetts

HAITI

Preview

Focus on the Main Idea
When people move to a new country, they blend parts of their old culture with parts of their new culture.

PLACES
Boston, Massachusetts
Haiti

VOCABULARY
immigrant
custom
ethnic group

Learning New Customs

 **You Are There** It's your first trip in an airplane. You strain to see out of the window. You cover your ears because the engines are so noisy. You're up in the air now! As you go higher, you can see the airport get smaller and smaller. Then you see the whole island far beneath the plane. It's getting farther and farther away.

Soon you don't see your home any more. You're going to a new home now. You know that people in your new country speak a different language. How will you make friends? What will you find?

 Compare and Contrast As you read, look for things that are the same and different in two communities.

Moving to a New Country

Hello! I'm Nicole. My family moved to **Boston, Massachusetts.** We're from **Haiti,** a country in the Caribbean Sea. In Haiti, we spoke Haitian Creole. We moved to a neighborhood where other immigrants from Haiti live. An **immigrant** is a person who moves into a country and lives there.

My new neighborhood friends helped us learn about living in the United States. They helped me learn English. We still follow some customs from Haiti. A **custom** is a way of doing things.

Some things here are the same as in Haiti. My school here is almost like my old school. I play soccer in the park, just like I used to. We ride buses and telephone our friends. My neighborhood now is different from where I lived in Haiti. Here I live in a city neighborhood, not a rural community like I did in Haiti.

▶ The mango and the plantain are fruits that grow in Haiti. The plantain looks like a banana.

REVIEW What is one way that Boston is like Nicole's community in Haiti? What is one way that they are different?

⟳ **Compare and Contrast**

79

There are many exciting places in Nicole's neighborhood. Let's explore!

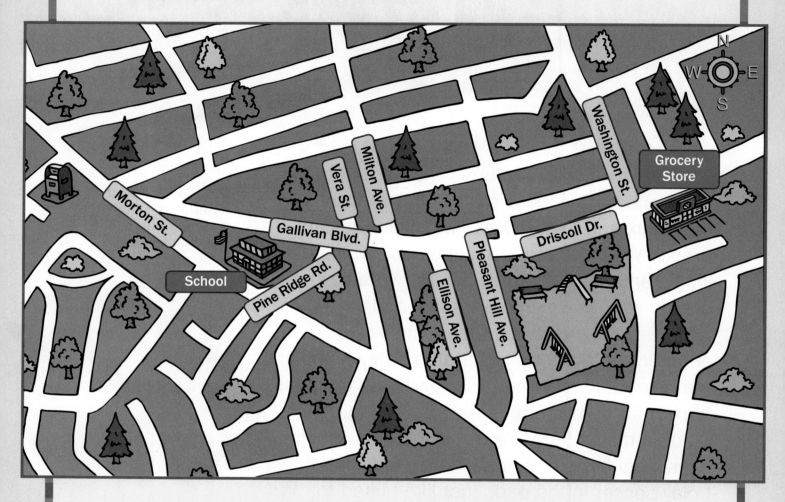

1. Nicole and her cousin are at school. Nicole wants to mail a letter to a friend in Haiti. Where would they go to mail it? What street would they take?

2. Then, they are going to the playground. What streets would they take?

3. Nicole needs to get something for her mother from the grocery store. What street is on the west side of the store and the east side of the playground?

Ethnic Neighborhoods

Nicole and her family are part of a Haitian ethnic group. An ethnic group is a group of people who have the same culture. In Nicole's ethnic neighborhood, people can speak in their home language. They can find stores that sell the foods they like to eat. They can follow the customs of their home culture. They can get used to a new culture while still being around things from their old culture.

REVIEW What things might a new immigrant to the United States have to learn? **Draw Conclusions**

Summarize the Lesson

- When people move to a new country, they often need to learn a new language and new customs.
- Some people who move to a new country live in ethnic neighborhoods.
- Ethnic neighborhoods can help people get used to their new country.

LESSON 2 REVIEW

Check Facts and Main Ideas

1. **Compare and Contrast** On a separate sheet of paper, fill in the diagram comparing Nicole's old community to her new one.

Compare/Alike	Contrast/Different

2. Why do you think Nicole's family moved to an ethnic neighborhood?

3. Give an example of how immigrants mix some of their old culture with their new culture.

4. What parts of their culture can immigrants find in an ethnic neighborhood?

5. Critical Thinking: *Apply Information* If you moved to a new country, what do you think would be the hardest thing to learn? What would be the easiest?

Link to Writing

Write a Letter How would you feel if you moved to another country? Write a letter to a friend telling about what you like about your new home. What do you miss about your old home?

A Country for Everyone

In the late 1800s, people came to our country from all over the world to live in freedom. Jane Addams wanted to help these immigrants get used to their new home.

BUILDING
CITIZENSHIP
Caring
Respect
Responsibility
★ Fairness
Honesty
Courage

Jane Addams's father taught her to treat everyone fairly. She knew that there were new immigrants to the United States who needed a fair chance to succeed. She opened a special place where immigrants in a neighborhood could get help so they could build new lives.

Jane Addams started Hull House in Chicago, Illinois, in 1889. Hull House quickly became an important part of the community. It had a health clinic, a child-care center, a kindergarten, and a playground. It had classes where people could learn English, art, music, and crafts. People who worked in Hull House also worked to get cleaner streets and better housing in the city.

Because of Jane Addams, many immigrants adjusted more easily to their new communities. Because of her work, Addams was given the Nobel Peace Prize in 1931. She was the first American woman to win this prize. The prize is given each year to a person who has worked hard to help world peace.

▶ Jane Addams worked to give immigrants a fair chance for a good life in the United States.

Fairness in Action

Link to Current Events As a class, find out about programs in your community that help people now. Who started them? How do they show that people think everyone should be treated fairly?

New York City, New York

Preview

Focus on the Main Idea
People came from all over the world to the United States.

PLACES
New York City, New York

PEOPLE
Mary Antin
Emanuel Gottlieb Leutze

VOCABULARY
ancestor
symbol

Where Did They Come From?

The year is 1919. A war in Europe has ended. You are finally able to leave Poland. Now, you are on a big ship on your way to the United States.

The ocean is rough, and the ship is rocking back and forth. You and your brother are exploring the ship. Your mother stays in the room with your little sisters.

You will be in New York City soon. You'll be happy to see the big statue in the harbor. But you'll be even happier to see your father. You haven't seen him for three years. Will he recognize you?

REVIEW As you read, look for details that tell why people move to the United States.
Main Idea and Details

They Came Long Ago

I'm Nancy. My grandma told me about how her family came to the United States. I love hearing stories about my **ancestors,** my relatives who lived long ago. My grandma's father came to the United States and worked to earn money to bring the family here later.

Other immigrants came here around the same time. My ancestors came from Europe many decades ago, in the early 1900s. A decade is ten years. Many other immigrants came here around the same time. The first thing they saw was the Statue of Liberty in the harbor of **New York City.** The statue was a symbol of freedom to these immigrants. A **symbol** is an object that represents something else. This statue meant that their long trip was over. They could now begin a new life in the United States.

▶ France gave the Statue of Liberty to the United States. It was completed in 1884.

REVIEW In the early 1900s, what part of the United States did many European immigrants reach first? **Main Idea and Details**

▶ Old photos show how families lived many years ago.

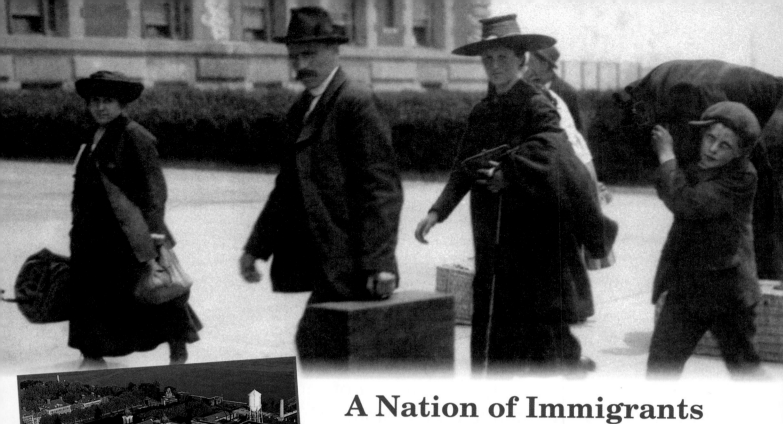

▶ Between 1892 and 1954, about 12 million immigrants passed through Ellis Island. They had to pass health tests, and their legal papers were checked. Now the main building on Ellis Island is an immigration museum.

A Nation of Immigrants

For decades, immigrants have come to the United States from almost every other country in the world. Some people wanted freedom or better opportunities. Some came because there was very little food in their home country. Others came to find jobs or to work on farms. Some came because they had no choice.

Many ships that came from Europe arrived first at Ellis Island in New York Harbor. Many immigrants from Asia arrived at Angel Island in San Francisco Bay. Immigrants also entered through other cities, such as Boston, Massachusetts; Galveston, Texas; and New Orleans, Louisiana.

The chart on the next page shows the decades in which large numbers of people came. It also shows the areas where some people came from.

REVIEW What were some reasons immigrants came to the United States?
Main Idea and Details

An Immigrant Writer

Some of the men and women who immigrated to the United States became famous writers. Their books and poems told their stories to people around the world.

One such writer was **Mary Antin.** Mary came to the United States from Russia when she was twelve years old. She and her family settled in Boston. Mary wrote about her experiences in Boston in a book called *The Promised Land.*

REVIEW How did people around the world learn about immigrants' stories?
Main Idea and Details

▶ Antin wrote about the first time she saw the Boston Public Library: "That I who was brought up to my teens almost without a book, should be set down in the midst of all the books that ever were written was a miracle as great as any on record."

FACT FILE

Times When Many Immigrants Came

Time Period	Where Many Were From
Before 1820	United Kingdom, countries of Western Africa such as those now known as Ghana, Togo, Benin, Nigeria, and Cameroon
1820–1860	Ireland, Germany, United Kingdom, France, Canada
1861–1890	Germany, United Kingdom, Ireland, Canada, Norway/Sweden
1891–1920	Italy, Austria/Hungary, Russia, United Kingdom, Germany
1961–1990	Mexico, Philippines, Canada, Korea, Cuba

▶ Many immigrants from Asia arrived at Angel Island in San Francisco Bay.

An Immigrant Artist

Some of the men and women who immigrated to the United States became artists. These people made beautiful paintings and wonderful statues. Like the immigrant writers, these artists shared their artwork with people all over the world. One such artist was German-born painter **Emanuel Gottlieb Leutze** (e MAN u ul GOT leeb lootz). Leutze came to America from Germany when he was nine years old. He lived and studied painting in Philadelphia. Perhaps his most famous painting was *Washington Crossing the Delaware.* He painted this scene in 1851.

▶ *Washington Crossing the Delaware* **was painted by Emanuel Gottlieb Leutze.**

Leutze's painting of George Washington during the Revolutionary War is known throughout the world. Visitors from all over the world have seen the figure of this famous American leading his troops into war. The painting is in the Metropolitan Museum of Art in New York City.

REVIEW How did Emanuel Leutze show the world a part of American history?
Main Idea and Details

Summarize the Lesson

- Immigrants came to the United States for many reasons.
- Immigrants have come to the United States from almost every part of the world.
- Immigrant writers and artists shared their talents with people around the world.

LESSON 3 REVIEW

Check Facts and Main Ideas
1. Main Idea and Details
On a separate sheet of paper, fill in the main idea.

```
┌─────────────────────────────────────────┐
│                                           │
└─────────────────────────────────────────┘
     ↑              ↑              ↑
```

| Immigrants came from Europe. | Immigrants came from South America. | Immigrants came from Africa and Asia. |

2. Why was the Statue of Liberty an important symbol to the immigrants?

3. Where have immigrants to the United States come from?

4. How have immigrant writers and artists shared their stories with the rest of the world?

5. **Critical Thinking:** *Interpret Visuals* Look at the painting on page 88. Which man is George Washington? How can you tell that he is the leader?

Link to ∞ Writing

Begin a Family History Ask your relatives where your family came from. Ask them if they know any special stories about how your family first came to this country. Write down the information. Share this history with your class.

Pittsburgh, Pennsylvania

Preview

Focus on the Main Idea
Immigrants to the United States had to start a new way of life.

PLACES
Pittsburgh, Pennsylvania

VOCABULARY
citizen
migration
Great Migration

A New Life in America

You Are There
Today is a very special day for you. Your grandparents are going to become citizens of the United States. They came to this country a long time ago. They have always wanted to be citizens. For the past months, they have studied hard and passed the test to become citizens. The ceremony is about to start. Your grandparents stand tall. They soon begin to say the oath, or promise, that all new citizens must say. "I hereby declare, on oath,...that I will support and defend the Constitution and laws of the United States of America...so help me God." You are so proud of your grandparents and of your country. You think about what it means to be a citizen.

REVIEW As you read this lesson, look for details about how people brought their culture to the United States from other countries. **Main Idea and Details**

A New Life

Immigrants who came to the United States in the early 1900s had to start a new way of life. Some people needed to learn a new language. Some needed to find homes and jobs. Some went to school to learn English or to learn skills to do new kinds of work.

Some immigrants moved into ethnic neighborhoods and lived in apartments in the cities. Others moved away from the cities to work on farms or live in small towns.

Most immigrants were eager to become citizens of the United States. A **citizen** is an official member of a community. In the United States, citizens can help make decisions that affect the community by voting.

REVIEW How can citizens help their community? **Main Idea and Details**

► Chinatown in San Francisco and Little Italy in New York are ethnic neighborhoods.

► These immigrants are taking the oath of citizenship.

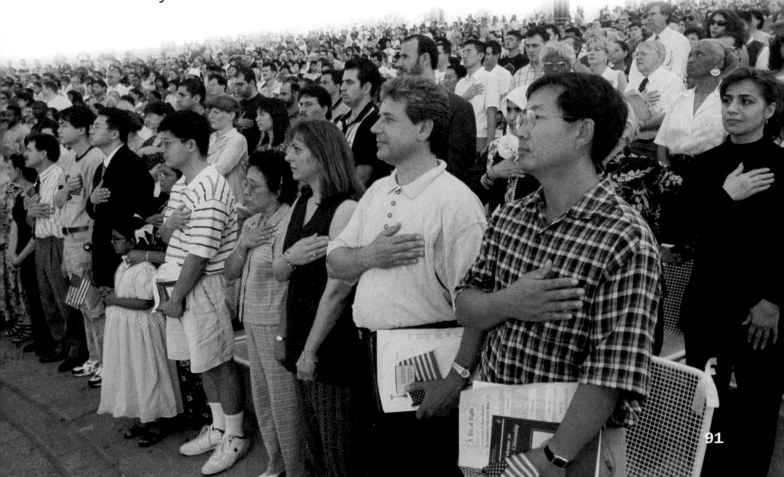

91

Education Past and Present

Some immigrants who came to the United States came from countries where the schools were very different. In some countries, children started at a younger age than children in the United States. In some places, the things that children learned were not the same things taught in the United States. They learned their native language. They learned about their country's history.

Immigrant children in the United States learned about the way of life and the government. They learned mathematics and science. Many children learned how to speak English for the very first time.

Today, education in the United States and in many countries around the world is still very different. Children who come to the United States from other countries today must still learn many of the things that children in the past had to learn.

REVIEW How is education in the United States and in other countries different in the past and today? **Compare and Contrast**

► Classrooms in Europe and in the United States around 1900 looked different from this present-day classroom in the United States.

92

The English were the first to play soccer. Today, soccer is a sport played in nearly every country in the world.

Sharing Cultures

In the early 1900s, ethnic neighborhoods grew, especially in cities on the oceans, such as New York City, Boston, and San Francisco. As neighborhoods grew, cities grew too. Each group of immigrants brought the customs of their culture with them.

As the cities grew, the cultures of the different groups started to blend. Gradually, the songs of one group were sung by others. Games and sports that one group brought were played by others. People started to eat foods that were introduced by people from other countries.

REVIEW Compare how countries around the world shared ways to have fun.

Compare and Contrast

The French created the game of tennis. Today, tennis is played around the world.

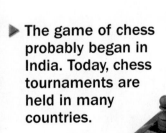

The game of chess probably began in India. Today, chess tournaments are held in many countries.

Moving North

At about the same time that many immigrants were coming from other countries, many African Americans left the South and moved to the North. Like the immigrants, they were looking for a better life. Moving in this way—from one part of a country to live in another part is called **migration.** Many African Americans moved to the North in the early 1900s. This was known as the Great Migration.

During the **Great Migration,** many African Americans left farms in the South. They moved into cities such as New York City, New York; Chicago, Illinois; and **Pittsburgh, Pennsylvania.** They were hoping to get good jobs in the factories there.

▶ Jacob Lawrence was an artist who painted a series of pictures about the Great Migration.

▶ This family is part of the Great Migration.

The African Americans brought their culture with them. Musicians, writers, and artists produced great works that have had lasting effects throughout the United States. You can read about Langston Hughes, who was one writer from this time, on pages 96-97.

REVIEW How was the Great Migration alike and different from immigration?
⟲ **Compare and Contrast**

Summarize the Lesson

- Immigrants that came to the United States had to start a new way of life.
- Communities around the world met their needs for education and recreation.
- Many African Americans moved from the South to the North during the Great Migration.

LESSON 4 REVIEW

Check Facts and Main Ideas

1. Main Idea and Details On a separate sheet of paper, fill in the main idea.

Immigrants had to learn a new language.

Immigrants had to learn new skills.

Immigrants had to find jobs and homes.

2. How can a citizen in the United States help make decisions for the community?

3. How were schools in other countries different from those in the United States?

4. Why did many African Americans move from the South to the North during the Great Migration?

5. **Critical Thinking:** *Draw Conclusions* Explain how people from different cultures can help make a community special.

Link to ⟟⟠ **Physical Education**

Make a Chart Find out information about sports that are played around the world. Make a chart that lists the sport and the country that each sport comes from. Share your information with the class.

Meet Langston Hughes

1902–1967 • Writer

Langston Hughes lived in many different places. He was born in Joplin, Missouri. Then he lived in the state of Kansas. When he was six years old, Langston, his mother, and his father lived in Mexico. Langston's father believed that African Americans could find good jobs there.

W. 132 ST.
ONE - WAY

Langston Hughes also lived in a part of New York City called Harlem.

For more information, go online to *Meet the People* at **www.sfsocialstudies.com**.

When Langston was in the second grade, he lived in Lawrence, Kansas. He felt lonely there, so he began to read books. He loved the beautiful language of books and the exciting characters. When he was thirteen, he lived in Lincoln, Illinois. His classmates there elected him Class Poet.

During the 1920s Langston Hughes became famous as one of the great writers of Harlem. Harlem is an area of New York City where many African Americans live. Much of Hughes's poetry was about the feelings of African Americans who lived in cities. Hughes also wrote short stories, plays, and novels. His work helped readers all over the world understand the hopes and dreams of African Americans.

Langston Hughes was called the Poet Laureate of Harlem. A Poet Laureate is a poet who is recognized as the best in what he or she does. Hughes was the best poet in Harlem.

BIOFACT

Learn from Biographies

Do you think that Langston Hughes's classmates helped him succeed as a poet? Why or why not?

Use Intermediate Directions

What? A **compass rose** shows you the **cardinal directions** on a map—north, south, east, and west. You use these directions to tell someone where you are going or to tell where you have been. Sometimes you are going somewhere in between one of these cardinal directions. Then you use an **intermediate direction**, or a direction that is in the middle of two cardinal directions. Then you can say, for example, that you are going **northwest** or **southeast.**

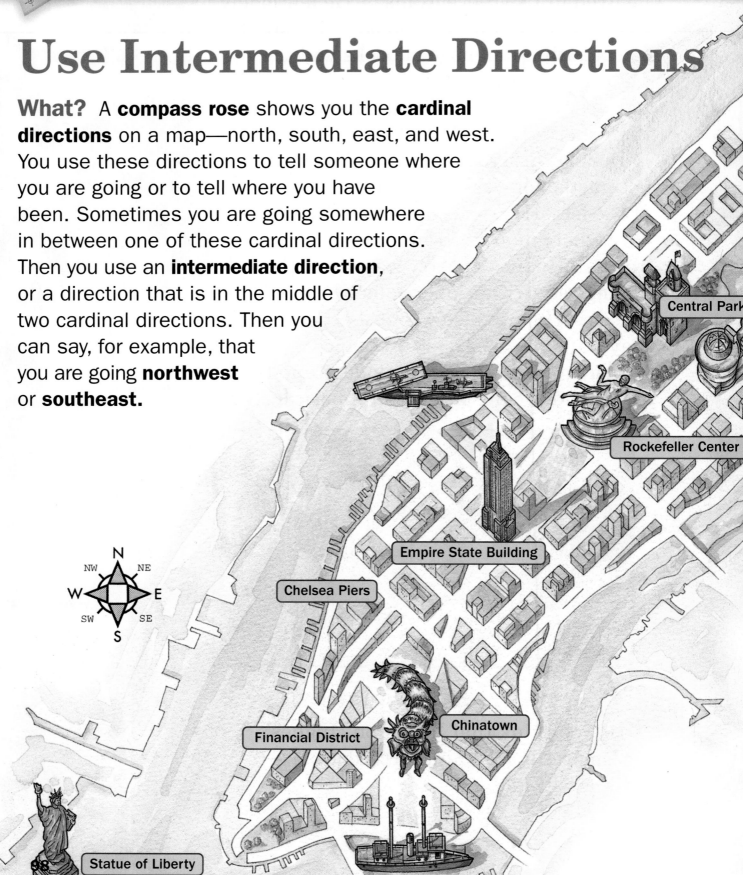

Central Park

Rockefeller Center

Empire State Building

Chelsea Piers

Financial District

Chinatown

Statue of Liberty

Why? Intermediate directions give you more choices when you try to explain where a place is located. You could say that the Statue of Liberty is south of the Empire State Building in New York, but that would not be exactly true. To be more exact, you can use intermediate directions. You can say that the Statue of Liberty is **southwest** of the Empire State Building.

How? To use intermediate directions, pick a place on a map. Imagine that the compass rose is directly over that place. Then trace along the arrows of the compass rose between that place and a second place.

To try it out, point to Chinatown on this map. If you traveled from Chinatown to Central Park, which way would you go? Trace along the compass rose in the same direction that you would go. You would go **northeast** to get to Central Park.

Think and Apply

1 Name the four cardinal directions.

2 Name the four intermediate directions.

3 Suppose you went southwest from Chinatown. What site in New York City would you see on the map?

4 If you went from Rockefeller Center to the Empire State Building, in which direction would you travel?

For more information, go online to the *Atlas* at **www.sfsocialstudies.com**.

Chapter Summary

 Compare and Contrast

On a separate sheet of paper, fill in the diagram. Compare and contrast why and how immigrants moved in the early 1900s or earlier times with why and how they move now.

Compare/Alike	Contrast/Different

Vocabulary

Fill in each blank with the vocabulary word that best completes the sentence.

1 Someone who moves into and lives in a country is an _____.

2 A _____ is an official member of a community.

3 An _____ is a chance that something better will happen.

4 Moving from one part of a country to live in another part is _____.

a. opportunity (p. 76)

b. immigrant (p. 79)

c. citizen (p. 91)

d. migration (p. 94)

Facts and Main Ideas

1. List some reasons why people move to a different community.

2. **Main Idea** How did a special culture grow in each community in the United States?

3. **Main Idea** How are ethnic neighborhoods helpful to people who live in them?

4. **Main Idea** Why did immigrants come to the United States in the late 1800s and early 1900s?

5. **Main Idea** How was the situation of African Americans moving to the North like the situation that new immigrants faced?

6. **Critical Thinking:** *Classify* each of the following items as a symbol or not a symbol: flag, an ancestor, freedom, the Statue of Liberty.

Internet Activity

To help with vocabulary, people, and terms, select the dictionary or encyclopedia from *Social Studies Library* at **www.sfsocialstudies.com.**

Apply Skills

Use Intermediate Directions

Answer the questions below the map.

1. What state is west of Pennsylvania?

2. What body of water is northwest of Pennsylvania?

3. What state is southeast of Pennsylvania?

Write About It

1. **Write a paragraph** about a restaurant in your community that serves a kind of food that came from another country.

2. **Write a journal entry** about moving to a new community. You might tell about how you think you might feel or how you felt if you actually did move.

3. **Write a newspaper article** about Jane Addams opening Hull House. Include an interview with Jane Addams.

Chapter 4 | Celebrations

Lesson 1

San Francisco, California

Communities celebrate cultures.

1

Lesson 2

New Orleans, Louisiana

Communities celebrate their histories.

2

Lesson 3

Washington, D.C.

Communities celebrate national holidays.

3

CANADA

UNITED STATES

San Francisco

Washington, D.C.

PACIFIC OCEAN

1

2

3

New Orleans

Gulf of Mexico

ATLANTIC OCEAN

MEXICO

Why We Remember

Celebrations are important to every culture. Families have celebrations. Communities have celebrations. And sometimes the whole country celebrates together. Celebrations help us remember important people and things that have happened in the past.

San Francisco, California

Preview

Focus on the Main Idea
Celebrations bring people of a community together.

PLACES
San Francisco, California

VOCABULARY
holiday
tradition

Celebrating Cultures

You Are There The streets in San Francisco are so crowded! The sound of the firecrackers is too loud! Smoke from the exploded firecrackers fills the air.

Then the parade passes. Big colorful paper dragons and lions dance around the marchers. When the gongs sound, you can almost feel the sidewalk shake.

When the parade is over, people leave to visit friends and relatives. You are going to celebrate Asian New Year with your family. As usual, your grandmother will have a big feast. Now you are really hungry!

Compare and Contrast As you read, think about ways celebrations are alike and different.

Families Celebrate Together

Families celebrate many different holidays together. A **holiday** is a special day for remembering an important person or event.

Often families celebrate holidays with special traditions. A **tradition** is a special way that a group does something. Traditions are repeated year after year as a part of celebrations. When people follow traditions, they feel that they are part of a community.

A tradition that many Asian families follow is to have a certain meal for Asian New Year. Some Asian communities also celebrate fall moon festivals. What special days does your family celebrate?

▶ Moon cakes are served as treats at Asian moon festivals.

You can read about a celebration in a Native American community in "End with a Poem" on page 128.

REVIEW How do traditions help keep cultures strong?

Main Idea and Details

▶ These children wear masks and carry star lanterns during an Asian moon festival.

Family Celebrations

Some holidays, such as Christmas and Hanukkah, are religious. Others, such as birthdays or anniversaries, are non-religious.

▶ Some people celebrate the birth of Jesus on Christmas. It is a tradition to go to church and light candles. Some families have a big holiday dinner. Some give gifts to members of the family.

▶ When Ramadan is over, Eid-al-Fitr (id ul FIT ur) is celebrated. Muslim adults do not eat or drink in the daytime during Ramadan. On Eid-al-Fitr they have a traditional holiday meal with special sweets. Children usually get gifts.

Many holidays have traditions, symbols, and music. A symbol is an object that represents something else. Cakes and candles are symbols that help people celebrate birthdays.

REVIEW What traditions of these family holidays are like yours? Which are different?

◎ **Compare and Contrast**

▶ Some families celebrate Hanukkah [HA-nuh-kuh], a Jewish holiday that lasts for eight days. People light a candle every night for eight nights. Some eat traditional foods and play special games. In some families, children get gifts.

▶ Some families celebrate Kwanzaa (KWAHN zuh) to honor their ancestors and their African American culture. The holiday is seven days long. People light candles. Each one stands for a special value, such as unity or responsibility.

Communities Celebrate Cultures

Many communities have celebrations that started in other countries. The celebrations honor the ethnic groups who helped build the community. These celebrations are sometimes called ethnic celebrations.

Cinco de Mayo (SIN ko day MY oh) means the fifth of May. It is a Mexican holiday that celebrates the victory of the Mexican people over the French who invaded their country. After a battle on May 5, 1862, the French left Mexico. For many people, the holiday is a symbol. It shows that the people of Mexico could become free of rulers from other countries.

Today many people in Mexico and other countries celebrate Cinco de Mayo. In the United States people dance in colorful clothes.

▶ These dancers are part of a Cinco de Mayo celebration in **San Francisco, California.**

They play music on guitars, and eat traditional Mexican food. They show that they are proud to be Mexican Americans.

St. Patrick's Day is celebrated in many communities around the United States and the world. The holiday started as a religious holiday in Ireland, a country in Europe.

On St. Patrick's Day both Irish and non-Irish people celebrate Irish culture. Some people honor Irish culture by wearing green clothing, watching parades, and eating green-dyed food.

REVIEW In what ways are Cinco de Mayo and St. Patrick's Day alike? How are they different? ⟳ **Compare and Contrast**

Summarize the Lesson

- People follow traditions when they celebrate holidays.
- Families celebrate religious and non-religious holidays.
- Communities celebrate to honor ethnic groups who helped build their community.

LESSON 1 REVIEW

Check Facts and Main Ideas

1. ⟳ **Compare and Contrast** On a separate sheet of paper, make a diagram like the one shown. Fill in the diagram with more facts to compare and contrast family celebrations and community celebrations.

Compare/Alike	Contrast/Different

2. Why do people celebrate holidays?

3. Why do groups of people follow traditions?

4. Tell how people in other countries and in the United States celebrate ethnic holidays such as Cinco de Mayo and St. Patrick's Day.

5. **Critical Thinking:** *Apply Information* Tell how you celebrate events that are important to you.

Link to ∞ Writing

Write a Journal Entry You were a guest at an ethnic celebration. Describe the celebration and what you did there.

Understand Hemispheres

What? Look at the picture of the globes below and on page 111. You can see Earth is really a sphere. A **sphere** is an object that is shaped like a ball. Look at the line drawn around the middle of the globe. This line is a symbol for the **equator.** At the equator, Earth can be divided into two parts. Each part is a **hemisphere.** *Hemi* means "half." The half of Earth north of the equator is called the **Northern Hemisphere.** The half of Earth south of the equator is called the **Southern Hemisphere.**

Another line on a globe runs north and south. It goes from the North Pole to the South Pole. This line is a symbol for the **prime meridian.** The prime meridian divides the Western Hemisphere from the Eastern Hemisphere. You can see these hemispheres in the globe pictures on the next page.

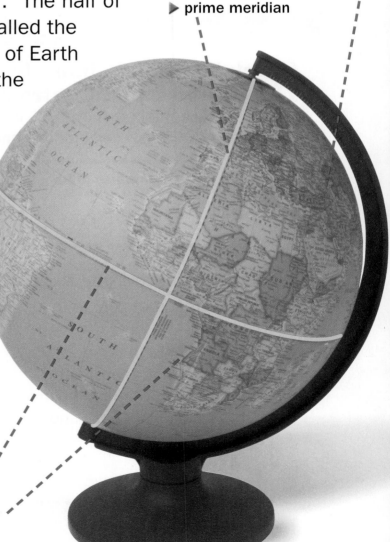

▶ Northern
Hemisphere

▶ prime meridian

▶ equator

▶ Southern
Hemisphere

110

Why? Thinking about the hemispheres of the Earth gives you a way to locate places on a map or globe.

How? To find out the hemisphere in which a place is located, first find the place on the globe. Then find the equator. Is the place north of the equator? If the place is north of the equator, it is in the Northern Hemisphere. If it is south of the equator, it is in the Southern Hemisphere. To find out if a place is in the Eastern Hemisphere or the Western Hemisphere, look at a map. For example, if a place is in North America, it is in the Western Hemisphere. If a place is in Australia, it is in the Eastern Hemisphere.

Look at the hemisphere globe pictures below. Find the continent of Australia. Is it closer to the North Pole or the South Pole? In which hemisphere is Australia?

Think and Apply

❶ Is the continent of North America in the Northern Hemisphere or the Southern Hemisphere? Is it in the Eastern Hemisphere or the Western Hemisphere?

❷ Find the continent of South America. Is it in the Eastern Hemisphere or the Western Hemisphere?

❸ Which continents are in both the Northern Hemisphere and the Southern Hemisphere? How do you know?

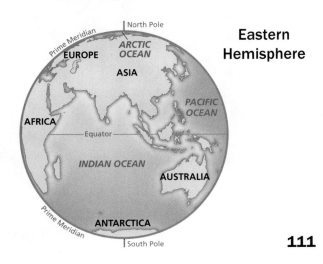

Western Hemisphere

Eastern Hemisphere

When groups of people dance together, they show that they are proud of their culture. Special costumes and symbols are traditional parts of many dances.

The dragon always has the traditional colors of bright yellow or gold.

The dragon dance is a part of the celebration of Chinese New Year.

People in northeast Spain do a special dance to celebrate the culture of their region.

Several dancers, one drummer, and one leader are needed for the dragon dance.

112

Mexican dancers wear feathers in special dances that celebrate their native culture.

The orissi dance is a tradition in eastern India.

This Ute chief is dressed for a competition in which the dances are taught to the younger people.

Gold, green, and white are the favorite colors in costumes for traditional Irish dances.

In Kenya, in east Africa, people perform Kikuyu dances for other people to watch.

New Orleans, Louisiana

Celebrating a Community's Past

Focus on the Main Idea
Communities have special celebrations to honor their people and their history.

PLACES
New Orleans, Louisiana

PEOPLE
David "Davy" Crockett

VOCABULARY
livestock

You Are There
All around you can feel the excitement of crowds and music. Today your family is going to the New Orleans Jazz and Heritage Festival!

Listen to the music of the trumpets and the drums! Look at the artwork of the craftspeople. Taste all of the different kinds of food sold in stands along the street.

You have been to some other festivals and fairs. Lots of communities have them. But you have never been to one like this!

Compare and Contrast As you read, compare one of these community celebrations to the community celebrations where you live.

▶ People enjoy special foods at community celebrations.

Community Celebrations

Many communities hold celebrations remembering important people or events. These celebrations bring the people of a community together.

Have you ever been to a fair? Community and state fairs bring people together to celebrate and share good times with friends. Some communities may hold a Founders Day, a day that remembers the people who started their community. Some communities, like **New Orleans, Louisiana,** hold a special heritage festival honoring the history and culture of the people who live there.

REVIEW Why do communities hold community celebrations?
Make Generalizations

▶ A vocal performer at a New Orleans Jazz and Heritage Festival

Busy Summer

by Aileen Fisher

State fairs usually take place during summer.
Here is a poem about other things that happen in summer.

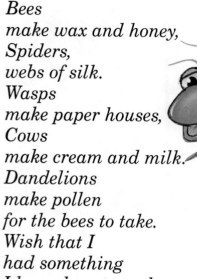

Bees
make wax and honey,
Spiders,
webs of silk.
Wasps
make paper houses,
Cows
make cream and milk.
Dandelions
make pollen
for the bees to take.
Wish that I
had something
I knew how to make.

Kansas State Fair

State fairs bring people together to celebrate the hard work they have done all year. People from all areas of Kansas bring the best examples of their work for others to see at the state fair in Hutchinson, Kansas. The fair is held in September, when the crops are ready to eat.

People bring many different things to display at the fair. Farmers show their livestock. **Livestock** are farm animals raised on local farms. On tables people spread out homemade arts and crafts items, homegrown plants and vegetables, and carefully prepared baked goods. Many of these displays are judged, and ribbons are passed out to the winners. Even the animals can win prizes!

REVIEW How is visiting the fair like going to a museum? ⟳ **Compare and Contrast**

Remembering Their Past

Some communities gather to remember events that happened long ago. In San Antonio, Texas, a celebration takes place every year to remember the Battle of the Alamo. It was fought by Texas settlers against the Mexican Army. Many tales have been told about **David "Davy" Crockett,** who led a group from Tennessee at the Battle of the Alamo.

REVIEW What did David Crockett do in San Antonio, Texas?
Main Idea and Details

Summarize the Lesson

- Fairs bring people together to celebrate the hard work they have done all year.
- Some communities have events to remember things that happened long ago.

LESSON 2 REVIEW

Check Facts and Main Ideas

1. **Compare and Contrast** On a separate sheet of paper, make a diagram like the one shown. Fill in the diagram with facts to compare and contrast kinds of community celebrations.

Compare/Alike	Contrast/Different

2. Why do some communities have a heritage festival?

3. When do state fairs usually take place?

4. What is one reason why state fairs take place?

5. **Critical Thinking: Apply Information** Why do communities celebrate their history?

Link to ⟷ **Mathematics**

Make Change Suppose that you are helping your parents at their booth at a state fair. A jar of your mother's jam costs $1.50. A customer gives you $5.00. How much change should you give?

Meet
David Crockett

1786–1836 Frontiersman

David "Davy" Crockett was born in 1786 in a territory that became the state of Tennessee. When Davy was 12 years old, his parents had him work for a farmer. Davy got paid for driving the farmer's cattle from Tennessee over the mountains to Virginia.

Davy did not get to go to school until he was thirteen years old. When his father sent him to work for another farmer, that farmer let Davy go to school. He learned skills that he would need later.

As an adult, Davy Crockett was in the United States Army. He also was elected to work for the state government of Tennessee and the U.S. Congress.

In 1835, Davy Crockett decided to travel to a new frontier called Texas. *Frontier* means the farthest part of the settled land. He had heard about battles there between Texas settlers and the Mexican government. When Davy Crockett arrived in San Antonio, he went to the Alamo. The Alamo was the fort for the Texas volunteer soldiers. Soon he became a leader of the soldiers when the Mexican Army began attacking the Alamo. After thirteen days, the Mexican Army won the battle. Davy Crockett probably died in that battle or shortly afterward.

Davy Crockett wore this vest. It is made of deerskin and decorated with beads.

BIOFACT

Learn from Biographies

Why was Davy Crockett considered a man of the frontier?

For more information, go online to *Meet the People* at **www.sfsocialstudies.com.**

Plymouth, Massachusetts

Washington, D.C.

Celebrations Across Our Nation

Preview

Focus on the Main Idea
National holidays are celebrated in communities across the country.

PLACES
Washington, D.C.
Plymouth, Massachusetts

VOCABULARY
Civil Rights Movement

EVENTS
Memorial Day
Veterans Day
Thanksgiving Day

You Are There
You are standing next to your grandfather at the Tomb of the Unknown Soldier near Washington, D.C. You watch as the President places flowers at the tomb. The tomb honors all of the American soldiers whose names we do not know who were killed in wars.

You know that these Memorial Day ceremonies honor people who fought and died for our country. You know that those who served the country deserve special honors. As the flag snaps in the breeze, you feel proud to be an American.

Main Idea and Details
As you read, find the main ideas behind the holidays that Americans observe.

Holidays for Freedom

Memorial Day is a national holiday. We celebrate it on the last Monday in May.

Veterans Day honors all who have served in the United States armed forces. We celebrate it on November 11.

Another national holiday, Martin Luther King, Jr., Day, also remembers a fight for freedom. Dr. King led the **Civil Rights Movement,** a drive for equal treatment of all citizens. He wanted fair treatment of African Americans. King did not believe in violence. He fought by using words to convince people to make changes.

In honor of Dr. Martin Luther King, Jr., the third Monday in January is a national holiday. People celebrate his life and the ideas that were important to him.

▶ **World War I veterans**

REVIEW How was the way Dr. King fought for freedom different from the way soldiers fight for freedom? How was it alike?

◎ **Compare and Contrast**

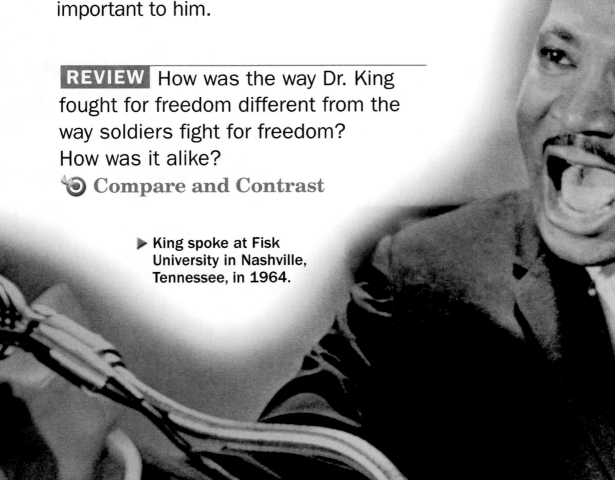

▶ **King spoke at Fisk University in Nashville, Tennessee, in 1964.**

Being Thankful

Thanksgiving Day is an American holiday that many families and communities celebrate. Across the country we give thanks for the good things that happened during the year.

In 1621, the settlers of **Plymouth, Massachusetts,** celebrated one of the first Thanksgivings. The settlers were known as Pilgrims. They had come from England because they wanted to be free to practice their religion.

Their first winter in Plymouth had been hard. The next fall, the Pilgrims wanted to give thanks to God for their good harvest and for living through the hard winter.

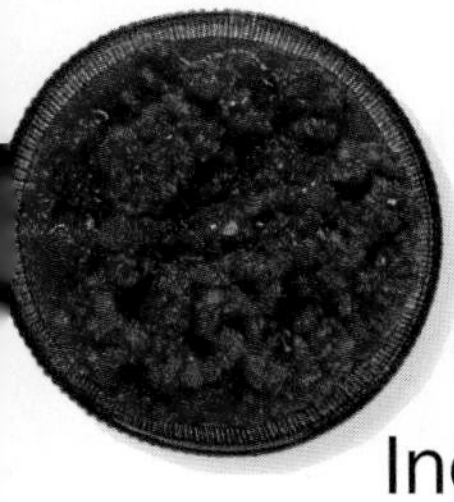

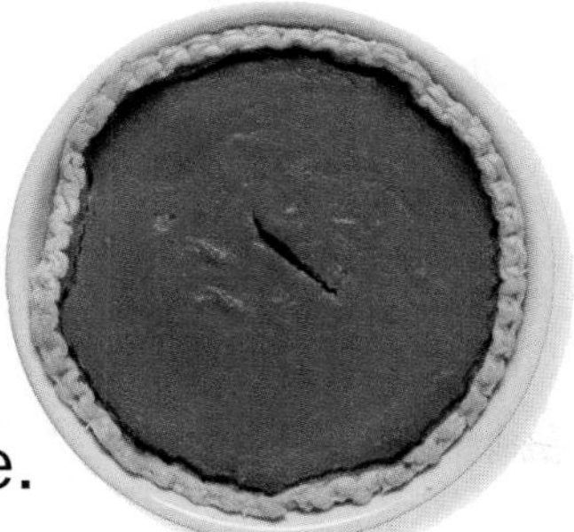

They also wanted to thank the Wampanoag Indians who welcomed them and helped them survive.

Today we celebrate by giving thanks for what we have. Families gather together and have a special meal. Do you eat special foods at Thanksgiving?

REVIEW How is the Pilgrims' Thanksgiving similar to the celebration of Thanksgiving today? How is it different?
Compare and Contrast

Summarize the Lesson

- Some national celebrations honor those who fought or died in wars to keep our country free.
- Martin Luther King, Jr., fought for fair treatment of everyone.
- Thanksgiving Day celebrates being thankful for good things.

LESSON 3 REVIEW

Check Facts and Main Ideas

1. **Main Idea and Details** On a separate sheet of paper, fill in the diagram to show more details about the main idea.

Americans have holidays to celebrate freedom.

Memorial Day honors people who fought and died in wars for freedom.

2. What was the Civil Rights Movement?
3. How did Dr. Martin Luther King, Jr., try to make changes in the United States?
4. Why did the Pilgrims come to America?
5. **Critical Thinking:** ***Make Inferences*** Why did the Pilgrims need help from the Wampanoag?

Link to Art

Sketch a Float Plan Suppose that you and your friends are going to build a float for a parade. Draw a picture that shows how your float will look.

N'cwala

An African Thanksgiving

Many people all over the world celebrate the harvesting of crops at the end of the growing season. They give thanks for a good harvest by holding a celebration. The Ngoni (na GO nee) people in Zambia (ZAM bee a) hold a celebration called N'cwala (enk WA la).

N'cwala is a harvest celebration that includes food, dancing, and music. Musical instruments such as drums, flutes, bells, and rattles are played. The festival is a way of showing thanks for a good yearly crop. To honor their king, the Ngoni people give the first fruits and vegetables from the harvest to him.

▶ **The Paramount Chief is the king of the Ngoni. He rules twelve local chiefs.**

▶ **Women from visiting villages make beef stew for the Paramount Chief during N'cwala.**

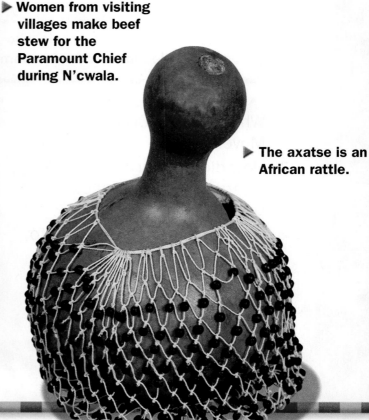

▶ **The axatse is an African rattle.**

124

▷ Each of the twelve groups of local men performs a warrior dance. The Paramount Chief decides which group is the best.

▷ The kora, African drum, and gourd shaker are traditional African musical instruments.

▷ Most Ngoni dancers wear costumes made of animal skins. They carry shields and warrior sticks.

125

Chapter Summary

 Compare and Contrast

On a separate sheet of paper, draw the diagram shown below. Fill in the boxes to compare and contrast community holidays and national holidays.

Compare/Alike	**Contrast/Different**
People take time from their work to remember special events.	The whole country celebrates national holidays.

Vocabulary

Fill in each blank with the vocabulary word that best completes the sentence.

1 On _____ we remember the people who died in our country's wars.

2 Having a special meal every year to celebrate a holiday like Thanksgiving is a _____.

3 Cinco de Mayo is an ethnic _____.

4 Farmers often raise _____ in addition to growing crops.

5 Dr. Martin Luther King, Jr., led the _____ in the United States.

a. holiday (p. 105)

b. tradition (p. 105)

c. livestock (p. 116)

d. Civil Rights Movement (p. 121)

e. Memorial Day (p. 121)

Facts and Main Ideas

1 What kind of music is part of New Orleans culture?

2 Whom did the Wampanoag help to survive many years ago in Plymouth?

3 **Main Idea** What kinds of things make a holiday special?

4 **Main Idea** How is a state fair like a holiday?

5 **Main Idea** What did Dr. Martin Luther King, Jr., believe in?

6 **Critical Thinking:** *Evaluate* Tell why Cinco de Mayo and Memorial Day are not religious holidays.

Internet Activity

To get help with vocabulary, people, and terms, select the dictionary or encyclopedia from *Social Studies Library* at **www.sfsocialstudies.com.**

Write About It

1 **Write a greeting card** for your favorite holiday. Your card should show and tell what you like about the holiday.

2 **Write about David Crockett** Why do many people in the United States think he is a hero? Do you think he is a hero to the people in Mexico? Tell why or why not.

3 **Write about Thanksgiving and N'cwala** How are they alike? How are they different?

Apply Skills

Look at the hemisphere maps on page 111 or use a globe. Choose a continent that you would like to visit. Find it on the map or globe. Then answer these questions.

- Is your continent above, below, or across the equator?

- Is it in the Northern Hemisphere, the Southern Hemisphere, or both?

- Is it in the Eastern Hemisphere, the Western Hemisphere, or both?

Celebration

Alonzo Lopez

*Alonzo Lopez was born in Arizona. In this poem
he writes about how celebrating with others
makes him feel like part of his community.*

I shall dance tonight.
When the dusk comes crawling,
There will be dancing
   and feasting.
I shall dance with the others
   in circles,
     in leaps,
       in stomps.
Laughter and talk
   will weave into the night,
Among the fires
   of my people.
Games will be played
And I shall be
   a part of it.

Test Talk

Locate key words in the text.

Main Ideas and Vocabulary

TEST PREP

Read the passage. Then answer the questions.

Communities change as people move from place to place. People today move for many different reasons. Some people have to move because of their jobs. Other people move because they want better schools for their children, better jobs for themselves, or nicer places to live. Some people move to feel safer. Other people move to have freedom.

The reasons people move today are the same as the reasons many of our <u>ancestors</u> came to America. The Pilgrims came for religious freedom. Some <u>immigrants</u> came to America for the opportunity to work or to own their own land. Becoming a United States citizen was important to many of them.

People from many different cultures and ethnic groups live in the United States today. We celebrate many different holidays and traditions from these cultures.

1 According to the passage, communities change because people

  A celebrate ethnic holidays.

  B become citizens.

  C move from place to place.

  D want to be safe.

2 What does the word *ancestors* mean in this passage?

  A parents

  B relatives who lived long ago

  C relatives who you live near

  D second cousins

3 What does *immigrants* mean in this passage?

  A people who belong to an ethnic group

  B people who move for religious freedom

  C new citizens

  D people who move to a country and live there

Vocabulary

Copy the sentences. Fill in each empty space with the vocabulary word or words that fit best.

a. custom (p. 79)

b. ethnic groups (p. 81)

c. Great Migration (p. 94)

d. symbol (p. 85)

1 The _____ was the movement of African Americans from the South to cities in the North.

2 Shaking hands when you meet someone new is an American _____.

3 A big city is often home to many _____.

4 The flag is a _____ of our country.

Apply Skills

Use Intermediate Directions Look at this map of a carnival. Find the compass rose. Then use intermediate directions to answer the questions.

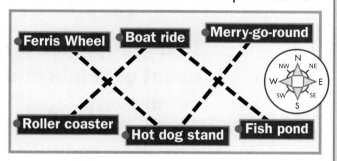

1 In what direction would you walk to get from the roller coaster to the boat ride?

2 In what direction would you walk to get from the merry-go-round to the hot dog stand?

3 In what direction would you walk to get from the fish pond to the boat ride?

Read on Your Own

Look for books like these in the library.

Write and Share

Research a Culture What holidays, symbols, traditions, and foods are important to people in that culture? Make a poster about the culture. Use drawings with captions to tell about it. Explain your poster to your classmates.

UNIT 2 Project

Celebrate!

In a group, give a report about an event or celebration in your community.

1 **Choose** a community event or celebration.

2 **Find out** about the history and reasons for the celebration. Write questions and answers about the celebration.

3 **Choose** a person who will play the role of TV news reporter. This person will interview group members.

4 **Make** a backdrop for your interview.

5 **Present** your eyewitness news report to the class.

Internet Activity

Explore celebrations on the Internet.
Go to www.sfsocialstudies.com/activities and select your grade and unit.

Where Are Communities?

Why do communities start and grow in certain places?

UNIT 3

Begin with a Poem

If I Built a City

by K. A. Singer

If I built a city
I'd build it on a river
I'd build it on a river
Not far from the sea.
I'd fill it with boats!
I'd fill it with trains!
I'd fill it with parks and schools
and all kinds of houses
And . . . the people would come.
And people would come and live near me.

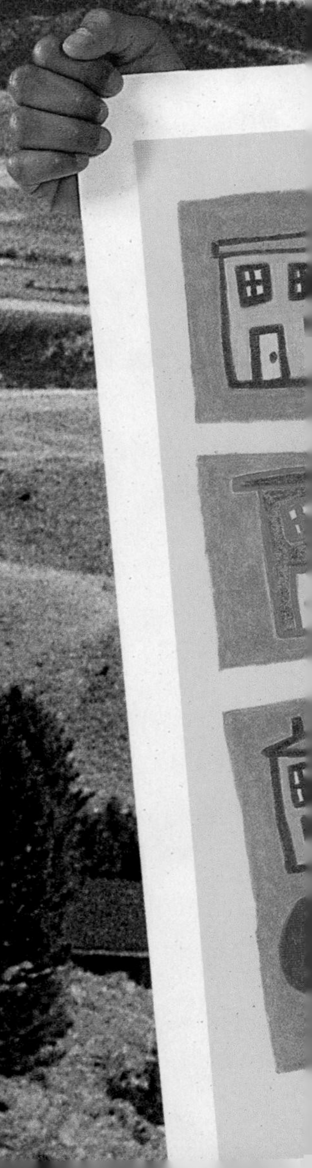

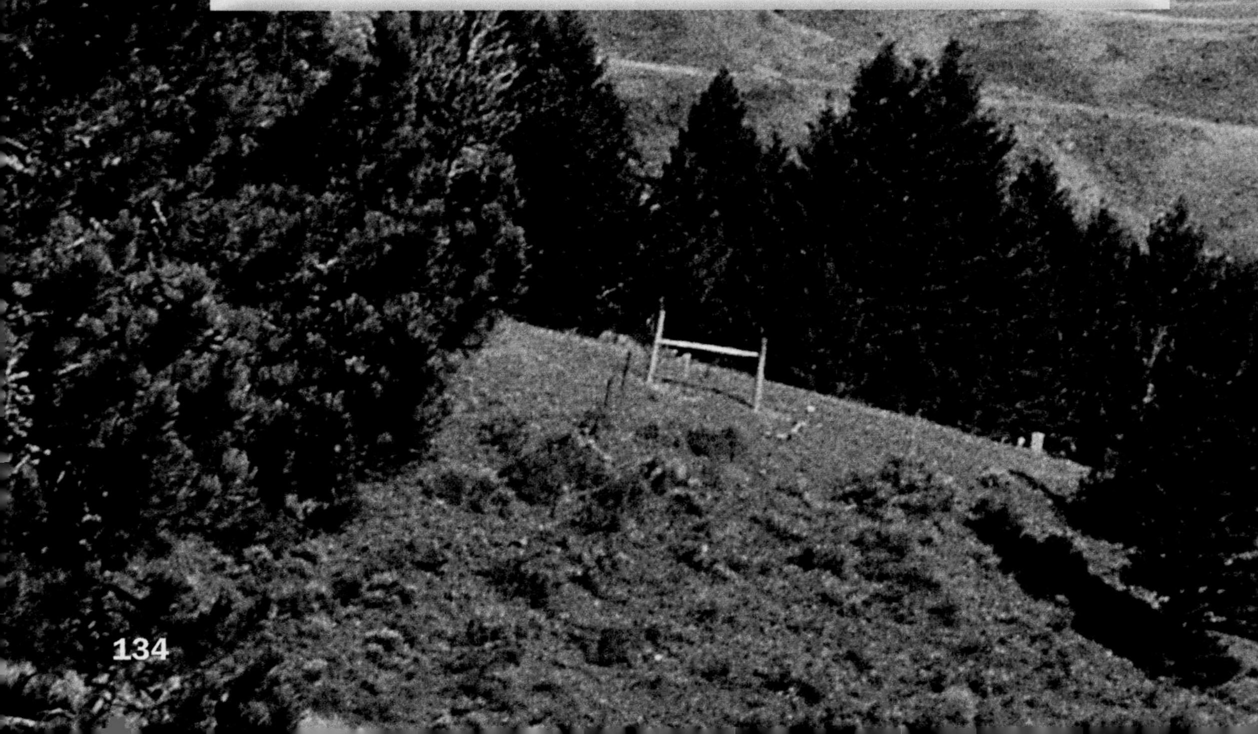

Welcome to My Community

Communities Across the Country

▶ Orchids grow on Kauai, an island in the state of Hawaii. A mountain on Kauai is the wettest place in the United States. It gets 450 to 460 inches of rain a year.

▶ Bozeman, Montana, is the home of the Museum of the Rockies. It contains many dinosaur bones and eggs found in Montana by Dr. Jack Horner, who works for the museum.

▶ After oil was discovered there in 1901, Beaumont, Texas, grew from a village to a community of 30,000 people in one month! You can visit the Spindletop-Gladys City Boomtown Museum.

▷ The National Institute for Fitness and Sport is in Indianapolis, Indiana. There you can learn about sports of all kinds, from golf to rock-climbing!

▶ The town of Barrow, Alaska, is the northernmost community in the United States. Because it is so far north, the sun rises in May and does not set for about three months. The sun sets in November and does not rise again for almost two months!

Weather in Some Communities

Draw Conclusions

Facts and details are small pieces of information.	**A conclusion** is a decision or opinion you make after you think about some facts and details.

- To draw a conclusion, you use details and facts as clues about what happens and why.

- You also use what you know to make a decision or form an opinion that makes sense of events.

Read this description of a natural hazard, a flood. Then look at another reader's conclusion below. The details that led to the conclusion are highlighted.

The rain began at 10:00 in the evening. It came down very, very hard. More than an inch fell each hour. By 6:00 the next morning, the river had overflowed its banks. Water rushed down the streets. People woke up to find that their living rooms looked like swimming pools.

Conclusion: The town flooded because the river overflowed its banks.

Drawing Conclusions About a Tornado

One spring day, the sky over Wichita, Kansas, began to look strange. Low, purple clouds hung down, and the wind blew hard. Suddenly a loud alarm sounded. People all over the city rushed for shelter.

A tornado touched down, rushing through a suburb, picking up objects and throwing them far and wide.

As the tornado moved through the community, trucks were picked up and tossed as if they were toys. The sound of the wind was like a train speeding by. Then, as quickly as it had come, the tornado was gone. A lot of damage had been done by this natural hazard, but no one was hurt.

Use the reading strategy of drawing conclusions to answer these questions.

1. What conclusion can you draw about the strength of the wind in a tornado? What sentences helped you draw this conclusion?

2. How might you know that a tornado is coming your way?

3. What conclusion can you draw about the destruction tornadoes can do?

Chapter 5 Community Environments

Lesson 1

Bozeman, Montana

Communities have different environments.

1

Lesson 2

Kauai, Hawaii

People in different areas adapt to different climates.

2

Lesson 3

Beaumont, Texas

Communities grow around natural resources.

3

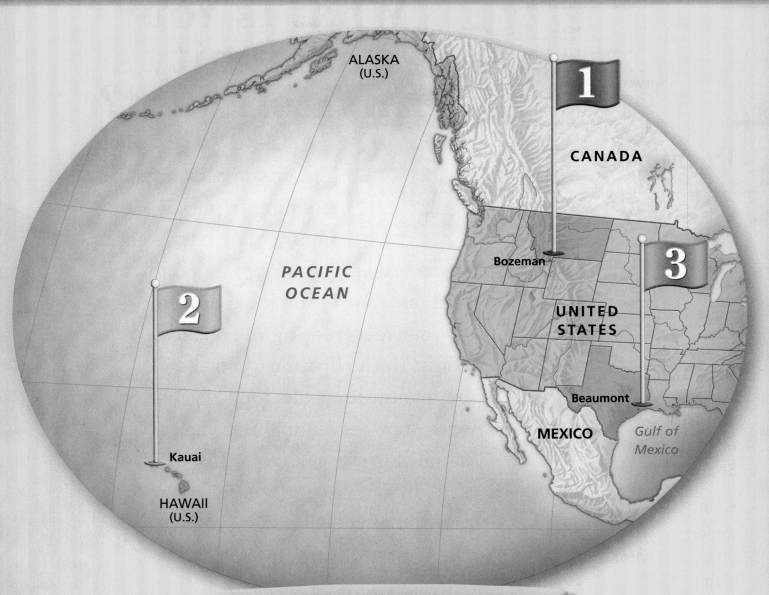

Why We Remember

A community's location, climate, and natural resources affect the people who live there. A community must have transportation to grow. Learning about all these parts of a community helps us understand its past, present, and future.

Bozéman, Montana
NORTHEAST
MIDWEST
WEST
SOUTHWEST   SOUTHEAST

Preview

Focus on the Main Idea
Communities are started in areas with different physical environments.

PLACES

West region
Northeast region
Southeast region
Midwest region
Southwest region

VOCABULARY

region
physical environment
climate
landform
ecosystem
adapt

What Is Your Community's Environment?

You Are There
You are on a fishing and camping trip with your family. Your tent is set up near a river. The water runs cold and fast. You stand knee-deep in it, your feet freezing in rubber boots. In the distance, you see big mountain peaks topped with snow—even in July! The smell of evergreen trees fills the air. You've caught a fish on the end of your line. Where in the United States are you?

Draw Conclusions
As you read, think about the details of the environment of each community. Details will help you draw conclusions about each environment.

Katrinka's Western Community

Hi! I'm Katrinka. I live in Bozeman, Montana. Montana is in the **West region** of the United States. I like to fish for trout, but I enjoy other outdoor activities too. I like to hike and ski in the mountains and paddle a kayak on the Gallatin River.

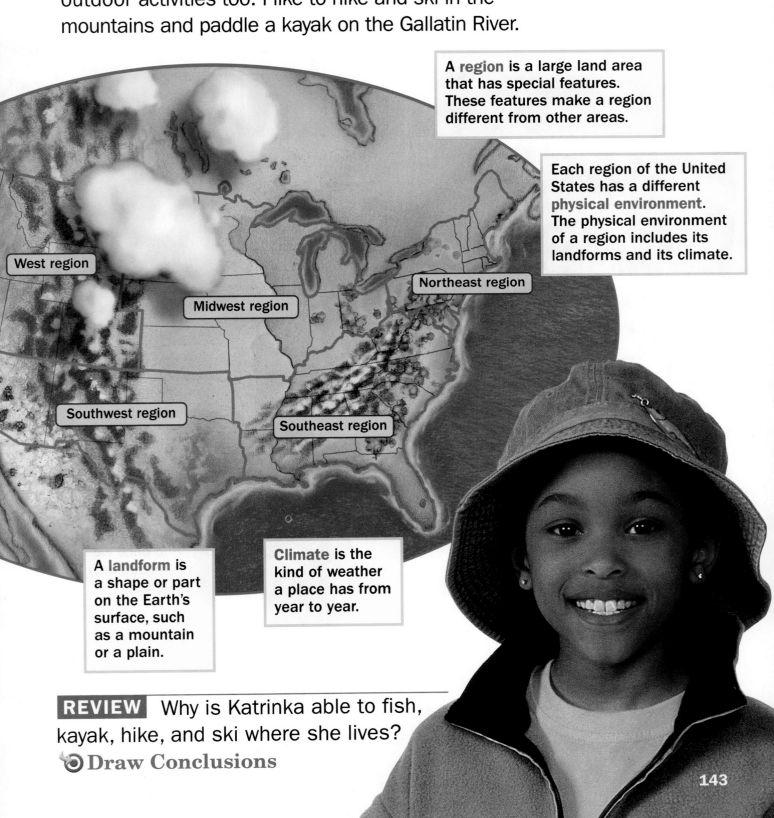

A **region** is a large land area that has special features. These features make a region different from other areas.

Each region of the United States has a different **physical environment**. The physical environment of a region includes its landforms and its climate.

West region

Midwest region

Northeast region

Southwest region

Southeast region

A **landform** is a shape or part on the Earth's surface, such as a mountain or a plain.

Climate is the kind of weather a place has from year to year.

REVIEW Why is Katrinka able to fish, kayak, hike, and ski where she lives?

Draw Conclusions

Communities in the Regions

People have started communities in all regions of the United States. Read to see how people use the physical environments of their communities. Are these communities similar to or different from yours?

Hi! I'm Kevin

from Stamford, Connecticut. My town is in the **Northeast region.** I love hiking in the hills and forests that are near the city. I've seen deer, fox, snakes, and turtles in the woods!

Hi! I'm Tonya

from Charleston, South Carolina in the **Southeast region.** When we go boating on the river, we pass rice fields and trees hung with Spanish moss. We usually see blue herons, and once we surprised an alligator!

The area around each community looks different. Each region has different landforms. Different kinds of plants and wild animals live in each region. Each physical environment and all the living things in it work together in a system called an **ecosystem.** Rivers, forests, and deserts are kinds of ecosystems.

REVIEW Suppose your family is looking for a new community in which to live. Your favorite activities are sailing and swimming. What type of physical environment would you look for? **⊚ Draw Conclusions**

Hi! I'm Nick, and I live in Omaha, Nebraska, in the **Midwest region.** I love to ride my bike on the flat bicycle paths. When I pedal along the banks of the Missouri River, I watch the water flow by. I sometimes hear coyotes in the distance.

Hi! I'm Winona from Tucson, Arizona, in the **Southwest region.** Around here you can see canyons, deserts, rivers, and mountains. I like to hike in Saguaro National Park and take photographs of cactuses, snakes, and desert toads.

145

Changes in People and Places

In every region, people adapt to the physical environment. To **adapt** means to change the way you do something.

When people adapt to their physical environment, they learn to change something about themselves in order to live in a certain place. In Bozeman, it is very cold in the winter. People adapt to living in cold places by heating their buildings and wearing warm clothes.

People also adapt by changing the environment to fit their needs. For example, people cut down trees to use for lumber to build houses. People have also cut down forests in order to have land to grow crops to eat and sell. They built roads to transport crops and other goods.

▶ How has Katrinka adapted to the cold climate?

People change the physical environment even more by building railroads and cities across the land. In some dry places in the Southwest region, many farmers have changed their environment by irrigating, or bringing in water for their crops. Many food plants that could not grow in the region now grow very well because of the water that the farmers bring in.

REVIEW Why do people change their environment? **⟳ Draw Conclusions**

Summarize the Lesson

- Each region in the United States has its own landforms and climate.
- People use the environment for a variety of activities.
- People have adapted to their physical environments.
- People have changed their environments in many ways.

LESSON 1 ⟩ REVIEW

Check Facts and Main Ideas

1. **⟳ Draw Conclusions** On a separate sheet of paper, draw a graphic organizer like the one shown. Choose a community from this lesson. Use the details you read about to draw a conclusion about how the physical environment affects life in the community.

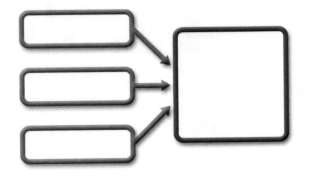

2. What makes up the physical environment of a region?
3. List five regions of the United States and tell about their physical environments.
4. How do people adapt to and change their environment?
5. **Critical Thinking: *Predict*** How might building a large new highway affect a rural community?

Link to ⟡ Science

Identify Trees Find out about one kind of tree found in each of the United States regions. Use an encyclopedia or almanac. Write a description of each tree.

147

The United States has many different geographical features. The United States has forests and deserts. Mountains stretch from north to south. You will find mighty rivers and enormous lakes across the nation. In the middle of the country, farmers grow enough food to feed millions of people.

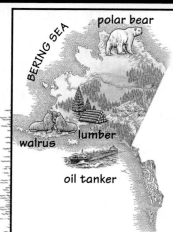

ALASKA
Alaska is the 49th state in our country. Like Hawaii, it is separated from the rest of the United States. Alaska lies in the northwestern part of North America.

polar bear
BERING SEA
walrus
lumber
oil tanker

salmon
WASHINGTON
harvesting wheat
MONTANA
skiing
Devil's Tower
OREGON
IDAHO
cougar
WYOMING
coyote
NEVADA
THE UNITED STA
Golden Gate Bridge
San Francisco
UTAH
COLORADO
CALIFORNIA
Grand Canyon
HOLLYWOOD
Hollywood
orange growing
ARIZONA
Los Angeles
Phoenix
Pueblo farmer
NEW MEXIC

Can you find San Francisco on the map? It is on the West Coast near the Golden Gate Bridge.

The Grand Canyon in Arizona is one of the largest canyons in the world. The Colorado River cut through the Rocky Mountains to form this natural feature. Look in the southwest part of the United States to find the Grand Canyon.

Hawaii is the 50th state in our country. This state is really a group of islands in the Pacific Ocean. On the big island of Hawaii you can see a volcano that sends out lava!

Kauai
Molokai
Oahu
Maui
Hawaii
HAWAII

Take a trip from the Golden Gate Bridge to the Statue of Liberty. In what state would you begin? In what state would you end?

Can you find a state that has a cattle rancher in it? That's the state of Texas. Cattle ranching is very important in Texas. Texas has large grassy areas where the cattle can get the food they need.

CANADA

bison

MINNESOTA

MICHIGAN

MAINE

VERMONT
NEW
HAMPSHIRE
Boston
MASSACHUSETTS
RHODE ISLAND
CONNECTICUT

TH DAKOTA

H DAKOTA
Mount Rushmore

WISCONSIN

MICHIGAN

car industry

Detroit

NEW
YORK

Statue of Liberty
New York

NEW JERSEY
PENNSYLVANIA

football

Chicago

OHIO

DELAWARE
MARYLAND
Washington, D. C.
(District of Columbia)

IOWA

NEBRASKA

ILLINOIS
INDIANA

U. S. Capitol
WEST VIRGINIA

VIRGINIA

ES OF AMERICA

MISSOURI

horse racing

KANSAS

KENTUCKY

TENNESSEE

NORTH
CAROLINA

OKLAHOMA

bald eagle
ARKANSAS

SOUTH
CAROLINA

Atlanta

tlesnake

armadillo

ALABAMA

GEORGIA

paddle steamer
MISSISSIPPI

FLORIDA

TEXAS

Austin

LOUISIANA

space
program

cattle
rancher

N

W   E

alligator

S

oil rig

New York City is the largest city in the United States. More people live here than in any other city in the nation. Here you can visit the Statue of Liberty.

Barrow, Alaska
Brattleboro, Vermont
Kauai, Hawaii
Taos, New Mexico

Preview

Focus on the Main Idea
Communities in the United States have many different climates.

PLACES

Barrow, Alaska
Kauai, Hawaii
Cape Cod, Massachusetts
Omaha, Nebraska
Brattleboro, Vermont
Taos, New Mexico

VOCABULARY

adobe

Living in Different Climates

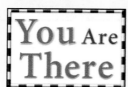

You Are There It is January 23 in Barrow, Alaska. You put on your warmest clothes and go out into the street. As the dark morning passes, other people come out too. It has been dark for a long time. Today, the whole town has a quiet feeling, as if it were waiting for something.

Suddenly, on the horizon, there is a glint of light. A loud cheer rings out. For the first time in more than two months, you can see the sun, but only for a short time!

 Draw Conclusions As you read, stop and think about the ways people adapt to the climate in their communities. Write down some of your conclusions as you read.

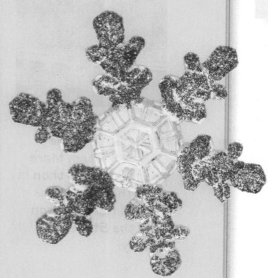

What Makes Up Climate?

The United States has many different climates. Climate is the weather that a place has over many years. In some places, the weather changes more throughout the year than in other places.

The climate of a place has several parts. Temperature is one part of climate. Temperature tells how hot or cold a place is. Another part of climate is how much rain or snow usually falls throughout a year. How strongly the winds blow is another part of climate.

Barrow, Alaska, has a cold climate. How can you describe the climate in your community?

▶ People in the past also lived in Barrow, Alaska. They learned to adapt to the cold climate there. They fished through the ice and built homes that would protect them from the cold.

REVIEW Compare the climate in your community with the climate in Barrow, Alaska. **Compare and Contrast**

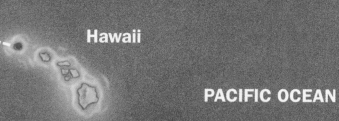

Hawaii

PACIFIC OCEAN

EQUATOR

▶ Certain plants can grow only in a warm, wet climate like Hawaii's.

United States Climates

The climate of a place depends on where it is located. You might wonder why Barrow, Alaska, has such a cold climate. It is very cold much of the year because Barrow is very far from the equator. Places that are far from the equator are colder than places that are close to the equator.

You wouldn't need to wear a heavy coat in **Kauai, Hawaii.** Kauai is an island. It has a very warm climate. Hawaii is close to the equator. The weather stays warm throughout the year.

How high a place is affects its climate. Very high places can be cold most of the time. That is why some very high mountains are covered with snow, even in the summer.

Omaha,
Nebraska

Cape Cod,
Massachusetts

ATLANTIC
OCEAN

▶ Cape Cod's climate is affected by its location near an ocean. The plants and animals here are different from those in Hawaii.

Being near an ocean or a large lake also affects a climate. Communities that are near a seacoast or close to a large lake can have milder climates than places that are inland. For example, Cape Cod, Massachusetts, is near the Atlantic Ocean. Omaha, Nebraska, is about the same distance from the equator, but it is in the middle of the country. Omaha is usually colder in winter and warmer in the summer than Cape Cod.

Climate affects people in many ways. People adapt to the climate in their communities. They wear clothes that keep them comfortable. They live in homes that protect them.

▶ Omaha, Nebraska

REVIEW Compare how you think people in Kauai and in Barrow have adapted to their climates.

Compare and Contrast

153

Homes of the Pueblo

The Anasazi Indians first settled in the Southwest region almost 2,000 years ago. Some of their homes were cliff houses built into the walls of canyons for protection. A cliff is a steep, rocky slope. The houses could be two, three, or even four stories high.

One group of Anasazi came to what is now Taos, New Mexico. This group is now known as Pueblo Indians.

The homes of the Pueblo are smaller than those of the Anasazi. But in many ways, the Taos Pueblo still live like their ancestors, the Anasazi.

Taos and Its Climate

Many Pueblo Indians live in the area that is now Santa Fe, New Mexico. Their ancestors lived there long before the Spanish explorers came.

The Pueblo Indian community in Taos, New Mexico, is located on a high plateau, or flat area, surrounded by huge mountains. The climate is dry, with warm days and cool nights in summer. In winter, the weather can be very cold and snow falls often.

The Pueblo have adapted to the climate by building adobe houses with thick walls that help keep them warm in winter and cool in summer. **Adobe** is a mixture of earth, straw, and water that is formed into bricks and dried.

You have read about some different climates in the United States. What kind of climate does your community have? How have people adapted to it?

REVIEW How did the Pueblo adapt to the climate in the Southwest region? **Main Idea and Details**

LESSON 2 REVIEW

Check Facts and Main Ideas

1. ⟳ **Draw Conclusions** On a separate sheet of paper, draw a graphic organizer like the one shown. Use details to draw a conclusion about how you adapt to the climate where you live.

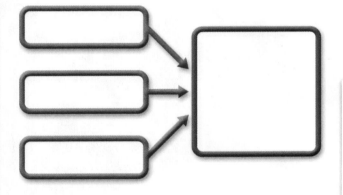

2. What are the different parts of the climate of a place?

3. What causes the climate of some places to be warm and other places to be cold?

4. How have people in the Pueblo Indian community in Taos, New Mexico, adapted to the climate?

5. **Critical Thinking:** *Evaluate* In which type of climate would you rather live? Why?

Link to ⟊⟊ Writing

Write a travel journal about traveling to communities with different climates. Describe what makes the climate different in each of the communities you describe.

Meet
Maria Martinez

1887–1980 • Pottery Artist

Maria Martinez was a Pueblo Indian. She made beautiful clay pots with traditional designs. Maria was born in San Ildefonso in New Mexico.

For more information, go online to *Meet the People* at **www.sfsocialstudies.com**.

As a child, Maria watched her aunt use clay to make pottery in the traditional Pueblo way. Her aunt would form the clay into a pot shape, then smooth and dry it. The clay pot was scraped, sanded, and painted. Then the pot was baked at a high temperature. Maria loved the traditional clay pots and began making her own.

Maria married Julian Martinez, an artist. They worked together using the designs of ancient pots from thousands of years ago. Maria shaped the clay, and Julian painted the designs.

Maria and Julian Martinez started a new pottery style known as black-on-black. The pots were a shiny black with a less shiny black design.

Mr. and Mrs. Martinez showed their work at the World's Fairs of 1904 and 1934. Soon, their black-on-black pottery was famous all over the world.

When Maria's pots were fired, they could easily crack or even explode. This made the pots that survived the process even more valuable.

BIOFACT

Learn from Biographies

Maria learned to make pots from her aunt. How was Maria's new pottery style different from the traditional style?

Use a Line Graph

What? A line graph shows how something changes over time. Look at the line graph below. It shows how the normal monthly daytime temperature in Brattleboro, Vermont, changes over six months. Brattleboro is in the Northeast region.

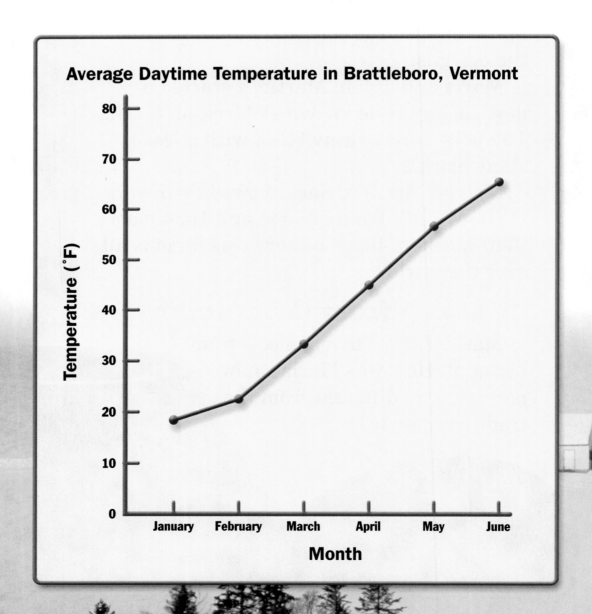

Average Daytime Temperature in Brattleboro, Vermont

Why? A line graph can help you understand how things change over time. Understanding changes can help you better understand events that have occurred.

How? When you read a line graph, look at the graph title. That tells you what the graph shows. Look at the words and numbers along the left side and the bottom. Those tell you what is measured and over what time period it is measured. Each dot on the graph shows an amount at a point in time. When you follow the line connecting the dots, you will see how the amount changes over time.

Think and Apply

1. What is the warmest month shown on the graph?

2. Between which two months did the temperature change the least?

3. About how many degrees warmer is the average temperature in June than in February?

Angels Camp, California

Beaumont, Texas

Preview

Focus on the Main Idea
The natural resources in an area help people live and communities grow.

PLACES

Angels Camp, California
Beaumont, Texas

VOCABULARY

natural resources
mineral
fuel
conserve
recycle

TERMS

Gold Rush

Communities and Resources

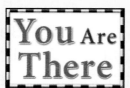 **You Are There** It is October 5, 1849. You are with your father in Angels Camp, California. You have been working here for several weeks. You are tired, and the food supplies are getting low. You are panning for gold in the creek. You sift the dirt from the creek bottom and pour it out, over and over again. Then, after about fifty tries, you see it—a glint of gold at the bottom. "Father!" you call out. "Look. Is it . . . ?" He looks, and then he stares at you. And then he smiles for the first time in a month.

 Draw Conclusions As you read, draw conclusions about the effects of natural resources on humans and the effects of humans on natural resources.

Our Natural Resources

Natural resources are useful materials that come from the earth. People need natural resources for food and for energy. We also use natural resources to build our homes, make our clothing, and make the many products we use every day. Communities have grown where natural resources are found.

REVIEW Why are natural resources so important for people? **Draw Conclusions**

▶ A **mineral** is a natural resource that has never been alive. Gold and salt are minerals.

▶ Trees are natural resources that are living.

▶ Fuels are also natural resources. A **fuel,** such as oil or gas, can be burned to produce heat, light, or other forms of energy.

▶ Two very important natural resources are water and soil. We need water to live. Crops grow in soil.

Mineral Resources

In 1848, gold was discovered in what is now the state of California. By 1849, more than 80,000 people had rushed to California to look for gold. This movement west was called the **Gold Rush.**

► **What do you think this painting, titled *Emigrant Party on the Road to California*, shows?**

Angels Camp, California, was one place where people looked for gold, using pans to sift the gold from muddy streams. Later, people dug deep into the earth. They dug mines where they found gold and brought it to the surface.

After the Gold Rush ended, many people stayed in California. In 1850 California became the thirty-first state. It is called the "Golden State," both for its sunny days and for the gold that brought thousands of people there.

Another valuable natural resource is oil. In 1901 in **Beaumont, Texas,** an oil-drilling machine hit a huge pocket of oil. Oil spouted out of the ground. Oil was so valuable that some people called it "black gold."

After oil was found, many people moved to Texas to work in the oil fields. The population of Beaumont grew very quickly. Oil is still a valuable natural resource. Texas and Alaska are two of the top oil-producing states.

REVIEW What changes occur when people discover a valuable natural resource like gold or oil?
⟳ **Draw Conclusions**

▶ Oil that comes from the ground is changed into many products that people use, including oil and gasoline for cars.

▶ A worker in an oil refinery checks the equipment.

Conserving Our Natural Resources

The earth has only a limited amount of some natural resources. We can conserve these natural resources so they will last a long time. We **conserve** resources when we use them carefully. One way to conserve natural resources is to use less of them.

Another way to protect natural resources is by recycling materials. When we **recycle** something, we use it again. Do you put cans and newspapers in a special place so they can be recycled? Some materials can be recycled and made into new products.

▶ Oil that is pumped from the earth is made into fuel and other materials.

▶ Plastics are made from oil and other natural resources. Plastic containers can be ground up and made into new materials.

▶ These plastic boards are made from other plastic items that have been recycled.

▶ Plastic boards can be used to make benches like this one.

We also need to take better care of our resources. When farmers did not take good care of the soil, much of it blew away. Farmers have now learned how to care for the soil, a very valuable resource.

Fuels are natural resources that can become used up. Scientists are trying to find new sources of energy. Meanwhile, we can all conserve fuel by using it carefully. What is one way that you can help protect our natural resources?

REVIEW Why is it important to conserve fuels? **Main Idea and Details**

Summarize the Lesson

- Many communities have grown because of their natural resources.
- Natural resources in the United States include water, soil, minerals, and fuels.
- It is important to conserve our natural resources.

LESSON 3 REVIEW

Check Facts and Main Ideas

1. **Draw Conclusions**
   On a separate sheet of paper, draw a diagram like the one shown. Use details you read about to draw a conclusion about the importance of conserving natural resources.

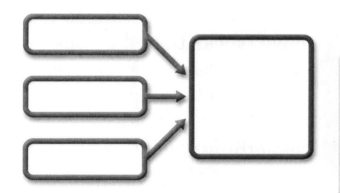

2. Describe some important natural resources.

3. How has the discovery of natural resources changed communities?

4. What are some ways that people can conserve resources?

5. **Critical Thinking: *Observe*** Why do you think the use of oil has increased since 1901?

Link to ⚬—⚬ **Art**

Make a poster that shows the recycling process. Do research to find out about other natural resources that are made into materials, then recycled.

Recycling

Anna, Megan, and Chris are third graders. They wanted to do something to help conserve resources in the environment. Anna pointed out that at home, her family recycles some things.

Megan's family recycles cans, bottles, newspapers, and cardboard boxes. Instead of throwing these items into the trash, the family puts them into special bags or bins. Trucks come and take the items to factories where they are made into new things.

The three students decided to start a school recycling program. They talked with teachers and students. Everyone agreed to put cans, bottles, and newspapers into bags. The school arranged to have trucks take the bags away to recycling centers. Reusing old materials to make new things is something we all can do as a community.

"Recycling is something everyone can do. If you recycle a newspaper, you can help save a tree!"

Chris

"I'm in charge of recycling in my family. I make sure all the items go into the right bags."

Megan

Issues and You

Find out if there is a recycling program in your community. If so, what items can you recycle? Make a list of the items. What can you and your classmates do to save our natural resources?

Chapter Summary

 Draw Conclusions

Read the "Land Resources" list on the left side of the diagram. On a separate sheet of paper, draw a conclusion about what would be a good use of that land.

river → flat land → good soil →

Vocabulary

Fill in the blank in each sentence with the vocabulary word that best completes the sentence.

a. fuel (p. 161)

b. landforms (p. 143)

c. climate (p. 143)

d. region (p. 143)

e. physical environment (p. 143)

f. adobe (p. 155)

g. ecosystem (p. 145)

h. natural resources (p. 161)

1 A _____ is a large land area that has special features.

2 The _____ in Hawaii is warm.

3 Landforms and climate make up the _____ of a region.

4 Mountains and plains are two types of _____.

5 Gas is a _____ that you can burn to produce energy.

6 The house was made with _____ bricks.

7 Trees and soil are _____.

8 A physical environment and the living things in it make up an _____.

Facts and Main Ideas

1 What are things found in nature that people can use?

2 What are some ways that people have changed the environment?

3 How have farmers changed their environment?

4 **Main Idea** What region of the United States do you live in?

5 **Main Idea** How does a climate affect how people live?

6 **Main Idea** Why should we conserve our natural resources?

7 **Critical Thinking:** *Draw Conclusions* Why did farmers want to live near a river when it came time to sell their crops?

Write About It

1 **Write a fact file** Tell three interesting facts about a natural resource in the region where you live.

2 **List features of the land** in the region where you live. Write a sentence about each telling why it is important to your region.

3 **Draw a picture** of what a Web page for your region might look like. Create symbols with the keywords someone would select to find out more about your region. List the information that would be found from that keyword. Include climate, natural resources, and landforms.

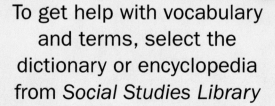

Internet Activity

To get help with vocabulary and terms, select the dictionary or encyclopedia from *Social Studies Library* at **www.sfsocialstudies.com**.

Apply Skills

Use a Line Graph

Look at the line graph on page 158. Answer the questions.

1 In what months is the average daytime temperature below freezing? Freezing is 32°F.

2 What is the average daytime temperature in June?

3 If 45° is a good temperature for planting trees, in what month should you plant trees?

169

Chapter 6 — Places Where Communities Start

Lesson 1

Glenwood Springs, Colorado

Communities grow in mountain areas.

1

Lesson 2

Seattle, Washington

Communities grow near water.

2

Lesson 3

Indianapolis, Indiana

Communities grow because of transportation.

3

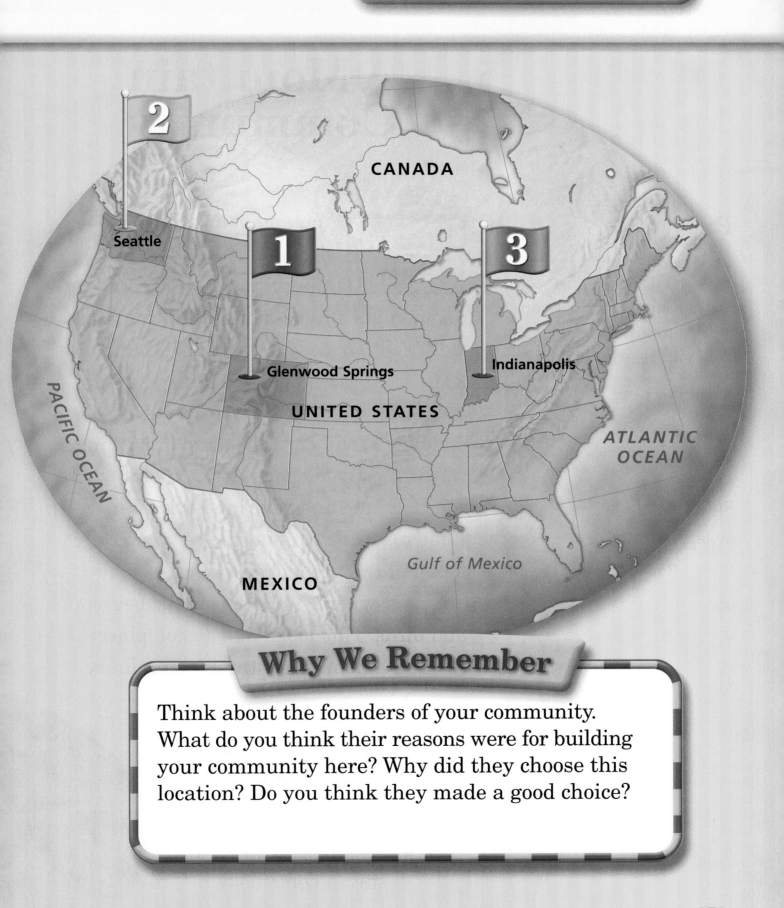

CANADA

2

Seattle

1

3

Glenwood Springs

Indianapolis

UNITED STATES

PACIFIC OCEAN

ATLANTIC OCEAN

Gulf of Mexico

MEXICO

Why We Remember

Think about the founders of your community. What do you think their reasons were for building your community here? Why did they choose this location? Do you think they made a good choice?

Glenwood Springs, Colorado

A Mountain Community

Preview

Focus on the Main Idea
Some communities develop in mountains because of their natural resources.

PLACES
Glenwood Springs, Colorado
Fort Defiance
Rocky Mountains

PEOPLE
Daniel Boone

VOCABULARY
miner

You Are There

You and your family are skiing in the Rocky Mountains. As you come to an opening, a huge mountain peak rises 4,137 feet above you. A gust of wind blows snow from the mountains into your eyes and nose. Suddenly, the trail begins to go downhill. You hear the sound of rushing water. A canyon opens up at a point where the Colorado and Roaring Fork rivers come together. Around the canyon is a forest of tall green trees. Wild animals are everywhere. You see rabbits, bears, and birds. This looks like a good place to build a home and start a community.

Draw Conclusions
As you read, decide why the location of Glenwood Springs, Colorado, made it a good place for people to start a community.

How Glenwood Springs Grew

Before there was a town named Glenwood Springs, Colorado, the land was settled by the Ute Indians. The Ute first discovered the hot water springs deep within Glenwood Canyon. These waters helped make their aches and pains feel better.

In 1879 other people came to live there. Some settlers came for the hot springs. Then miners came. A miner digs materials from the earth. Here, the miners dug out coal buried within the area's caves.

A short while later, in 1881, Captain Isaac Cooper and others set up Fort Defiance. They later changed the town's name to Glenwood Springs.

After much hard work laying a track through the Rocky Mountains, the Colorado Midland Railroad chugged into Glenwood Springs in 1887. Now the miners had a way to send out their coal. Many people also rode the train to visit the hot springs.

REVIEW What was the effect of the railroad on Glenwood Springs?
⟳ Draw Conclusions

► This Ute chief is wearing the traditional clothing of his people.

MAP ADVENTURE

Many visitors go to Pioneer Cemetery in Glenwood Springs. They want to visit the graves of settlers and the famous people who are buried there. People can visit cemeteries to get information about their community and the people who lived in it. The map shows the location of the cemetery.

1. Suppose you want to go from downtown Glenwood Springs to Pioneer Cemetery. What is the shortest way to get there?

2. Find and use the map scale. About how long is Cemetery Road from Bennett Avenue to the cemetery?

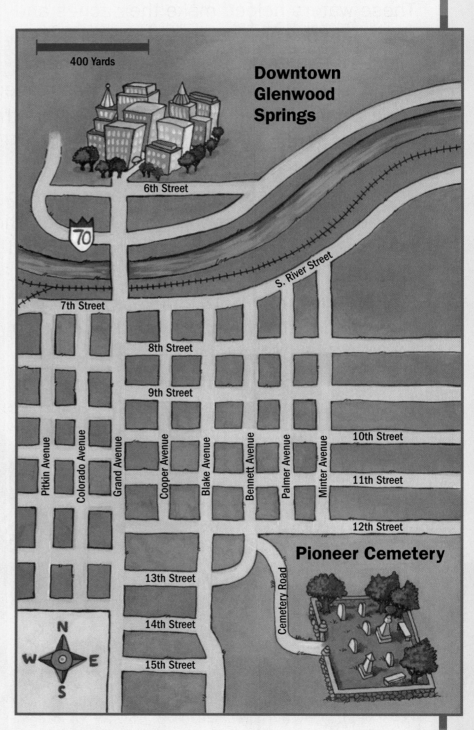

400 Yards

Downtown Glenwood Springs

6th Street

S. River Street

7th Street

8th Street

9th Street

Pitkin Avenue
Colorado Avenue
Grand Avenue
Cooper Avenue
Blake Avenue
Bennett Avenue
Palmer Avenue
Minter Avenue

10th Street

11th Street

12th Street

Pioneer Cemetery

Cemetery Road

13th Street

14th Street

15th Street

N
W E
S

174

Living in Mountain Communities

Even though communities in places like the Rocky Mountains had many natural resources, they were hard places in which to live. Traveling through the mountains was difficult, and it was hard to grow food. People tried starting mountain communities in other parts of the United States too.

REVIEW Why would it be difficult to have a large farm in a mountain community?

> **Draw Conclusions**

LESSON 1 REVIEW

Check Facts and Main Ideas

1. **Draw Conclusions** On a separate sheet of paper, draw a diagram like the one shown. Use the details you read about Glenwood Springs. Draw a conclusion about why people settled there.

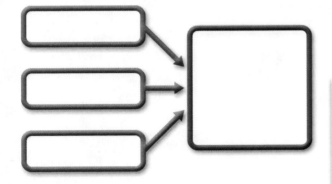

2. What events changed Glenwood Springs over time?

3. What natural resource brings visitors to Glenwood Springs?

4. What made it difficult to live in mountain communities?

5. **Critical Thinking: *Compare and Contrast*** Why did the Utes and the settlers come to the Glenwood Springs area? How were their reasons similar and different?

Link to ⟶ Mathematics

Solve a problem The mountain peak by Glenwood Falls rises 4,137 feet above the town. The town of Glenwood Springs is 5,758 feet above sea level. How high above sea level is the mountain peak?

175

Meet
Daniel Boone
1734–1820 • Pioneer

Daniel Boone was a pioneer who spent his life exploring and settling new parts of the country.

As a child, Daniel Boone grew up outside of Reading, Pennsylvania. When he was ten years old, he and his mother went to live near a pasture each summer so he could tend the cows. Daniel did not go to school very often because of the work he did to help his family.

When Daniel was about sixteen years old, his father moved the family to what is now the state of North Carolina. Daniel spent much of his time hunting and trapping animals. He traded their fur for salt and other items his family needed.

Daniel Boone heard about the land of Kentucky beyond the mountains. He found a trail through the mountains that went to the area around the Kentucky River. Few settlers lived there.

Then he helped other people settle areas of Kentucky. He and 30 other men built up this trail to make it easier for settlers to travel. This new trail was called the Wilderness Road.

Because of Daniel Boone's work, many settlers came to live in Kentucky.

This is Daniel Boone's house in Defiance, Missouri.

BIOFACT

Learn from Biographies

Daniel Boone had many adventures as he explored new places and built new settlements. How did Daniel Boone's courage affect the growth of our country?

For more information, go online to *Meet the People* at **www.sfsocialstudies.com**.

Seattle, Washington

Preview

Focus on the Main Idea
Towns grew along bodies of water because of their resources. Boats could carry goods to places where they could be sold.

PLACES
Seattle, Washington
Puget Sound

VOCABULARY
logging
lumber
port
industries

A Water Community

You Are There
You are standing on one of the rolling hills in the city of Seattle, Washington. To the west lies the sparkling water of Elliot Bay and Puget Sound. Fish seem to be jumping out of the water, and there are miles and miles of trees. Beyond the bay stand the mountains of Olympic National Park. The Cascade Mountains rise to the east. To the south you can see Mount Rainier, almost three miles high, with snow on its peak.

It's time to get off that hill and head downtown. You can't wait to see the view of the city from the top of the Space Needle!

Draw Conclusions As you read, try to figure out why the city of Seattle today looks so different from when it was founded.

The Early Days of Seattle

Before the city of Seattle grew, the area was full of tall trees, and the waters were full of fish. The city started to grow in 1851. A group of settlers built a town on Alki Point, which was on **Puget Sound.** The Pacific Ocean is connected to Puget Sound.

When the settlers arrived, they found Duwamish (Du-WA-mish) and Suquamish (Su-KWA-mish) Indians living nearby. They already knew about the area's natural resources—water, trees, and fish.

One of the Native American leaders was Chief Sealth. He was friendly, and he helped the settlers. The settlers named their town Seattle to honor Chief Sealth.

▶ Georgia George is the chair and executive director of the Suquamish tribe.

REVIEW What natural resource was used to build the town of Alki Point?

○ Draw Conclusions

▶ Chief Sealth

Seattle Today

Logging—cutting down trees to use for wood—became an important business in Seattle. One main use for wood is **lumber,** which is wood that is cut into boards so it can be used for building.

The loggers who cut down the trees told tall tales about a character named Paul Bunyan. According to legend, he was a giant logger who traveled across the country with a giant blue ox named Babe.

▶ Loggers sometimes used rivers for transportation. Logs moved along the river to places where they were cut into lumber.

Literature and Social Studies

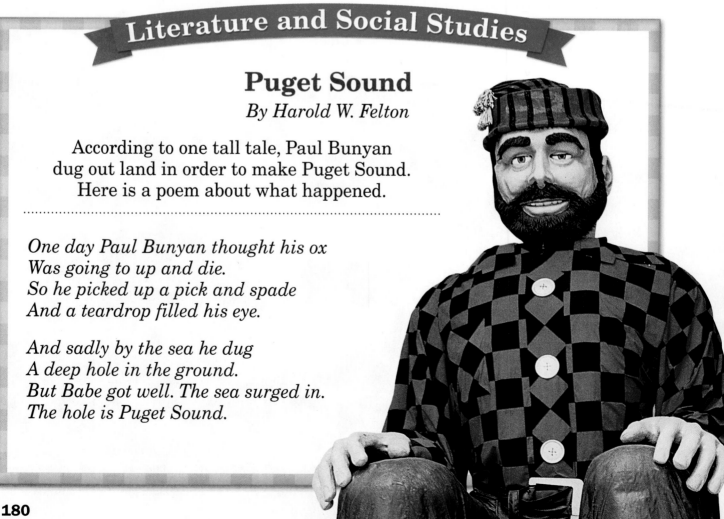

Puget Sound
By Harold W. Felton

According to one tall tale, Paul Bunyan dug out land in order to make Puget Sound. Here is a poem about what happened.

One day Paul Bunyan thought his ox
Was going to up and die.
So he picked up a pick and spade
And a teardrop filled his eye.

And sadly by the sea he dug
A deep hole in the ground.
But Babe got well. The sea surged in.
The hole is Puget Sound.

Seattle grew into an important city because of its port. A **port** is a place where ships can load and unload things. Lumber and other goods were shipped to and from places all over the world.

New **industries,** or kinds of businesses, have come to the city. Airplane making and computer companies have grown. In fact, one of the largest builders of airplanes is in the Seattle area. The largest maker of computer software is there too. Some people now wonder what will happen to Seattle's natural resources.

REVIEW Why does the city take up so much more space now than it did when it was first settled? ⟳ **Draw Conclusions**

LESSON 2   REVIEW

Check Facts and Main Ideas

1. ⟳ **Draw Conclusions**
   On a separate sheet of paper, draw a diagram like the one shown. Use the details you read about Seattle. Draw a conclusion about the good and bad effects of Seattle's growth.

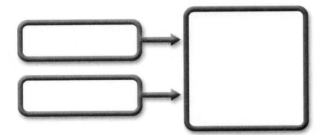

2. Describe a person and an event that changed Seattle.

3. Describe the physical environment and the natural resources around Seattle.

4. In what way were wood and water important natural resources in the growth of Seattle?

5. **Critical Thinking:** *Predict* How do you think Seattle will change if its population continues to grow quickly?

Link to ∽ **Writing**

Compare Cities Look at a map of the United States. Try to find a major city that is not on some kind of water. What makes this city different from other large cities? Write about what you find.

181

World Climate Regions

North Pole

Arctic Circle · A · *Needleleaf Forest*

Tundra

Broadleaf Forest

EUROPE

NORTH AMERICA

Needleleaf Forest

Mediterranean

Broadleaf Forest

MEDITERRANEAN SEA

Tropic of Cancer

Hot Desert

RED SEA

CARIBBEAN SEA

A T L A N T I C

AFRICA

Dry Woodland

Tropical Grassland

Equator

Tropical Rain Forest

Broadleaf forest
It doesn't get too hot, too cold, or too dry in temperate climates. Forests have broadleaf trees such as oaks that lose their leaves in the fall.

SOUTH AMERICA

Tropical Rain Forest

Dry Woodland

Tropical Grassland

O C E A N

Dry Woodland

Mountain

Tropic of Capricorn

OCEAN

Mountain
Plant life varies on a mountain. At lower heights, trees and plants grow. The higher you go, the colder and windier it gets. Fewer plants grow in this climate. Mountain peaks may be snowy even when it is warm at the bottom.

Tundra

Tundras are found in the Arctic Circle and on mountains. The ground is frozen about ten months of the year. The only plants that grow are mosses, lichens, and low-growing bushes.

Needleleaf Forest

Much of northern North America, Europe, and Asia are covered with needleleaf forests. These are forests of evergreens. Evergreens can survive the long frozen winters in these regions.

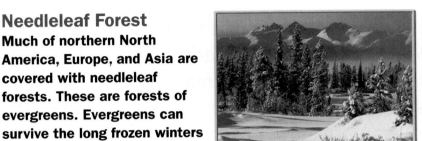

Mediterranean

A Mediterranean climate is the climate of countries around the Mediterranean Sea. Some of these countries have forests. Others have thinly-spread bushes. It is hot and dry in the summer and warm and wet in the winter. Parts of southern Africa, the Americas, and Australia have Mediterranean climates.

Dry Woodland

Some areas of the tropics have dry, hot seasons. Some plants that live in these areas can store water. Trees grow far apart with lots of grassland between them.

Hot Desert

Few plants and animals can live in a hot desert. There is little rain. It can be over 104°F in the daytime. Then it can be freezing cold at night. High winds and shifting sands are desert hazards.

Weather Extremes

Extreme weather can be dangerous. Heat waves, hurricanes, blizzards, tornadoes, sandstorms, droughts, and floods are examples of natural hazards.

Tropical Rain Forest

Tropical rain forests are found near the equator. The weather is hot and rainy. Many different plants and animals live in rain forests.

Drought is a long period without rainfall. Plants die, and the soil blows away.

Tropical Storms have high winds, heavy rain, thunder, and lightning. They can cause much damage to coastal communities.

Write a Letter for Information

What? To find out information about a town, you can write a letter to the town's Visitor Center. These places have lots of information about a town. As you read, try to figure out what the student wants to know.

Visitor Center
Glenwood Springs, CO

Dear Glenwood Springs Visitor Center,

My name is Gary, and I'm in the third grade in North Carolina. For a class activity, we need to write about spending one day in a new town. I picked Glenwood Springs, Colorado.

I have used the Internet to find out facts about Glenwood Springs, but I need to know other things.

Can you tell me the best things to eat at some of the restaurants in town? What is the inside of a coal mine like? Finally, where is the best place to get a good view of the sunset? Those kinds of things will make it seem like I actually came to visit. Thank you.

Sincerely,
Gary Dugger

Why? In a letter, you can ask very specific questions. With email, writing a letter has become even easier. Also, you can get a response much faster because your letter gets there in seconds.

How? When writing to get information, first make sure you explain who you are. You are more likely to get an answer if you identify yourself. Remember to tell your return address. Then, tell why you want this information. If you have a good reason, then the person is more likely to want to help you.

Next, you need to tell exactly what you want to know. Look back at the letter to the Visitor Center. Gary asked about human characteristics of Glenwood Springs. Before you begin writing, ask yourself the questions you want to ask in your letter. Be sure they make sense. Finally, write your letter to get the information you need.

Think and Apply

1. Why is Gary writing to the Visitor Center in addition to using the Internet?

2. If Gary's report is due in a week, how can he get the information in time?

3. Do you think Gary's report will be interesting? Why or why not?

Indianapolis, Indiana

Preview

Focus on the Main Idea
Communities sometimes are built where many roads, railroads, and air routes come together in one place.

PLACES
Indianapolis, Indiana

PEOPLE
Harriet Tubman

VOCABULARY
state capital
state government
crossroads

TERMS
Underground Railroad
National Road

A Crossroads Community

You Are There You are standing at a place where many different roads come together and cross one another. You could take a road north to Chicago, Illinois, or south to Nashville, Tennessee. Heading on a road going west takes you to St. Louis, Missouri, but turning east finds you facing Philadelphia, Pennsylvania. As you stand there deciding, you look around at the miles and miles of cornfields.

You are on the Till Plains, a large area of farmland. The land outside the city is flat. The White River flows through the city. Where are you? You are standing in Indianapolis, Indiana—a community known as the "Crossroads of America."

Draw Conclusions As you read, try to figure out why Indianapolis is known as the "Crossroads of America."

Forming the Crossroads

The Miami and Delaware Indians knew that the farmland and climate in the area were good for growing crops. The first white settlers who came to what is now the city of **Indianapolis, Indiana,** were farmers too. Later, people decided that the area along the White River in the middle of the state would be perfect as a state capital.

▶ The National Road brought changes to the community.

Indianapolis, as shown below, was chosen as the state capital in 1820. A **state capital** is a city in which the state government is located. People in the **state government** make and carry out the state's laws.

A **crossroads** is a place where many different roads meet one another. Indianapolis started to become a crossroads center in the 1830s. At that time, the first United States highway came through Indianapolis. This highway was named the **National Road.** It helped people from the East move west.

REVIEW What is the main idea in the last paragraph on this page?
Main Idea and Details

187

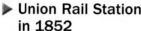 **Union Rail Station in 1852**

Roads and Railroads

Indianapolis is one of the biggest cities in the country that you can't get to by boat. About seven important highways lead out of the city. They help trucks carry products from the city to the rest of the country.

With the arrival of the railroad in 1847, more and more people came to Indianapolis. The Union Rail Station was built in 1852. Indianapolis became an important stop for many different railroad lines.

The **Underground Railroad** also stopped in Indianapolis, but it was not a real railroad. It was a route that helped African American slaves escape from the South to find freedom in the North. It was made up of a network, or connected group, of places called *stations.* One of the stations was the Bethel AME Church in Indianapolis. Some of the people of the church helped many escaping slaves.

REVIEW Which city is the capital of your state? Why do you think it was chosen as the capital? ⊙ **Draw Conclusions**

Summarize the Lesson

- Indianapolis was chosen to be the capital of Indiana.
- It was an important stop on the National Road and the Underground Railroad.
- Because of its central location, Indianapolis is known as the Crossroads of America.
- Many highways and railroads cross through Indianapolis.

LESSON 3 REVIEW

Check Facts and Main Ideas

1. ⊙ **Draw Conclusions** On a separate sheet of paper, draw a diagram like the one shown. Use details from the lesson. Draw a conclusion about the importance of Indianapolis in the past and present.

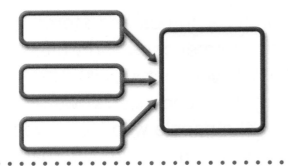

2. Why is Indianapolis known as the "Crossroads of America"?

3. What events were important to Indianapolis's early growth?

4. What made Indianapolis an important stop on the Underground Railroad?

5. **Critical Thinking:** *Evaluate* Why do you think so many roads were built through Indianapolis?

Link to ⚭ Geography

Look at a road map of the United States. Find out what major highways pass through Indianapolis. With what other cities do they connect Indianapolis?

"I would make a home for them in the North, and the Lord helping me, I would bring them all there."

Leading People to Freedom

Do you feel a responsibility, or duty, to help other people? **Harriet Tubman** did. She helped members of her family escape slavery. Slavery is the owning of a person by another person. Harriet Tubman risked her own life to lead hundreds of people to escape from slavery to freedom.

Harriet Tubman was born into slavery in Maryland around 1820. When she was about twelve years old, she started working in the fields. There she heard other slaves talk about wanting to be free.

Harriet Tubman had heard of the Underground Railroad. It wasn't a real railroad with trains and stations. The "trains" were the people who were running to freedom. The "stations" were churches and the homes and stores of free African Americans and white people who believed that slavery was wrong. The "conductors" were the people who led slaves on their journey to parts of the northern United States and Canada.

BUILDING
CITIZENSHIP
Caring
Respect
Responsibility
Fairness
Honesty
★ Courage

Harriet Tubman used the Underground Railroad to escape from slavery. She did this by walking through the cold woods at night and by getting help from people at the stations. She reached freedom in Philadelphia.

Once Harriet Tubman was free, she risked her life to help her family and others. She showed courage by facing danger without fear. She became the greatest "conductor" in the history of the Underground Railroad. She did so by using her courage and intelligence to outwit the slave owners chasing her. Harriet Tubman felt that she had a responsibility to help all people who were slaves.

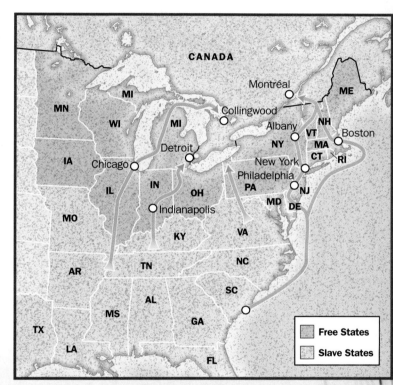

▶ Routes of the Underground Railroad

Courage in Action

Think of another person in history who showed courage and helped many other people. It could be a United States President or a citizen like Harriet Tubman. Read about this person and write down how he or she showed courage and intelligence.

Chapter Summary

 Draw Conclusions

On a separate sheet of paper, draw the diagram shown at right. Fill in a conclusion based on the details.

> Several major highways join around the city. →

> It is a city in the center of a state, and many railroad lines go through it. →

> [ ]

Vocabulary

Match each word with the correct definition or description.

a. chopping down trees for wood

b. businesses that make things

c. people who make and carry out the state's laws

d. city in which a state government is located

e. wood used for building

❶ logging (p. 180)

❷ lumber (p. 180)

❸ industries (p. 181)

❹ state capital (p. 187)

❺ state government (p. 187)

Facts and Main Ideas

1 Why do people go on vacation to Glenwood Springs?

2 How did its geography make people decide to make Indianapolis the state capital?

3 **Main Idea** Why do industries grow in certain areas?

4 **Main Idea** Explain how geography affects development of a city.

5 **Main Idea** How has transportation affected the development of an area?

6 **Critical Thinking** *Compare and Contrast* In what ways are Indianapolis and Seattle alike? In what ways are they different?

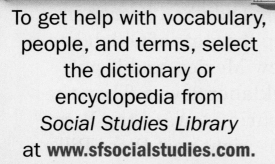

Internet Activity

To get help with vocabulary, people, and terms, select the dictionary or encyclopedia from *Social Studies Library* at **www.sfsocialstudies.com.**

Write About It

1 **Write a description** of the area around your town or city.

2 **Make two lists** for the Visitor Center Web site for your town. First, list reasons why people should visit your town. Second, explain why people should move to your town.

3 **Write a pamphlet** for the local museum. Your pamphlet should explain the history of your town.

Apply Skills

Write a Letter for Information

Pick a place in the United States that you would like to visit. Find it on a map or globe. What do you know about its geography and climate?

Write to the Visitor Center of that location. Ask about things you want to do on your visit.

Pecos Bill Rides a Tornado

In the Southwest, people told stories about a mythical hero named Pecos Bill. He was very strong and did many amazing deeds. Here is one of his adventures.

Everybody knew that Pecos Bill was the best cowboy in the West, but nobody ever thought that Bill would have to ride a tornado. This is the way it happened.

One day, a big storm roared in from the west. About that same time, another storm came up from the south. These two storms turned into the biggest tornado anybody had ever seen. This tornado picked up the state of Oklahoma and put it down in New Mexico, and it put New Mexico where Oklahoma was. Then the tornado came roaring toward the Pecos River in Texas, right past Pecos Bill's house. The tornado took Bill's house, barn, and the Pecos River.

Bill decided to catch that tornado. As he was galloping across Texas, he ran into a rattlesnake.

"You're in a mighty big hurry," the rattlesnake said.

Pecos Bill was surprised to hear a snake talk. But that didn't stop him from asking the snake if it had seen a tornado go past there. Just then, Bill saw the tornado rushing toward them. Quickly Bill began to spin his lasso. The lasso pulled Bill high in the air. He climbed up the lasso and began to ride the tornado like a wild horse.

Well, that tornado couldn't throw Pecos Bill. Finally the tornado got tired. Bill made the tornado put Oklahoma back below Kansas, and New Mexico back next to Arizona. Then he made it carry his house and his barn and the cottonwood trees and the Pecos River back to Texas.

Bill grabbed the tornado's last bolt of lightning and slid down to the ground. After Bill arrived home, his wife Sue heard a noise outside. They looked out the window and saw that the tornado had turned into a spring breeze.

"Well, let's keep it," Sue said. "It'll be nice to have a breeze of our own when the weather gets hot this summer."

Review

Narrow the answer choices. Rule out answers you know are wrong.

Main Ideas and Vocabulary

TEST PREP

Read the passage below. Then answer the questions.

Why do people choose to live in a certain place? When the English first settled in the Americas, they settled in what is now the Northeast Region. They settled near the seacoast.

As settlements began to move inland, people often searched for places with the right climate for farming. The Midwest has many farms because it has enough rainfall and regular seasons.

Some people choose an area because of its natural resources. Seattle grew in part because of water. People used the rivers for fishing and logging, and the ocean for trade. Indianapolis grew because the rich soil produced good crops. Also, railroads could be built quickly on the flat land. Many people moved to California because of its gold.

No matter where people live, they depend on natural resources. We need to <u>conserve</u> natural resources so they can last for a long time.

1 According to the passage, which of these is not a reason people choose to live in a certain place?

  A environment
  B government
  C natural resources
  D climate

2 In this passage, the word *conserve* means—

  A save   **B** use
  C store   **D** sell

3 According to the passage, climate is very important to people who are—

  A loggers **B** miners
  C farmers **D** sailors

Vocabulary

Use one of the following terms to complete each sentence below.

a. miner (p. 173)
b. adapt (p. 146)
c. state capital (p. 187)
d. Underground Railroad (p. 189)
e. port (p. 181)

1 A _____ digs minerals from the earth.

2 Many people escaped from slavery on the _____.

3 People _____ to their environment by wearing suitable clothes and building homes.

4 Some people in Seattle work at loading ships in the _____.

5 Indianapolis was chosen to be the _____ of Indiana.

Read on Your Own

Look for books like these in the library.

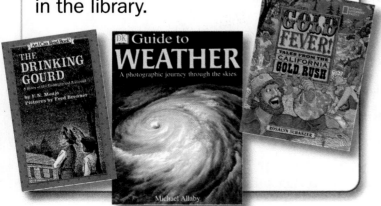

Apply Skills

Make a Line Graph

Keep track of the temperature at noon every day for a week. Then make a line graph to show how the temperature changes from day to day. Put the temperature scale on the left side. Write the days of the week across the bottom. Then plot the temperatures on your graph. Connect the dots with a line. Label your graph.

Write and Share

Make a Travel Brochure

Pick a place in a region that you want to visit. Find out ways to get there. Also find out what you can do there and how much things cost. Include this information in your brochure. Use words and phrases that will make people want to visit. Add pictures to make the brochure attractive. Remember to write complete sentences. Use the correct end marks. Check your spelling and punctuation.

Read a classmate's brochure. Think of questions to ask about that location. Discuss the travel plans you would like to make.

Use and Reuse

Recycling and reusing are good ways to help the earth. You can make something new from something you have already used.

1 **Choose** something that could be made into something else.

2 **Think** of what you want to make. Create the product that uses what you chose.

3 **Make** an advertisement to sell your product. Include five sentences that tell about where the materials came from.

4 **Present** your product to the class.

5 **Ask** the class what price it should be.

Internet Activity

Learn more about geography in the United States on the Internet. Go to www.sfsocialstudies.com/activities and select your grade and unit.

History of Communities

Why is the history of communities important?

History!

by Lindy Russell

Is history
A mystery?
Let's start small
And learn it all!

First look at your family.
Who is in your family tree?
Where did they come from?
Where did they go?
These are things you ought to know.

Next look at your community.
Just how did it come to be?
Who all lived there long ago?
How did they live? Do you know?

Then find out about your state.
What about it makes it great?
Is it the weather? Is it the scenery?
Is it the farmland? Is it the factories?

All these little histories
Help to solve the mystery
Of just what is the U.S.A.—
Our country, our home, today.

Welcome to My Community

Communities Past and Present

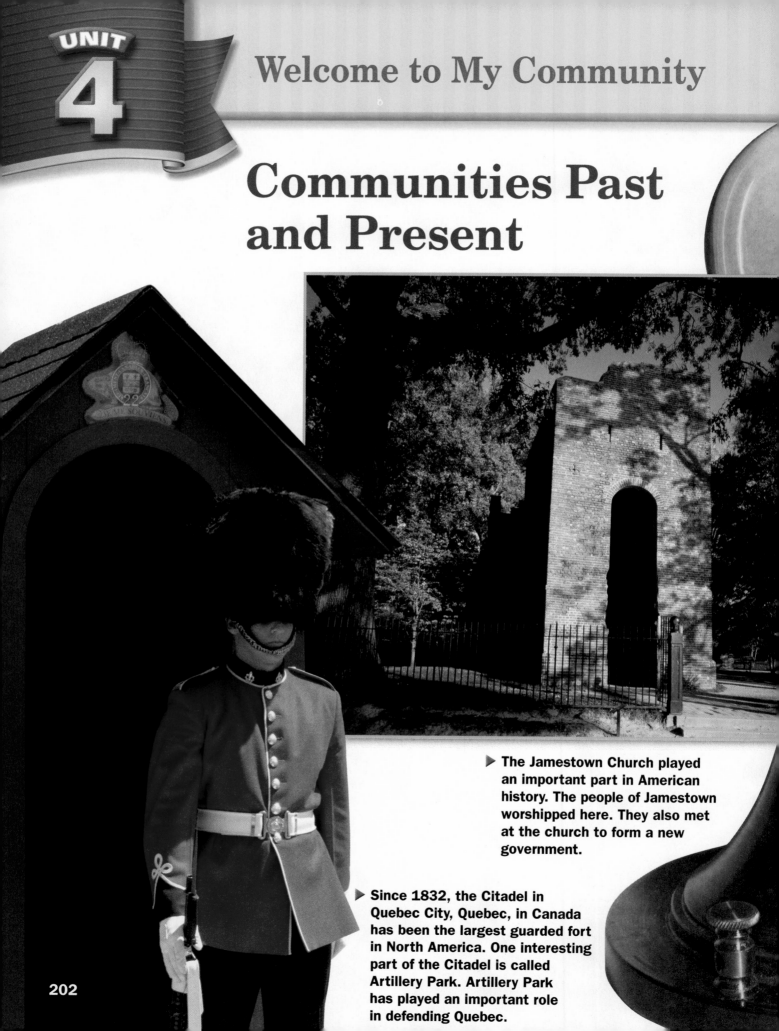

▶ The Jamestown Church played an important part in American history. The people of Jamestown worshipped here. They also met at the church to form a new government.

▶ Since 1832, the Citadel in Quebec City, Quebec, in Canada has been the largest guarded fort in North America. One interesting part of the Citadel is called Artillery Park. Artillery Park has played an important role in defending Quebec.

From November to January, the city of St. Augustine, Florida, celebrates the holiday season. The people of this community hang more than a million white lights on buildings, bushes, and trees in the historic downtown area. These white lights sparkle at night after dark.

Thomas Edison lived in Menlo Park, New Jersey. He invented the light bulb. One of his first light bulbs is shown here.

203

What Caused People to Move West

Cause and Effect

Cause	→	Effect

A cause makes something happen.	→	**An effect** is the outcome or the result of the cause.

- Sometimes writers use the words *cause* and *effect* in the information that you are reading.

- Other times words such as *because, if, then, now,* and *since* might be used to talk about cause and effect.

- Remember that an effect can come before a cause when you are reading.

Read the following paragraph. Cause and effect have been highlighted for you.

Seattle has become an important city because of its port. The ability to move goods easily attracts businesses. Airplanes are manufactured in the area. Seattle is also home to computer companies.

Moving West

When the United States first became a country, many people lived on the East Coast. Improvements in transportation helped other parts of the country grow. New ways of getting from place to place helped people move westward.

Meriwether Lewis and William Clark explored the West in boats, canoes, and on horseback. Settlers followed this route by horse and by wagon. Soon tracks were laid, and trains steamed westward. The population of the West grew quickly.

Use the reading strategy of cause and effect to answer these questions.

1 How did Lewis and Clark make it easier for others to travel westward?

2 What improvement in transportation made traveling across the country easier?

3 What was the effect of transportation on the population of the western part of the United States?

Chapter 7

Communities and Their Histories

Lesson 1

Oneida County, New York

The Iroquois live in New York.

1

Lesson 2

St. Augustine, Florida

The Spanish come to the New World.

2

Lesson 3

Quebec City, Quebec, Canada

The French come to North America.

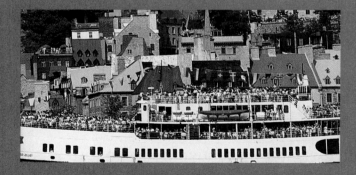

3

Lesson 4

Jamestown, Virginia

English settlers arrive in Virginia.

4

North
America

Oneida County

Quebec City

Atlantic
OCEAN

Jamestown

PACIFIC
OCEAN

St Augustine

Gulf of
Mexico

Why We Remember

Every community has a history that is shaped
by the people who first arrived there. Your
community might be remembered for Native
Americans who lived there first. Perhaps your
community celebrates its early explorers or
settlers. Your community is special because of
its past as well as its present.

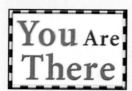

Oneida County, New York

Explorers Come to North America

Preview

Focus on the Main Idea
Native Americans and European explorers built the first communities in North America.

PLACES

Oneida County, New York
Portugal
Spain
France
England

PEOPLE

Christopher Columbus
Hernando de Soto
Juan Ponce de León
Jacques Cartier
Samuel de Champlain
John Cabot
Henry Hudson

VOCABULARY

explorer

You Are There Grab a load of branches. You are just in time to help build a new longhouse. A longhouse is a large, wooden building where many families live together.

You cut the wood in the spring when it is green and easy to bend. Then you use your ax to sharpen the ends of the branches into points. Then you cut some elm bark into rectangles to make the roof and walls. After you do this, you can put the longhouse together. You had better hurry up! There's a lot of work to do.

 Cause and Effect As you read, look for the effects that the exploration of the Americas had on the people who already lived there.

The Iroquois

Long before European explorers arrived, many people already lived in the Americas. An **explorer** is a person who travels to little-known places looking for land or other new discoveries. When explorers arrived in what is now **Oneida County, New York,** and Quebec, Canada, a Native American tribe called the Iroquois lived there.

▶ This Iroquois mortar and pestle were probably used to grind spices.

The Iroquois women were very good farmers. Their main crop was corn. The men were very good hunters.

The Iroquois set up a government. They had a set of rules that protected the rights of groups within the Iroquois world. It also protected religious ceremonies.

In time, explorers came to the Americas from Spain, England, and France. These explorers had customs and ideas different from the Native Americans. These differences sometimes led to conflicts.

REVIEW What differences between the Native Americans and the explorers caused conflicts?
⟳ Cause and Effect

Literature and Social Studies

Hiawatha's Sailing

Henry Wadsworth Longfellow learned about Onondagan stories and legends to write *The Song of Hiawatha*. This part of that poem tells about Hiawatha's search for a tree to make a canoe.

Give me of your bark, O Birch-tree!
Of your yellow bark, O Birch-tree!
Growing by the rushing river,
Tall and stately in the valley!

Early Explorers

Portugal, **Spain**, **France**, and **England** all traded for goods from China and India. Traveling to China and India by land took a very long time. Explorers from each country wanted to be the first to find a water route. They thought a water route would be faster and safer.

▶ People in Europe wanted spices from India and China.

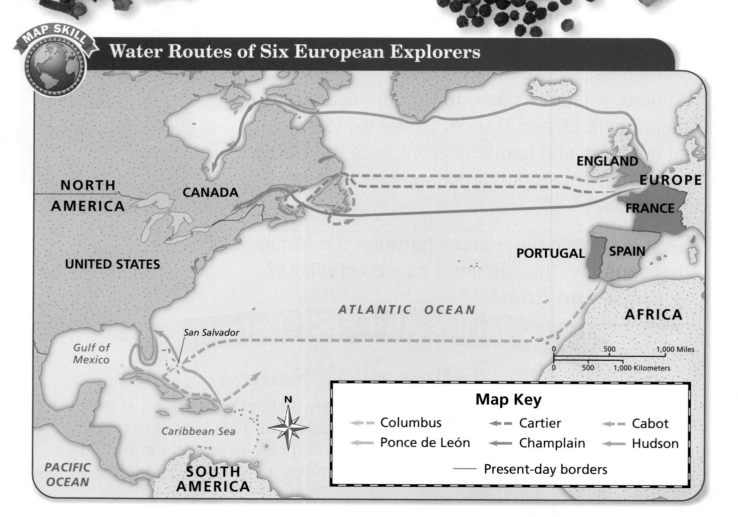

Water Routes of Six European Explorers

ENGLAND
EUROPE
NORTH AMERICA
CANADA
FRANCE
PORTUGAL   SPAIN
UNITED STATES
ATLANTIC OCEAN
AFRICA
San Salvador
Gulf of Mexico
Caribbean Sea
PACIFIC OCEAN
SOUTH AMERICA

0   500   1,000 Miles
0   500   1,000 Kilometers

Map Key
◄-- Columbus   ◄-- Cartier   ◄-- Cabot
◄— Ponce de León ◄— Champlain   ◄— Hudson
—— Present-day borders

▶ Explorers from England, France, Portugal, and Spain took different routes across the Atlantic Ocean.

MAP SKILL Movement: *Some of these explorers wanted to travel to China and India in the East. Why did they sail west?*

Portugal led the way by sailing to the East around Africa. Spain sent explorers across the Atlantic Ocean. **Christopher Columbus, Hernando de Soto,** and **Juan Ponce de León** explored North America for Spain. Some built settlements.

The French soon followed. **Jacques Cartier** and **Samuel de Champlain** landed in what today is called Canada. They created settlements and traded with Native Americans. The English sent **John Cabot** and **Henry Hudson** in hopes of catching up with the Spanish and French in claiming land in the Americas.

REVIEW Why did some countries in Europe send out explorers? **Cause and Effect**

Summarize the Lesson

- The Iroquois lived in North America before the explorers arrived.
- The Iroquois had a set of rules that protected the rights of their people.
- The explorers had different customs than did the Iroquois.
- Portugal, Spain, France, and England sent out explorers to find a water route to China.

LESSON 1 REVIEW

Check Facts and Main Ideas

1. Cause and Effect On a separate sheet of paper, fill in the effects for each of the causes.

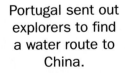

Explorers had different ideas from Native Americans. →

Portugal sent out explorers to find a water route to China. →

2. Why did the Iroquois cut wood for their houses in the spring?

3. What rights did the Iroquois' form of government protect?

4. Name four countries that sent explorers to the Americas.

5. Critical Thinking: *Draw Conclusions* Why do you think that the countries that traded with China and India wanted a water route to those countries?

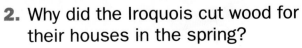

Link to **Art**

Make a Poster Choose Portugal, Spain, France, or England. Do research to find the flag of the country. Make a poster that shows the flag and other facts about the country.

Use the Library

What? To get information about a topic you want to know more about, you can visit your local library.

Why? Libraries have all the resources that you need to do your research. They carry **periodicals,** which are magazines that are printed regularly. Libraries have **reference books,** such as almanacs, dictionaries, atlases, and encyclopedias. They have computers for doing **Internet searches.** Libraries also have stacks of nonfiction books on just about any topic you can imagine. Let's head to the library right now!

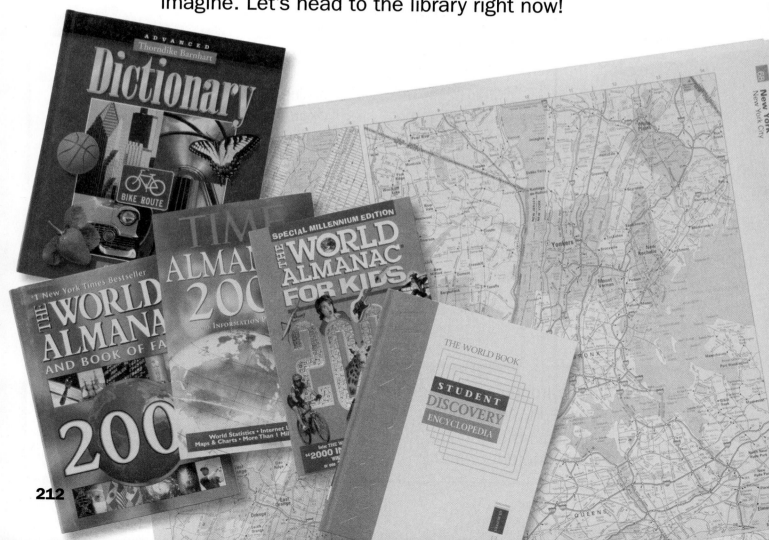

How? Let's start with your own community or a nearby community that you want to know more about.

- First, let's do an Internet search to see if there is information about the history of your community. To use the Internet, you'll need to do a **keyword search.** The name of your community might be a good keyword. After that, you can search for information about your community's history, geography, or whatever else you want to learn.

Search New York City

- Use an atlas to learn about your community's geography.
- An article in your local newspaper might be helpful, especially if it has pictures.

Your library may have people who can come to your school to talk to you about your community. These people can share information about the geography and history of your community.

The more sources that you use, the better the information that you will get. Using only one or two sources may not give you all the information that is important about a topic.

Think and Apply

1. What keyword would you use to get information about your community from the Internet?

2. What resource would be the best place to find information about the geography of your community?

3. What kind of information do you think might be important to gather about your community?

St. Augustine, Florida

A Spanish Community

Preview

Focus on the Main Idea
Spanish explorers came to present-day Florida and established communities.

PLACES
St. Augustine, Florida

PEOPLE
Juan Ponce de León
Don Pedro Menéndez de Avilés

VOCABULARY
fleet

You Are There Your ship has been tossed and turned by wind and waves for weeks now. Half your crew is sick from disease and hunger. If you don't find land soon, you don't know what you will do.

This afternoon you heard the call from the top of the ship that land has been sighted. Finally, you have reached your destination, the Americas. Surely gold must be here somewhere. You have traveled so far to find it. Your men can't wait to touch solid ground again. You wonder what you will find in this new place.

Cause and Effect As you read, look for the effects the Spanish had on the southern part of the present-day United States.

The Spanish in Florida

Juan Ponce de León landed north of present-day **St. Augustine, Florida.** He named the place where he landed *La Florida,* which means "land of flowers." He and his crew hoped to find Native American cities full of riches. Instead they found only a beautiful land that was perfect for farming. Disappointed, Ponce de León left. He went to Puerto Rico and then back to Spain.

Ponce de León came back to the northern coast of Florida in 1521. Bringing about 200 settlers with him, he hoped to build a city there. Unfortunately, the Spanish who first arrived attacked the native people. When Ponce de León returned, his crew was attacked, and he was killed by an arrow.

REVIEW What caused Ponce de León to leave Florida soon after exploring it?
◉ **Cause and Effect**

▶ Esteban was an enslaved African who traveled with Spanish explorers through present-day Florida, Louisiana, Texas, Arizona, New Mexico, and Mexico.

3 Terreplein

5 Sally Port

1 Moat

2 Curtain

4 Bastion

▶ Castillo de San Marcos at St. Augustine

▶ Sculpture of Spanish explorer Don Pedro Menéndez de Avilés

The Fight for Florida

The French also decided to build a settlement in Florida. In 1564 they set up a fort and a colony on the St. John's River. Fort Caroline was near where the Spanish had first landed. The French settlement threatened the safety of the Spanish treasure ships that sailed along the Florida coast on the way home to Spain from South America.

King Philip II of Spain sent **Don Pedro Menéndez de Avilés,** [AH vee lace] Spain's most experienced admiral, to be governor of Florida. The king told him to explore and settle Florida. Menéndez was also told to drive out any pirates or settlers from other countries.

216

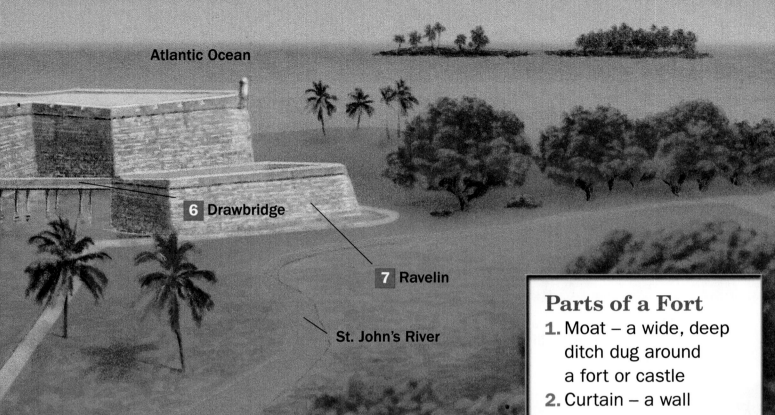

Atlantic Ocean

6 Drawbridge

7 Ravelin

St. John's River

Parts of a Fort

1. Moat – a wide, deep ditch dug around a fort or castle
2. Curtain – a wall that connected two bastions
3. Terreplein – a broad, flat, raised area
4. Bastion – a part built out from a corner of a fort
5. Sally Port – an opening in the wall of a fort
6. Drawbridge – a bridge that could be raised to keep people out and lowered to allow people to cross the moat
7. Ravelin – a building in front of the main gate

Menéndez arrived in Florida in 1565. Menéndez and his soldiers and settlers built a fort, Castillo de San Marcos. The area was sheltered from the ocean. It could be defended easily. The Spanish called the settlement St. Augustine.

Menéndez then defeated the French at Fort Caroline. With the help of a hurricane, he defeated the French fleet in the Atlantic Ocean. A **fleet** is a large group of ships. The coast of Florida was finally controlled by Spain. St. Augustine became the first permanent European settlement in North America.

REVIEW Why did Menéndez decide to build a community at St Augustine?

↻ Cause and Effect

St. Augustine Today

Hi, my name is Kevin and I live in St. Augustine, Florida. If you come to my city, we could visit the beaches and go to the historic sights in town. We can see the oldest standing house in the United States. We can explore the oldest stone fort in the country, Castillo de San Marcos. We can visit Fort Mose, which protected Africans from slavery.

▶ The Oldest House is now a museum. It shows what life was like long ago.

▶ Many people come to the fort to see how the soldiers lived. People dressed as soldiers give tours of the fort.

My city, St. Augustine, is one of the oldest communities in the United States. Our history is important, and the people here in St. Augustine have kept the Spanish culture of the community alive. What is the history of your community?

REVIEW Why do parts of St. Augustine still look like an old Spanish town?

⦿ **Cause and Effect**

▶ **Doubloon of Phillip II, King of Spain**

Summarize the Lesson

- Ponce de León hoped to find gold in Florida. Instead he found beautiful land for farming.
- The French came to Florida and threatened Spanish ships.
- After the Spanish defeated the French in Florida, St. Augustine became a permanent settlement.
- The community of St. Augustine has kept its history alive.

LESSON 2 ⟩ REVIEW

Check Facts and Main Ideas

1. ⦿ **Cause and Effect** Copy the chart on a separate sheet of paper. For each cause, fill in the effect in the correct box.

Ponce de León hoped to find gold in Florida.	→	

The Spanish found a perfect location for a community.	→	

2. What does *La Florida* mean in English?

3. Why did Ponce de León come back to Florida in 1521?

4. What two countries fought over Florida in the 1500s?

5. **Critical Thinking:** *Draw Conclusions* How can you tell that people who live in St. Augustine today are proud of their history?

Link to ⚭ **Geography**

Make a Map Use a map of the United States to trace Florida. Place a dot where St. Augustine is today. Put other cities that you know are in Florida on your map too. Label the cities. Write a title for your map. Explain what you know about those cities to a friend.

Cádiz, Spain

St. Augustine, Florida, is one of the oldest communities in the United States. Cádiz, Spain, is one of the the oldest communities not only in Spain, but in all of Europe.

The first group of people who came to Cádiz was called the Phoenicians [fo NEE shins]. They built the city around 1130 B.C.

For the next 2,000 years, different countries fought over the city. Finally, in 1262, Cádiz became a part of Spain.

For more than 200 years, Cádiz seemed just an ordinary port city. But one event changed Cádiz forever. In 1492, a man named Christopher Columbus sailed west and arrived in the Americas. Cádiz suddenly became the major port city for the Spanish. It became one of the richest cities in all of Europe.

Cádiz and St. Augustine are both port cities on the Atlantic Ocean.

▶ Spanish coins minted in 1814

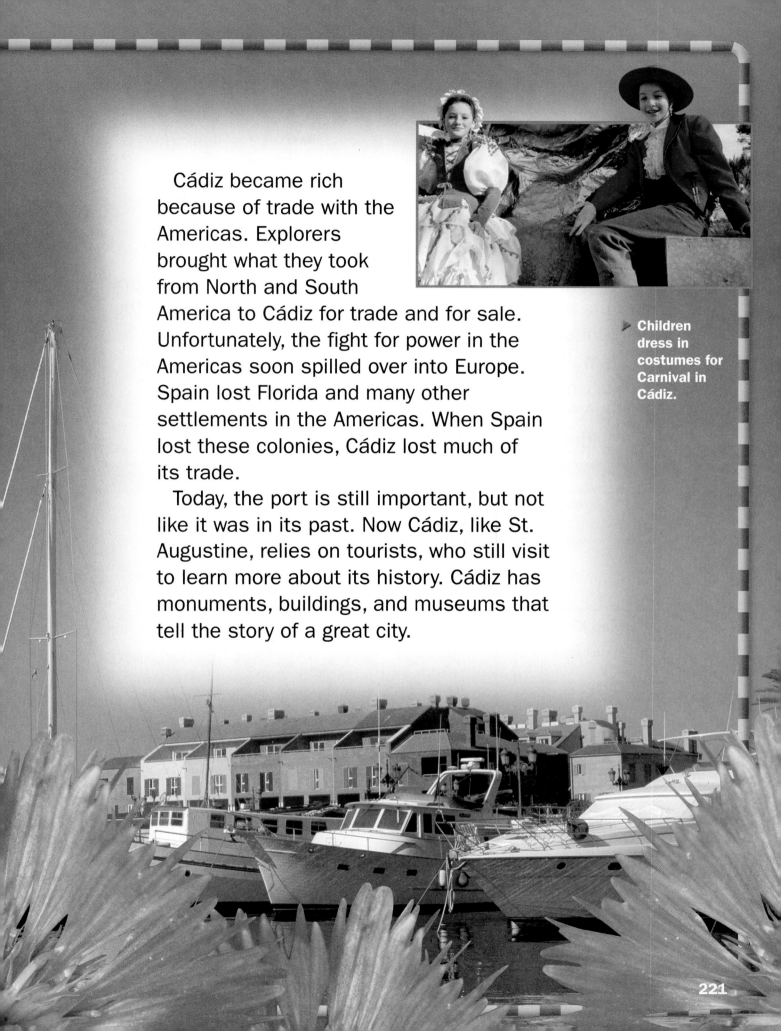

Cádiz became rich because of trade with the Americas. Explorers brought what they took from North and South America to Cádiz for trade and for sale. Unfortunately, the fight for power in the Americas soon spilled over into Europe. Spain lost Florida and many other settlements in the Americas. When Spain lost these colonies, Cádiz lost much of its trade.

Today, the port is still important, but not like it was in its past. Now Cádiz, like St. Augustine, relies on tourists, who still visit to learn more about its history. Cádiz has monuments, buildings, and museums that tell the story of a great city.

▶ Children dress in costumes for Carnival in Cádiz.

Use a Locator Map

What? You have been learning about Ponce de León who explored Florida. These two maps show how this area looks today. The large map shows the entire state of Florida. The smaller map shows the United States. A box is placed around Florida. The smaller map is called a locator map. A **locator map** is an inset that shows how a place fits into a bigger place. This locator map locates the state of Florida within the United States.

MAP SKILL

Florida with an Inset of the United States

Map Key
★ State capital

▶ Florida is a peninsula. It is surrounded by water on three sides.

MAP SKILL Use a Locator Map *In what region of the United States is Florida located?*

Why? A locator map gives you the "big picture" of a place, even though it's a small map! In the locator map on page 222, you see that Florida is one state in the United States. The larger map gives you lots of details. You can see some major cities in Florida. You wouldn't be able to put all those cities on the small map.

How? When you see a locator map, you should look for two things.

First, look for the big picture. Is the locator map showing you the world, hemispheres, continents, countries, states, or cities? Second, look for the place on the locator map that has a box, circle, or some kind of shading or symbol that sets the area apart. That box, circle, or shading will tell you that this area of the locator map will be shown in greater detail on a larger map.

Think and Apply

Look at the two maps and answer the questions.

1. What area is the locator map showing?

2. What area is the larger map showing?

3. Near which ocean is St. Augustine?

For more information, go online to the *Atlas* at **www.sfsocialstudies.com**.

CANADA

St. Lawrence R.

Quebec City

UNITED STATES

Preview

Focus on the Main Idea
French explorers came to present-day Canada and built communities.

PLACES
Quebec City, Canada

PEOPLE
Jacques Cartier
Samuel de Champlain

VOCABULARY
fortification

A French Community

You Are There You stand on a high bluff and look out over the city and the St. Lawrence River. This is one of the most beautiful places in all of Canada. The city is very old and has a rich history. The province of Quebec is the only place in Canada where French is the main language of most of the people.

You can understand why the French explorers chose this place to settle. Samuel de Champlain must have realized that this location was the perfect place to build his city. High above the river, the city was protected from attack. The river provided a way to trade with other parts of the Americas. What is this place, you ask? Why, it's Quebec City, in Canada!

Cause and Effect As you read, think about what effects the French had on life in Quebec City and throughout Quebec.

Etching of Jacques Cartier meeting with Native Americans at Hochelaga, which is now Montreal, a city in Quebec, Canada.

Samuel de Champlain

The French in Canada

Portugal had found a water route to the East. The French thought that it might be faster to travel by inland waterways to the North and West. In 1534 **Jacques Cartier** (car tee A) landed on the coast of present-day Newfoundland.

Cartier explored the area and realized that this could not be the direct route to China that he was seeking. Rapids and waterfalls blocked his path west. He returned home to France.

In 1608 **Samuel de Champlain** sailed from France to present-day Canada. At Stadacona, an Iroquois village, he built a permanent French settlement called **Quebec City.** During the next 150 years, many battles were fought over Quebec City. In 1759, the English broke through the wall of Quebec City, and French rule in Canada ended.

REVIEW What caused Cartier to realize that he had not found the northwest route to China? ↻ **Cause and Effect**

Nautical telescope and compass

Bienvenue au Québec!

Quebec City Today

I am Marie. If you speak English, I will translate for you. "Welcome to Quebec!"

First we'll go to Old Quebec. That is the area you see behind the old stone walls, or **fortifications,** on the top of the hill. This is where the French built their fort and held out against the English for so long.

At the heart of Old Quebec proudly stands Le Chateau (sha TOE) Frontenac. Since 1893, this castlelike hotel has sat on a hilltop overlooking the St. Lawrence River. From here you can see for miles.

The park in the middle of the old part of the city fills with musicians, jugglers, mimes, cartoonists, artists, and people who just want to relax after walking around.

Quebec's culture makes the city a special place to live and a special place to visit. French is spoken throught the city. French customs and traditions are celebrated in Quebec all year long.

REVIEW What makes Quebec City a special place? **Draw Conclusions**

LESSON 3 REVIEW

Check Facts and Main Ideas

1. **Cause and Effect** Copy the chart on a separate sheet of paper. Look at the cause. Fill in the effect in the box.

> The French controlled Quebec early in history. →

2. Why did Champlain build a permanent settlement at Quebec City?

3. Where did Cartier first land when he arrived in the Americas?

4. What culture makes Quebec City special?

5. **Critical Thinking:** *Make Inferences* Why would rapids and waterfalls cause Cartier to turn back from his search for a route to China and India?

Link to **Writing**

Write a Paragraph Describe old Quebec. Include the fort, the hotel, and the park. Remember to use complete sentences. Share your paragraph with your class.

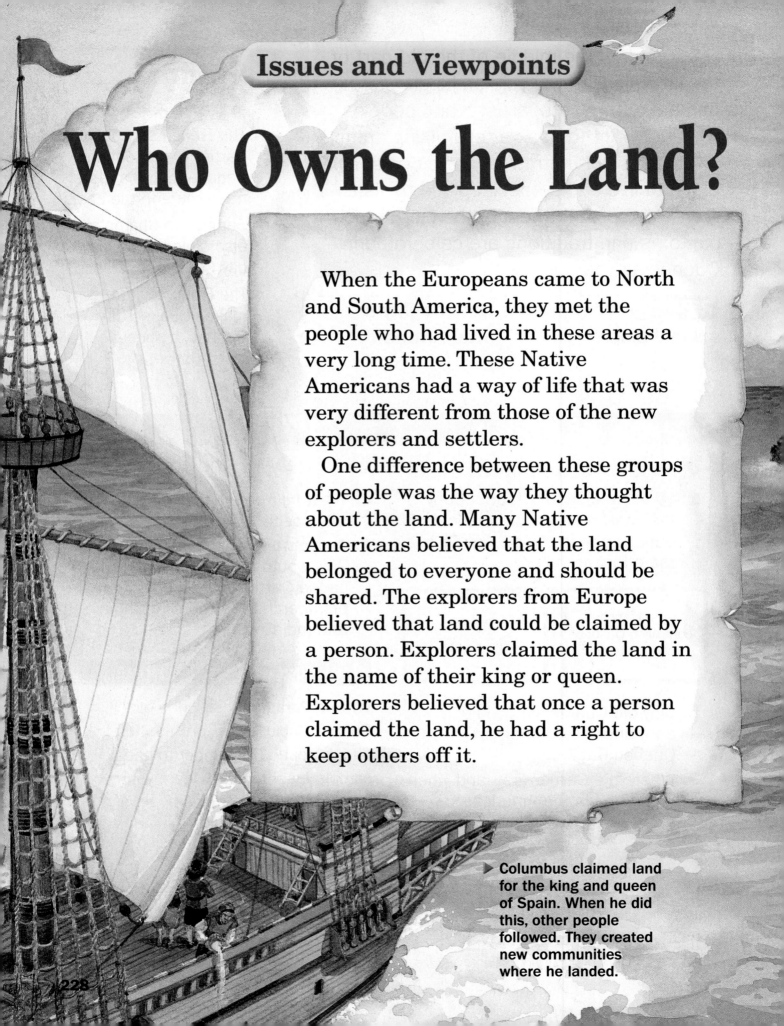

Who Owns the Land?

When the Europeans came to North and South America, they met the people who had lived in these areas a very long time. These Native Americans had a way of life that was very different from those of the new explorers and settlers.

One difference between these groups of people was the way they thought about the land. Many Native Americans believed that the land belonged to everyone and should be shared. The explorers from Europe believed that land could be claimed by a person. Explorers claimed the land in the name of their king or queen. Explorers believed that once a person claimed the land, he had a right to keep others off it.

▶ Columbus claimed land for the king and queen of Spain. When he did this, other people followed. They created new communities where he landed.

"Sell a country! Why not sell the air, the great sea, as well as the earth? Did not the Great Spirit make them all for the use of his children?"

Tecumseh, *1810*

"We sweat and toil to live; their (Native Americans) pleasure feeds them, I mean their Hunting, Fishing, and Fowling...."

William Penn, *1683*

"The Admiral called upon the two captains, and the rest of the crew who landed, to bear witness that he before all others took possession of that island for the King and Queen, which are set down here in writing.

Journal of Christopher Columbus, *1492*

Issues and You

Native Americans and European explorers had different views about who could own land. What viewpoints do people have about owning land today? How are these views alike or different from the views of the Native Americans or European explorers?

Jamestown, Virginia

An English Community

Preview

Focus on the Main Idea
English explorers came to present-day Virginia and built communities.

PLACES
Jamestown
James River

PEOPLE
Christopher Newport
John Smith
Powhatan
Pocahontas

VOCABULARY
representative government

You Are There The bright sunshine feels warm on your face. You come here to the river as often as you can. You love to fish and swim.

What's that floating up the river? You've never seen a boat that big before. The boat stops right in the middle of the river. The men and boys coming to the shore are not from here. Their skin is very pale. They are wearing strange clothes. You look at the tools they are taking off the boat. Do they think they can farm in this swamp, you wonder? Are they just here for a visit? How long will they stay?

Cause and Effect As you read, think about how the English arrival in Jamestown affected the Native Americans who lived there.

The English in Virginia

Around May 13, 1607, the first English settlers arrived in present-day **Jamestown** to seek their fortune. Long before the English came, however, the Native Americans there had planted crops and built villages.

Captain **Christopher Newport** dropped off about 105 people from his ship. The settlers named their settlement Jamestown, and they called the river the **James River** after King James I.

Soon the settlers were running out of food. **John Smith,** a leader in the settlement, led a search to find more food. The Native Americans in the area captured his group and brought him before their chief, **Powhatan.** The chief's daughter, **Pocahontas,** watched as Powhatan agreed to help the settlers. Smith returned to Jamestown. Only about 38 of the 105 people were still alive. The rest had died of hunger and disease.

REVIEW What caused so many settlers to die? ↻ **Cause and Effect**

▶ Engraving of Powhatan being crowned head of the Powhatan Confederacy

First Sermon Ashore was painted by Jean Leon Gerome in 1621.

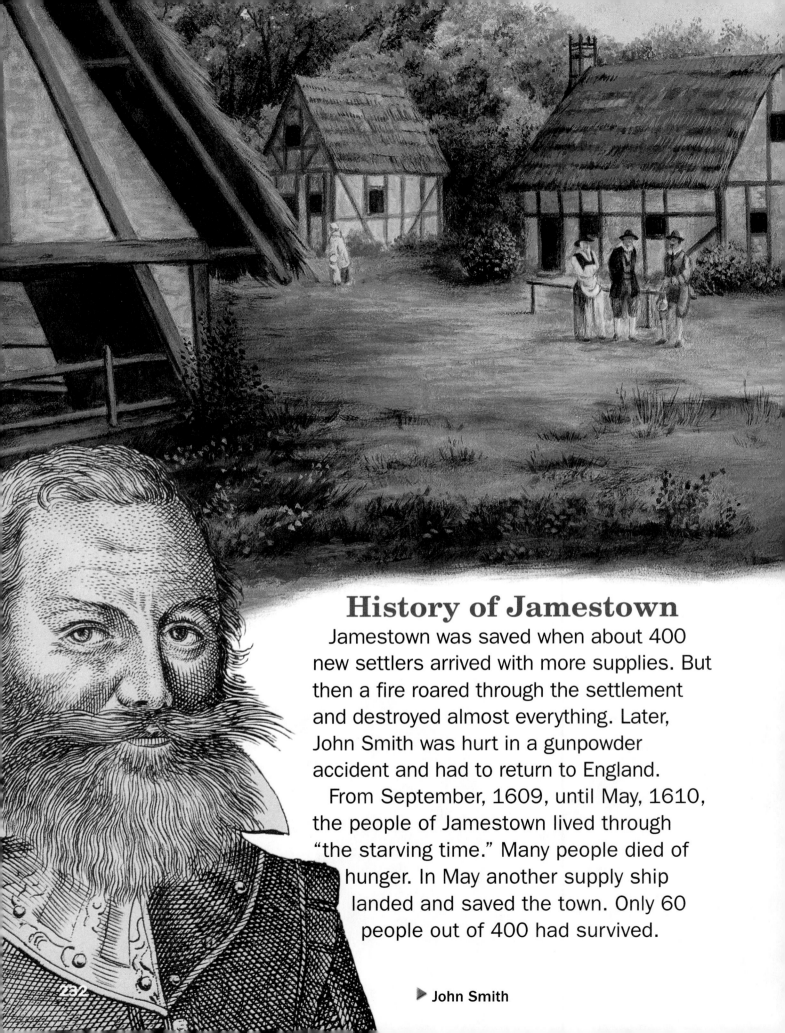

History of Jamestown

Jamestown was saved when about 400 new settlers arrived with more supplies. But then a fire roared through the settlement and destroyed almost everything. Later, John Smith was hurt in a gunpowder accident and had to return to England.

From September, 1609, until May, 1610, the people of Jamestown lived through "the starving time." Many people died of hunger. In May another supply ship landed and saved the town. Only 60 people out of 400 had survived.

▶ John Smith

Community life in Jamestown

Many of the men who went to Jamestown were English citizens. They had the same rights that they had when they lived in England. One of these rights was the right to have a voice in how they were governed.

On July 30, 1619, the first representative assembly in the New World met in a Jamestown church. In a **representative government,** voters elect people to speak for them. The job of the assembly was to form a government that would work for all of Virginia.

REVIEW What was the job of the first representative assembly?
Main Idea and Details

Jamestown Today

Today, Jamestown is a national historic site. Every year people from all over the world come to Jamestown to learn the history of this important settlement.

Historic Jamestown

A statue of John Smith overlooks the James River.

Barracks Soldiers live in barracks.

North Bulwark A bulwark is a wall made of earth.

South Palisade A palisade is a fence made of long wooden stakes.

Powder Magazine A powder magazine is a building for storing gunpowder.

John White's Place was the first building made of brick. All buildings before 1620 were made of wood.

Locations of some places are estimates based on historical information.

▶ This jar and pitcher are from the historic Jamestown site.

People no longer live in historic Jamestown. Present-day Jamestown is located several miles from historic Jamestown.

REVIEW How is historic Jamestown alike and different from when it was first founded? **Compare and Contrast**

Summarize the Lesson

- Captain Christopher Newport and other settlers founded Jamestown.
- John Smith was a leader of the Jamestown settlement.
- Disease and hunger killed most of the people in Jamestown.
- The first representative assembly in the New World met in a Jamestown church.

LESSON 4 REVIEW

Check Facts and Main Ideas

1. **Cause and Effect** Copy the chart on a separate piece of paper. For each cause, fill in the effect in the correct box.

John Smith was hurt in an accident.	→	

First representative assembly met.	→	

2. How did Christopher Newport help found Jamestown?

3. What was "the starving time"?

4. What was one right that some of the men brought with them to Jamestown?

5. **Critical Thinking:** *Make Inferences* Do you think that the settlers who came to Jamestown were well prepared? Why or why not?

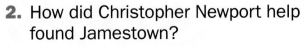

Link to — **Art**

Make an Ad Your ad should help someone decide to visit historic Jamestown. Show scenes of early Jamestown. Tell about people and places you will learn about there. Share your ad with your class.

235

Meet Pocahontas

About 1595–1617

Pocahontas was one of Powhatan's daughters. Powhatan was the leader of at least 30 Native American groups in Virginia. When she was 12, Pocahontas saw some of the first Englishmen to arrive in that part of the country.

For more information, go online to *Meet the People* at **www.sfsocialstudies.com**.

Pocahontas played an important role in the Jamestown colony. John Smith said that she saved his life when her father wanted to kill him. She often visited the Jamestown colony. There she learned about English customs and brought food to the settlers.

After John Smith returned to England, Pocahontas was captured by the settlers. She lived with a minister and changed her religion. She also changed her name to Rebecca. During this time she met John Rolfe and they were married.

In 1615 Thomas was born to Rebecca and John Rolfe. One year later the Rolfe family traveled to England. There she met an old friend, John Smith.

In 1617, before she could come back to her home, she became very ill. She died when she was about 21. Pocahontas was buried in England.

Pocahontas is remembered for her courage and her kindness. Without her, Jamestown might not have survived.

Learn from Biographies

Do you think Jamestown could have survived without Pocahontas's help? Why or why not?

Her family called Pocahontas by her given name, Matoaka. Pocahontas was her nickname. It means "playful."

BIOFACT

▶ **Portrait of John Rolfe**

Chapter Summary

 Cause and Effect

On a separate sheet of paper, fill in the cause or effect of the exploration of the Americas.

Native Americans and European explorers had different cultures and ideas.	→
	→ Even today Spanish culture is important in St. Augustine.

Vocabulary

Match each word with the correct definition or description.

1. explorer (p. 209)
2. fleet (p. 217)
3. fortifications (p. 226)
4. representative government (p. 233)

a. a large group of ships

b. voters elect people to speak for them

c. stone walls

d. a person who travels to little-known places

Facts and Main Ideas

1 Name one group of people that lived in New York before European explorers arrived.

2 **Main Idea** What were early explorers from Europe looking for on their travels?

3 **Main Idea** How did the Spanish treat Native Americans in Florida? What happened because of this?

4 **Main Idea** Why did France send Jacques Cartier and Samuel de Champlain west?

5 **Main Idea** What two things caused most of the people in Jamestown to die?

6 **Critical Thinking:** *Compare and Contrast* How did many Native Americans feel about who should own land? How did European explorers feel about it? Compare and contrast.

Write About It

1 **Write a Journal Entry** Describe what Florida must have looked like to one of Juan Ponce de León's explorers.

2 **Write an advertisement** that you could put up around London. You need people who want to go to Jamestown. Give reasons why people should make the trip to North America.

3 **Write a list** of questions that you would like to ask one of the people you read about in this chapter.

Apply Skills

Use the Library Columbus explored the island community of San Salvador. Tell which library resources you would use to find information about San Salvador's geography, history, and famous people.

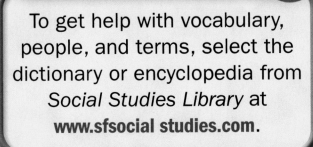

Internet Activity

To get help with vocabulary, people, and terms, select the dictionary or encyclopedia from *Social Studies Library* at **www.sfsocial studies.com**.

Chapter 8

Technology Changes Communities

Lesson 1

Kitty Hawk, North Carolina

Transportation improves over time.

1

Lesson 2

St. Joseph, Missouri

Communication allows people to keep in touch.

ST.JOSEPH

2

Lesson 3

Menlo Park, New Jersey

Technology affects communities.

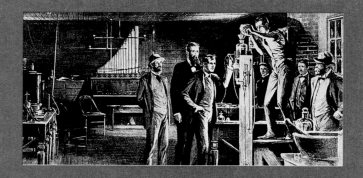

3

Lesson 4

Paris, France

Medicine improves the health of people.

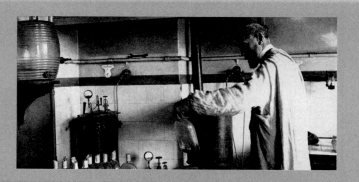

4

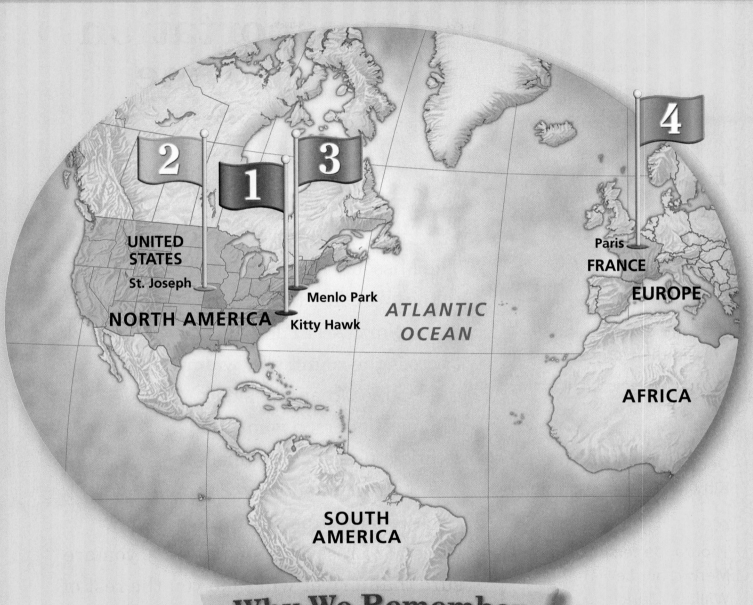

Why We Remember

In the early 1800s cities and towns lined the eastern part of the United States. Few people had moved past the Mississippi River. Why? No one could imagine how to travel that far. Wagons and trains opened the way west. Soon communities sprang up along wagon routes and train tracks. These brave travelers helped our country grow.

Detroit
Kitty Hawk

Preview

Focus on the Main Idea
New forms of transportation allowed people to move across the United States and around the world.

PLACES
Mississippi River
Detroit, Michigan
Kitty Hawk, North Carolina

PEOPLE
Thomas Jefferson
Meriwether Lewis
William Clark
Sacagawea
Gottlieb Daimler
Karl Benz
Henry Ford
Orville and Wilbur Wright

VOCABULARY
Transcontinental Railroad

Transportation Over Time

You Are There
You are traveling with William Clark and Meriwether Lewis in 1804. The Missouri River is your road to the West. You have followed it in search of the Northwest Passage. It is a way to cross the country by water to get to the Pacific Ocean. President Thomas Jefferson wants you to find a passage like this.

Tall, proud, and snowy, the Rocky Mountains stand in your way. Once you cross these mountains, you are sure that a river will take you the rest of the way. After all, if you can't go by boat, how can you travel west?

Cause and Effect As you read, look for how new forms of transportation affected the growth of communities in the western part of the United States.

Trails Across America

In 1804, **Meriwether Lewis** and **William Clark** explored the land west of the **Mississippi River.**

Lewis and Clark traveled along the Missouri River until it ended. They crossed over the Rocky Mountains on foot and horseback. A Native American translator and peacemaker, **Sacagawea,** traveled with them part of the way. Lewis and Clark finally made it to the Pacific Ocean after a long, hard trip. They brought back stories that made people want to move west in search of a better life. Because of Lewis and Clark, new communities sprang up all over the West.

In 1842, on a trail that was first used by Native Americans and fur traders, settlers came in covered wagons pulled by oxen. The trip along the Oregon Trail took six months, and it was full of hard work and danger. There had to be a better way to get to this new land!

REVIEW What caused people who lived in the East to begin to travel west?
Cause and Effect

► Sacagawea (sack uh juh WE uh) was a Shoshone. This sculpture of her stands in Bismarck, North Dakota.

Westward Expansion

▶ The final spike joining the tracks of the Union Pacific and Central Pacific Railroads was driven in at Promontory, Utah, on May 10, 1869.

Chinese immigrant workers lay track for the Transcontinental Railroad.

Even though the trip west proved difficult, plenty of people were willing to go. Some people wanted to go west to seek their fortunes. Families joined together in wagon trains. Wagons rolled west with everything a family owned. But a safer, faster way west was needed.

British engineers James Watt and Richard Trevithick developed and improved steam engines. Their inventions led to a brand new form of transportation, the steam locomotive, that changed the way people around the world traveled. Soon railroad companies began laying miles of tracks across the country.

In 1869 the **Transcontinental Railroad** linked the eastern United States to the West. Now a family could travel safely from Omaha, Nebraska, all the way to Sacramento, California, in just a few days!

REVIEW What effect did the Transcontinental Railroad have on the way people traveled west?
⟳ **Cause and Effect**

MAP ADVENTURE — Traveling West

Suppose your parents traveled west on the Oregon Trail in 1869. Twenty years later you are taking the Transcontinental Railroad. Your trip will be faster and easier than your parents' trip.

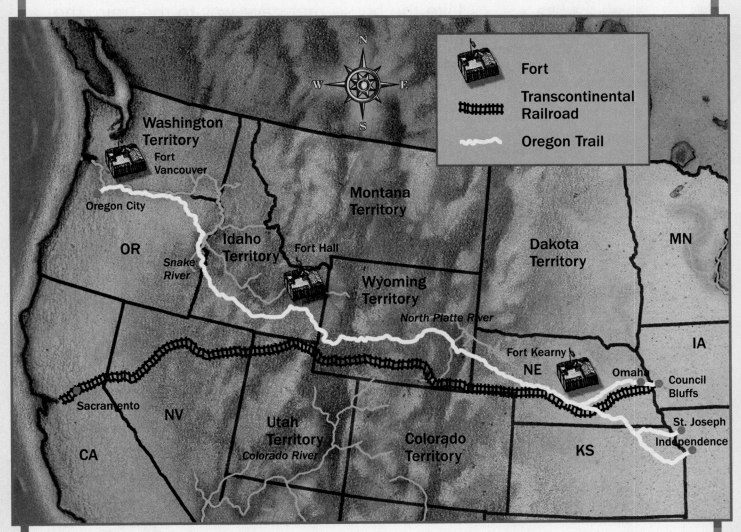

1. What state and territory will you pass through that your parents passed through?

2. Which river do both routes west cross?

3. Which fort is near both the Oregon Trail and the Transcontinental Railroad tracks?

► Karl Benz with his assisstant Josef Brecht in 1886

Trains, Cars, Planes, and Space Shuttles

The first year that people could ride on trains in the United States was 1830. There were 23 miles of track in the United States. By 1917, train tracks extended over 250,000 miles. The Iron Horse, as the locomotive was called, was replacing the real horse as a way to travel.

Like the horse that gave way to the train, the train now had to give way to the car. In 1885 and 1886 German inventors Karl Benz and Gottlieb Daimler built the first gasoline-powered cars. American Henry Ford started making cars in Detroit, Michigan, in 1903. Soon other car makers came to Detroit to build cars. Detroit became known as the Motor City. At the same time, new roads and highways were built across America.

► Henry Ford

► The Lincoln Highway, started in 1913, was the first highway to run from coast to coast.

In 1903, two brothers, Orville and Wilbur Wright, flew the first airplane. Its longest flight was about 852 feet from a hill at Kitty Hawk, North Carolina. From propeller planes to jets, air travel again made transportation faster. Cars and trains made our country seem smaller. Airplanes made the whole world seem smaller.

Today, rockets, satellites, and space shuttles soar into space. Who knows what the future of transportation will be?

Summarize the Lesson

- Because of Lewis and Clark, new communities grew throughout the West.
- The Transcontinental Railroad made travel to the West safer and faster.
- Transportation inventions include cars, trains, and airplanes.

REVIEW How have the automobile and airplane changed the world?

⊙ **Cause and Effect**

LESSON 1 REVIEW

Check Facts and Main Ideas

1. ⊙ **Cause and Effect** Copy the chart on a separate piece of paper. For each cause, fill in the effect in the correct box.

Lewis and Clark explored the West.	→	

The Transcontinental Railroad linked the East and West coasts.	→	

2. Which group of people first traveled along the Oregon Trail?

3. How did families traveling to the West on the Oregon Trail move their belongings?

4. What new form of transportation was the result of an invention by Orville and Wilbur Wright?

5. **Critical Thinking:** *Make Inferences* Why do you think the Iron Horse replaced the real horse as a way to travel to the West?

Link to ⚭ Mathematics

Measure the Distance The Wright brothers' airplane flew about 120 feet on its first flight. Use a yardstick to measure 120 feet of string or yarn. Stretch out the string or yarn to show the distance the Wright brothers' first airplane flew.

Use a Time Line

What? A time line shows when events occurred. The time line can be divided into sections of single years, decades, and even centuries. A **decade** is 10 years. A **century** is 100 years. The events are placed on the time line in the order, or sequence, that they occurred. Look at the time line showing when certain areas of the United States became states.

Why? Time lines can act as a reference for you to find when something happened in history. They can also be good sources for comparing when events happened.

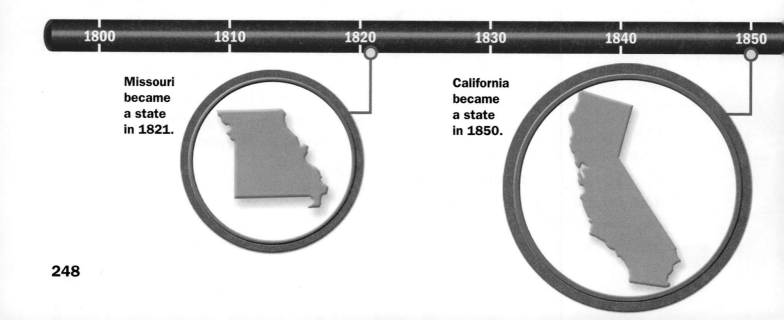

Missouri became a state in 1821.

California became a state in 1850.

How? Time lines can be very helpful as you read a social studies book. Before you start reading, make your own time line. First, write in the date of 1803. That's when Lewis and Clark began their journey west. Go back to the first lesson and see if any other dates seem important. Keep a list of dates as you read through this chapter. At the end of the chapter put all your dates together in order. Make a time line that shows these dates.

Look at the time line on these pages and answer the questions.

1 In what decade were most states on this time line admitted to the United States?

2 Which of the states was admitted in 1890?

3 How many centuries are shown on this time line?

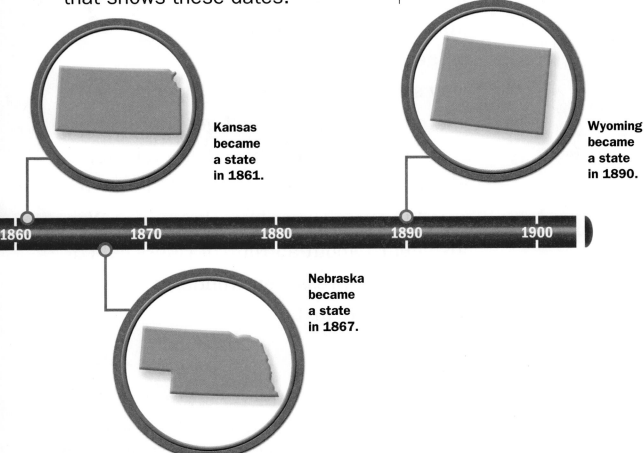

Kansas became a state in 1861.

Wyoming became a state in 1890.

Nebraska became a state in 1867.

1860   1870   1880   1890   1900

Sacramento • St. Joseph

Preview

Focus on the Main Idea
New forms of communication help people keep in touch with one another.

PLACES
St. Joseph, Missouri
Sacramento, California

PEOPLE
Benjamin Franklin
Samuel Morse
Alexander Graham Bell
Guglielmo Marconi
A. A. Campbell Swinton

VOCABULARY
Pony Express
invention
Morse code
broadcast

Communication Over Time

 You live in Boston in 1860, and you write a letter to your cousin in Baltimore. The letter arrives in about ten days. The riders the Post Office uses must be very fast.

It is much farther from Boston to San Francisco. You think there may be a stagecoach heading that way soon, but even then a letter you write to your uncle won't get there for several months. You have been told you can send a letter by ship, but that has to go all the way around South America. You also heard about a group of riders called the Pony Express. You wonder if they would be any faster.

 Cause and Effect As you read, look for how new forms of communication affected the way people kept in touch with one another.

Mail by Horseback

What if you couldn't pick up the phone or send an email inviting your cousin to come spend the weekend? What if you had to write a letter, and the letter wouldn't get there for weeks? That was what it was like for people in the United States in the early 1800s. The only way for mail to get anywhere was on horseback or by wagon train.

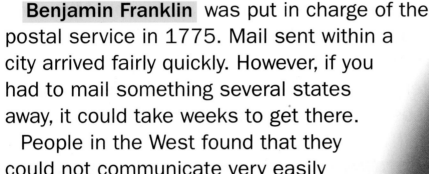

▶ Benjamin Franklin

Benjamin Franklin was put in charge of the postal service in 1775. Mail sent within a city arrived fairly quickly. However, if you had to mail something several states away, it could take weeks to get there.

People in the West found that they could not communicate very easily with their families and friends back in the East. Something had to be done, but what?

REVIEW Why did people in the West have a difficult time communicating with people in the East? **Draw Conclusions**

▶ Franklin Post Office,
Philadelphia,
Pennsylvania

Mail by Pony Express

If you sent a letter west in the early 1800s, you never knew if it would get there. Bandits often attacked the wagons loaded with mail. Weather also caused delays. In order to make sure the mail was delivered faster and safely, a group of business people set up the Pony Express in 1860.

The **Pony Express** was made up of riders who rode 75 miles per day from **St. Joseph, Missouri,** to **Sacramento, California.** Rest stations were built along the route. Riders would get food and water at these stations. They would also change horses. The Pony Express cut mail delivery time in half.

▶ This plaque is on a marker on the route used by the Pony Express.

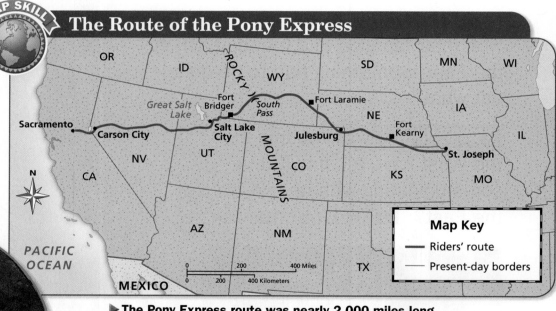

The Route of the Pony Express

▶ The Pony Express route was nearly 2,000 miles long.

MAP SKILL Location *In which state did the Pony Express route cross the Rocky Mountains?*

After the start of the Transcontinental Railroad, the postal service began sending letters across the country on the train. This way was faster and safer.

REVIEW What was the effect of bandits and bad weather on mail delivery?
⟳ **Cause and Effect**

▶ The telegraph received signals in a series of dots and dashes on paper. This series of signals was called the **Morse code.**

The Telegraph and Telephone

In 1837, **Samuel Morse** invented a way to send and receive signals through a thin wire. He called this invention the telegraph. An **invention** is something that is made for the first time.

In 1861, the first transcontinental telegraph wire was put up. Messages could be sent across the country in seconds.

Alexander Graham Bell thought that if messages could be sent through these wires, why not the human voice? In 1876, Bell invented the first telephone. Soon people in different places could talk to each other easily. Before too long, people across the nation were talking to one another on the telephone.

REVIEW What effect did the telegraph and telephone have on communication?
↺ **Cause and Effect**

▶ Marconi and his radio

Radio and Television

In fewer than 100 years, Americans went from sending letters by wagon to calling a number and hearing a voice on the telephone. In 1896, italian inventor **Guglielmo Marconi** found a way for voices to travel without wires.

Marconi sent radio signals a distance of more than a mile. Since radio waves could travel through the air and did not need to go through wires, there was no limit to how much information could be sent. People all over the world listened to radio programs for the first time.

In 1908, **A. A. Campbell Swinton** used a special tube to build a television. Words were **broadcast,** or sent out, with black and white pictures. By the late 1940s, the news of the world in pictures came to you right in your home. Now televisions are in color.

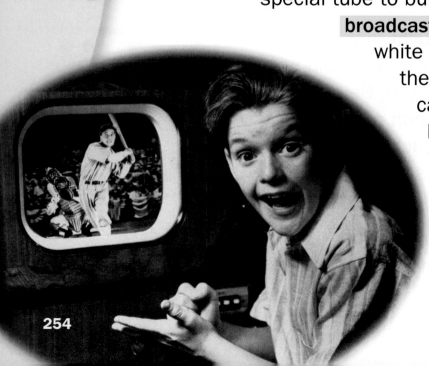

▶ **1939 television set**

254

In the last 20 years, communication has changed even more. Many telephones no longer need wires. Satellites and cables can send us hundreds of television channels. Thanks to the Internet, we write letters on computers. Email letters arrive in just a few seconds.

REVIEW How was radio alike and different from the first telephones? **Compare and Contrast**

Summarize the Lesson

- Benjamin Franklin was put in charge of the first postal service in 1775.
- People sent mail by horseback or stagecoach in the early 1800s.
- The Pony Express cut the time to deliver mail across the country in half.
- The telephone and telegraph made communication faster and easier.
- Radio and television bring news of the world into homes.

LESSON 2   REVIEW

Check Facts and Main Ideas

1. **Cause and Effect** Copy the chart on a separate sheet of paper. Look at the effect. Fill in the cause in the box.

| | | Mail could be delivered in half the time it once took. |

2. Why was the Pony Express set up in 1860?

3. How did Samuel Morse and Alexander Graham Bell change the way people communicated?

4. Why was radio such an important invention?

5. **Critical Thinking:** *Draw Conclusions* Why is it important to be able to communicate easily?

Link to **Writing**

Write a Paragraph Choose one kind of communication that you read about in this chapter. Write about why this kind of communication was important in communities both in the past and today.

▶ Ben

▶ Tricia

Ben and Tricia Wymore

Bike Riders Through Virginia

Virginia is a state with an important past. Ben and Tricia Wymore took a bike ride through Virginia to help students understand and respect the history of this state.

Ben and Tricia began in Jamestown, Virginia, and ended in Rosedale, Virginia. Ben built a bicycle that both he and Tricia could ride together. Ben and Tricia thought it would be a great idea if they could put this trip on the Internet. They wanted students to learn about the people and places they visited.

▶ The Virginia countryside

BUILDING
CITIZENSHIP
Caring
Respect
Responsibility
Fairness
Honesty
Courage

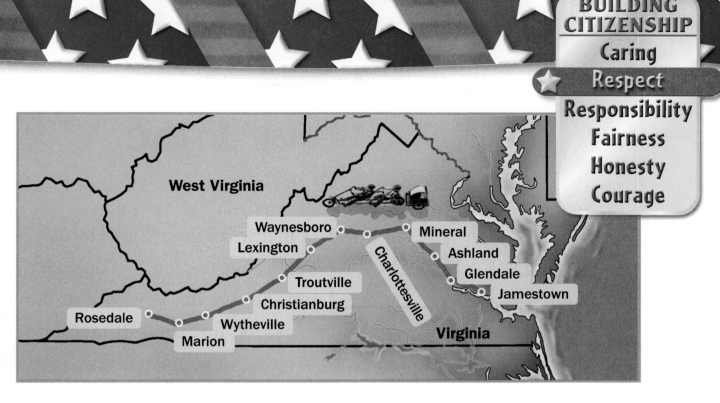

For 13 days, Ben and Tricia traveled through Virginia. The map shows the route that they took. Each day they used special equipment to put their trip on a Web site on the Internet so students all over the world could learn more about the state of Virginia. Ben said that he wanted to share with others what he and Tricia saw every day.

▶ Ben and Tricia's bike

Ben was also interviewed by the Voice of America. The Voice of America is a radio show that reaches 100 million people in Africa, Asia, and Europe. This show tells the world about the United States, our freedom, and our way of life. Ben talked about his trip to people all over the world.

Respect in Action

Ben and Tricia want students in Virginia and in every state to respect their state's special history. As a class, research the special history of your state. What special hero do you respect most?

257

Menlo Park, New Jersey

Inventions Over Time

Preview

Focus on the Main Idea
Inventors and their inventions made the lives of people in communities easier.

PLACES
Menlo Park, New Jersey

PEOPLE
Thomas Edison
Lewis Latimer
Cyrus Hall McCormick
Louis Daguerre
George Eastman

VOCABULARY
reaper

You Are There
It is a warm night in Menlo Park, New Jersey. You decide to take a walk. It is late at night and dark as ink, but the full moon allows you to see where you are going. As you walk, you pass the laboratory of Thomas Edison. You notice light in one of the windows. Edison seems to be working late these days.

The window is open. You stare more closely at Edison's light. It doesn't flicker like a candle. It just sits in a ball of glass and lights up the night. What kind of light has Edison made?

 Cause and Effect As you read, think about the effects of inventions on people's lives.

Inventions at Work

If you worked indoors during the day, sunlight streamed through the windows. At night candles and oil or gas lamps provided light. Although these might give off light, they weren't very bright and also caused fires. A better way to light homes and factories was needed.

Thomas Edison's light bulb changed the way people lived. His invention provided light and yet there was little danger of fire. Factories and offices could now stay open around the clock.

Lewis Latimer was a famous African American inventor. He did special drawings of a telephone for Alexander Graham Bell. Lewis Latimer also worked with **Thomas Edison.** The lamps and the light bulbs that we use today use many of the parts that Latimer invented when he worked in Edison's company. Latimer helped New York City; Philadelphia; Montreal, Canada; and London, England light their communities.

REVIEW How did Thomas Edison and Lewis Latimer change the way people lit their factories and homes? **Draw Conclusions**

▶ Lewis Latimer, African American inventor

▶ Thomas Edison in his studio

259

Inventions in Farming

In the 1700s and 1800s, many people worked on farms. The work was hard, the hours were long, and the work never ended.

Cyrus Hall McCormick saw that harvesting crops was hard work. A person would walk through a field with a sharp blade on a long handle. He would cut off the stalks of the ripe grain with the blade.

In 1831, McCormick created the reaper, a machine that cuts grain. It could be tied behind a horse. The horse then walked across a field as the reaper harvested the crops. McCormick's invention made work on the farm easier.

In farming communities today, farmers use many machines. Farms are larger in size. Each farmer can farm more land.

▶ Pioneers in the Midwest in 1870 cut their crops using a McCormick reaper.

REVIEW How did Cyrus McCormick's invention change the way farmers worked?
Draw Conclusions

▶ This daguerreotype is a portrait of Louis Daguerre taken by Charles Meade.

▶ This early camera was in use in 1870.

Smile for the Camera

Two inventors, Frenchman **Louis Daguerre** (da GARE) and American **George Eastman,** changed the way people remembered their favorite times. These men invented a way to take pictures and develop them.

Louis Daguerre made his first photographs in 1831. He invented a way to develop a picture. He used thin pieces of silver, chemicals, and a certain amount of light. The picture then appeared on a piece of metal with a silver surface. This type of picture was called a daguerreotype (da GARE a tipe). His invention was the first step toward modern photography.

In 1888, George Eastman invented a simple camera. He put everything a person needed to take a picture into a box. Anyone could take a picture with this simple camera.

▶ Digital still camera

REVIEW Why was Eastman's camera popular? **Draw Conclusions**

FACT FILE

New Technologies

New products are being invented every day. Below are four inventions that people long ago could never have imagined. What new inventions might be around when you grow up?

Computers with DVD players
Invented 1997

Handheld computers
Invented 1993

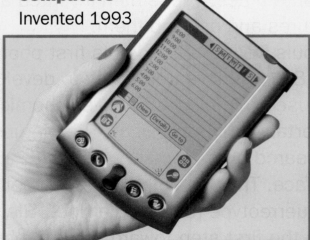

Cellular phones
Invented 1979

Compact Discs
Invented 1982

The Information Age

In the last 20 years, inventors have changed the way people around the world work and play. DVD players, compact discs, CD players, cellular phones, and tiny handheld pocket computers are used every day. Your parents and grandparents have seen so many changes in just a short time.

The Fact File on page 262 shows when some of these inventions were introduced. Look at the list. Which of these inventions have you used? Can you think of other inventions that are important to you?

REVIEW Name some inventions that have changed the way people work and play. **Main Idea and Details**

LESSON 3 | REVIEW

Check Facts and Main Ideas

1. **Cause and Effect** Copy the chart on a separate sheet of paper. For each cause, fill in the effect in the correct box.

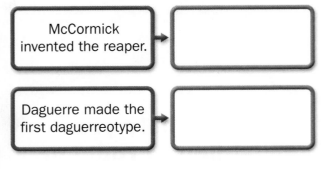

McCormick invented the reaper. →

Daguerre made the first daguerreotype. →

2. How did Lewis Latimer help New York City and Philadelphia?

3. How did farmers harvest crops before McCormick invented the reaper?

4. What current inventions were made possible by the inventions of Daguerre and Eastman?

5. **Critical Thinking:** *Evaluate* What computer inventions do you use every day? Which do you think is the most important? Why?

Link to ∞ Mathematics

Make a Bar Graph Each day of the week keep track of the number of minutes or hours that you use a computer. Make a bar graph with your information. Share this information with your class.

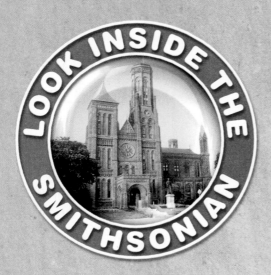

Sound Over Time

What if you could not listen to your favorite CD because CD players were not yet invented? Read on to find out how communication has changed over the years.

Phonograph
In 1900, Thomas Edison invented a machine that played music. It is called a phonograph.

It's for You...
In March 1876, Alexander Graham Bell invented the telephone.

What would you do without a radio or a television?

264

Radio Days

These radios were first available in 1938. People listened to comedies, baseball games, and the President.

Antique Phones

This collection of telephones shows what they looked like over the last 100 years.

Dots and Dashes

The telegraph, invented by Samuel Morse in 1837, sent electrical signals over long distances.

Top Forty!

This machine, called a jukebox, was built in 1946. You put a coin in the machine and played your favorite song.

Paris
FRANCE

Medicine Improves Over Time

Preview

Focus on the Main Idea
New medicines and ways to fight diseases have improved the health of people around the world.

PLACES
Paris, France

PEOPLE
Edward Jenner
Louis Pasteur
Jonas Salk
Gertrude Elion

VOCABULARY
pasteurization
vaccine

You Are There
You live on a farm. Your chore is to take care of the cows. One morning you wake up sick. You've got cowpox. In time you get over this disease and go back to doing your chores.

Another terrible disease has struck. People around you are getting sick, yet you feel just fine. Other people who have had cowpox don't get sick either. You wonder if the cowpox that you had has protected you from this disease. They are calling this awful sickness smallpox.

Cause and Effect As you read, look for ways that new medicines and ways of fighting diseases have made our communities healthier.

Edward Jenner and Louis Pasteur

Smallpox was a terrible disease that killed millions of people. In 1796, **Edward Jenner** of England found a way to protect people from smallpox. He learned this from people who had once had cowpox. These people never seemed to get smallpox. He gave patients a very weak form of cowpox. Then a person's body learned to fight off smallpox. This prevented the disease from killing the patient.

Louis Pasteur of **Paris, France** discovered that many diseases are caused by germs. If those germs could be kept out of the body, then those diseases could also be kept out. He developed one way to kill off certain germs by heating milk. Today we call this process **pasteurization,** after Louis Pasteur. He made milk safe for us to drink.

▶ Edward Jenner

REVIEW What was the impact of Louis Pasteur's ideas on communities around the world?
Draw Conclusions

▶ Most milk sold today is pasteurized.

▶ Louis Pasteur in his laboratory

Jonas Salk and Gertrude Elion

In 1952, **Jonas Salk** made a vaccine for polio. A **vaccine** is a weak or killed form of a disease that is given to people. Polio is a disease that can damage a person's spinal cord. Some people who have had polio are unable to walk. Salk used Edward Jenner's ideas. He gave patients a dead form of polio. This prevented people from getting polio. This vaccine saved the lives of many people.

If a person already has an illness, then a doctor tries to treat, or cure, that disease. In the 1940s, **Gertrude Elion** figured out how to make medicine to attack diseased cells. The medicines she created traveled to the diseased cells and killed them. The medicine did not harm the healthy cells.

▶ Jonas Salk

▶ Gertrude Elion

▶ Jonas Salk vaccinates a young girl against polio.

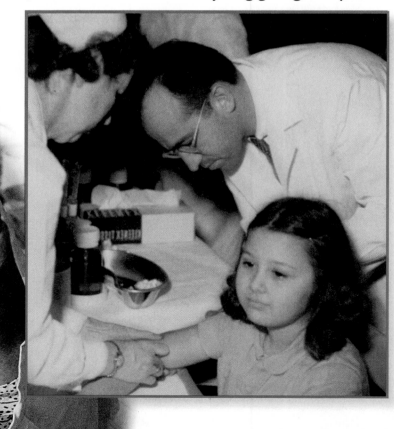

Elion's medicines helped treat people with diseases such as leukemia and malaria. Elion's medicines saved many lives that would have otherwise been lost. She was given the Nobel Prize for her work in medicine. She was also a member of the National Inventors Hall of Fame.

Today, medicines save people's lives every day. Many diseases that once killed millions of people are nearly wiped out. In the 21st century, people are living longer, healthier lives.

REVIEW How did Edward Jenner's ideas influence Jonas Salk? ⊙ **Cause and Effect**

Summarize the Lesson

- Edward Jenner found a way to prevent people from getting smallpox.
- Louis Pasteur invented a way to kill germs in milk.
- Gertrude Elion created medicines to fight leukemia.

LESSON 4 REVIEW

Check Facts and Main Ideas

1. ⊙ **Cause and Effect** Copy the chart on a separate sheet of paper. For each cause, fill in the effect in the correct box.

| Pasteur created a way to kill off germs in milk. | → | |
| Salk invented a vaccine for polio. | → | |

2. Describe the most important step in the process of pasteurization.

3. How is polio prevented?

4. What prize did Gertrude Elion earn for her work?

5. **Critical Thinking: *Draw Conclusions*** How did Edward Jenner figure out how to prevent smallpox?

Link to ⫘ Science

Do Research Other people also made important discoveries in the field of medicine. Find out information about Charles Drew. Share this information with a classmate.

Solve Problems

What? A problem is a difficult question or something to be worked out. You have been reading about inventors and scientists who saw problems. These men and women worked very hard to solve these problems.

Why? Inventors and scientists work to solve problems that can help people all over the world. You might be asked to help solve a problem at home or at school. Your problem could be very important to you and others.

How? Inventors and scientists often follow a step-by-step plan to solve problems. You can follow this same process to help solve your problems. Read about how scientists solved a problem about people getting sick from drinking milk.

Step 1 Identify a problem. People were getting sick when they drank milk from cows.

Step 2 Gather information. Louis Pasteur had discovered that germs could cause diseases and make people sick. Scientists looked at the information that he had gathered to see if the same could be true of germs in milk. They also read about experiments that other scientists had done.

Step 3 List and consider options. Scientists studied milk and the process that was used to make milk ready for people to drink. They made a list of all of the things that they thought might be causing people to get sick after they drank milk. One of the things on the list was germs in the milk.

Step 4 Consider advantages and disadvantages. The scientists thought about advantages and disadvantages of each possible solution. They decided which things were the most likely to be causing the diseases. They found that the diseases were caused by certain kinds of germs, just as Pasteur had learned earlier.

Step 5 Choose and try a solution. The scientists decided to try Pasteur's solution. They heated milk to a certain temperature to see if it would kill the germs, but not harm the milk.

Step 6 Decide if the solution works. People stopped getting sick when they drank pasteurized milk. The scientists solved the problem.

Think and Apply

① What are the six steps in solving problems that scientists used to make milk safer to drink?

② What solution did the scientists find to solve the problem?

③ How does the work of these scientists in the past affect you today?

1. There were germs in milk.
2. People did not wash hands.
3. Equipment was not clean.
4. Bottles were not clean.
5. Cows were sick.

Meet
Helen Keller
1880–1968 • Writer

Helen Keller lost her eyesight and her hearing before she was two years old. Helen had already learned a couple of words before she got sick. After her illness, words meant nothing to her. She couldn't see, she couldn't hear, and she couldn't tell anyone how that made her feel.

Anne Sullivan came to teach Helen in 1887. She taught Helen the words for things by spelling the letters into Helen's hand. One of the first words that Helen learned was W-A-T-E-R. Once Anne Sullivan showed Helen that she could learn, there was no stopping her.

"I gain a little, I feel encouraged, I get more eager and climb higher and begin to see the widening horizon. Every struggle is a victory. . . ."

When she was six years old, Helen Keller met Alexander Graham Bell. He recommended Anne Sullivan as her teacher.

BIOFACT

The more Helen learned, the more she understood that many people with problems like hers didn't get the chances she did. She started traveling around the country and talking to people about what it was like to be blind and deaf. She worked with the American Foundation for the Blind to help people without sight become part of their community.

Helen Keller knew there were many more people in the world with the same problems as she. She wanted to help them get a fair chance in life, just as Anne Sullivan had helped Helen get her chance.

Learn from Biographies

Learning how to speak without being able to hear or see was very difficult for Helen Keller. What do you think might have been some other challenges for Helen Keller?

For more information, go online to *Meet the People* at **www.sfsocialstudies.com**.

Chapter Summary

 Cause and Effect

On a separate sheet of paper, fill in the effects that were caused by each invention.

Edison invented the light bulb.	→	

Salk created the vaccine for polio.	→	

Vocabulary

Fill in the blank with the correct word.

1. Something that has never been made before is an _____.

2. The process of killing germs by heating is called _____.

3. The riders who delivered the mail were called the _____.

4. A series of dots and dashes used to send messages is called the _____.

a. Pony Express (p. 252)

b. invention (p. 253)

c. Morse code (p. 253)

d. pasteurization (p. 267)

Facts and Main Ideas

1. How did radio and television change the way people got news?

2. **Main Idea** How did the Transcontinental Railroad change the way people moved west?

3. **Main Idea** How did the telegraph and telephone change communication over time?

4. **Main Idea** How did Daguerre and McCormick change the world?

5. **Main Idea** How did discoveries by Pasteur and Salk change the world?

6. **Critical Thinking:** *Compare and Contrast* How is farming today alike and different from farming in the past?

Internet Activity

To get help with vocabulary, people, and terms, select the dictionary or encyclopedia from *Social Studies Library* at **www.sfsocialstudies.com**.

Write About It

1. **Write a letter** to a friend. Describe the different ways that mail used to be delivered in the United States. Compare that with how mail is delivered today.

2. **Write a paragraph** telling about a person you read about in this chapter. Explain why that person is special.

3. **Take a survey** to see which invention your classmates think is most important—cellular phones, personal computers, CD players, or digital cameras. Make a bar graph to show the results.

Apply Skills

Use a Time Line Look at the inventions and the dates that they were introduced. Make a time line. Put these inventions on it.

a. compact discs 1982

b. cellular phones 1979

c. handheld computers 1993

d. computers/DVD players 1997

The Railroad Cars Are Coming

Author Unknown

The great Pacific railway
For California hail!
Bring on the locomotive,
Lay down the iron rail.
Across the rolling prairies,
Through mountain valleys grand,
The railroad cars are coming, humming,
Through the prairie land.

The prairie dogs in dog town,
The rattlesnake and quail
Will see the cars a-coming,
Just flying down the rail.
Amid the purple sagebrush,
The antelope will stand
While railroad cars are coming, humming,
Through the prairie land.

Review

Test Talk

Look for details to support your answer.

Main Ideas and Vocabulary

TEST PREP

Read the passage. Then answer the questions.

The United States has changed a great deal. When the first European explorers came to North America, Native Americans already lived here. Spanish explorers traveled to Florida. French explorers traveled to Canada. English explorers first went to Virginia.

After Lewis and Clark explored the western part of the country, people began moving westward.

Inventors improved transportation, communication, work, and health. Trains, cars, and airplanes made travel easier. The telephone, telegraph, radio, and television helped people communicate faster and easier. The electric light, photography, and the reaper changed the way people worked and played. New medicines and ways to treat illnesses helped people live longer.

1 In the passage, which two people explored the western part of the United States?

A Columbus and Clark
B Ponce de León and Lewis
C Lewis and Clark
D Franklin and Jefferson

2 In the passage, the word *inventors* means people who

A discover new places.
B make things for the first time.
C travel across the country.
D begin new communities.

3 What is the main idea of the passage?

A The Native Americans were here first.
B The United States has changed a great deal.
C Lewis and Clark explored the West.
D Communication and transportation are better today.

Vocabulary

Write a journal entry that describes the importance of the following discoveries and inventions.

1 Transcontinental Railroad (p. 244)

2 pasteurization (p.267)

3 reaper (p. 260)

4 vaccine (p. 268)

Apply Skills

Use a Locator Map Look at the maps below. Which of the two maps shows you the United States? Which shows you the location of St. Augustine within the state of Florida?

St. Augustine, Florida

Write and Share

Write an advertisement to air on a radio program. Choose one of the inventions described in this unit. In your ad, describe what the invention is, how it is used, and why you think it is important. Record the advertisement. Play it for the class.

Read on Your Own

Look for books like these in the library.

Discovery CHANNEL SCHOOL

UNIT 4 Project

Making Tracks

Create a presentation about traveling with an explorer.

1 **Form** a group and choose a route taken by one of the explorers you studied in this unit.

2 **Research** the part of the route you chose and write descriptions about the geographical features. Make a travel brochure that includes your descriptions.

3 **Tell** what it is like to travel along the route. Draw pictures. You may also tape sound effects and bring in costumes or props.

4 **Draw** a map of the route.

5 **Present** your travel adventure program to the class.

Internet Activity

Explore historic places on the Internet.
Go to www.sfsocialstudies.com/activities and select your grade and unit.

Communities at Work

What choices do people make when spending money?

Making Choices

by Megan Molloy

**Sung to the tune of "Take Me Out
to the Ballgame"**

How do you use your money?
You have choices to make.
You could take lessons or buy a bat.
If you spend it for this,
You can't spend it for that.
You can save it up for the future,
What do you want to do?
For it's earn, save, spend just a bit,
It's all up to you!

Communities Meet Needs and Wants

▶ For about 50 years, the casts and crews of plays in New York City have played softball together. They started a league called the Broadway Show League. Each team plays a 10-game schedule, followed by playoffs. They have All-Star games, Old-Timer games, and games for charity.

The Pacific Ocean and trees have always been important to Portland, Oregon. The official seal of the city shows a female figure representing commerce. *Commerce* means "buying and selling." She stands next to the ocean and points to a forest of pine trees.

Some farmers around Phoenix, Arizona, sell their produce at farmers markets. There, farmers can sell directly to customers. People meet and talk as they shop for food. This can help bring communities closer together.

The town of Ellicottville, New York, is near the border with Pennsylvania. For many years, trees have been cut from forests near Ellicottville to use for wood. Fruit is grown in Ellicottville, and milk and cheese are made nearby.

What Happens Next?

Target Skill

Sequence

Learning to put things in order—or sequence—will help you understand many kinds of writing. Sequence is especially useful when you are reading about history. Look at the chart.

Clue Word	Date	Event
first	1895	Duryea Brothers open factory to make cars.
next	1901	Ransom Olds begins mass producing cars.
finally	1913	Henry Ford uses a moving assembly line.

- Sequence is the order in which events take place.

- Sometimes you do not have dates to help you find sequence.

- Words such as *first*, *second*, *then*, *after*, *next*, *finally*, and *later* can help you find the sequence of events.

Read the following paragraph. Words that help show sequence have been highlighted in blue. Dates are highlighted in yellow.

Making cars improved over time. The Duryea Brothers opened the first car factory in the United States in 1895. Next, in 1901 Ransom Olds started mass producing cars in his factory. Finally, Henry Ford started using a moving assembly line to make cars in 1913.

Opening a Savings Account:
A Sequence of Events

Many children save money. Have you thought about opening a savings account in a bank? You could open an account by following five easy steps.

First, you must save some money. Often ten dollars is enough to open an account.

Second, go with an adult in your family to a bank in your community. Explain to the teller that you want to open a savings account.

Next, fill out the new account form the teller gives you. The adult can help you.

When you finish, give the form back to the teller.

Next, the teller will give you a signature card to be signed. After the card is signed, return the card to the teller.

Finally, the teller will open a savings account for you. Give the teller your money. The teller will give you a piece of paper. It will show your account number. It will also show how much money you have in the bank.

That is all there is to it. Happy saving!

Use the reading skill of sequence to answer the following questions.

1 What clue word helps you find the second step?

2 What is the third step?

3 How many steps are there? What are two ways you can tell?

Chapter 9 Making Choices

Lesson 1

Indianapolis, Indiana

People earn, spend, and save money.

1

Lesson 2

Indianapolis, Indiana

People make economic choices.

2

Lesson 3

Indianapolis, Indiana

Businesses provide communities with goods and services.

3

CANADA

1
2
3

UNITED STATES

Indianapolis

PACIFIC OCEAN

ATLANTIC OCEAN

Gulf of Mexico

MEXICO

Why We Remember

In the United States, we believe that people can own businesses. A business can provide you with goods and services you need. You can earn and save your money. Then you can spend your money to buy goods or services. The way we do business in the United States has made our nation the wealthiest in the world.

289

Indianapolis,
Indiana

Earning, Spending, and Saving

Preview

Focus on the Main Idea
People make choices about how money is earned, spent, and saved.

PLACES
Indianapolis, Indiana

VOCABULARY
earn
budget
income
spending
savings

You Are There

You are in third grade now. In just seven weeks, you are going to play softball for the first time. Your old T-ball bat will not do.

You saw some great softball bats at the sporting goods store in your community. But they cost more than you have to spend.

How can you pay for a bat? What can you do to earn money?

 Sequence As you read, look for how money is earned, spent, and saved.

Feed neighbor's cat.

Run errands for grandfather.

Earning Money

My name is Robin. I live in **Indianapolis, Indiana.** Lots of people here like softball. This year I will be playing softball for the first time. My old T-ball bat is too small. I need a new bat.

I like listening to music too. There are two great new CDs that I want.

My mom and dad say I have to earn the money for the bat or the CDs. I **earn** money when I work and get paid. My parents say that softball bats cost around $20 to $35. That's about what the two CDs would cost. I am going to think of ways to earn money.

REVIEW What must Robin do before she can buy the bat or the CDs? ◑ **Sequence**

I could earn money doing these jobs.

How I Can Earn Money!
things I can do each week

Walk neighbor's dog............

Weed the garden.

Keeping Track of Money

After Robin thought of ways to earn money, she made a budget to help her buy the bat. A **budget** is a plan that shows income, spending, and saving. Look at Robin's budget.

Income is all the money a person earns from a job or other places. For Robin, it includes the money she is paid for her jobs plus her allowance. Robin's budget has a row for every week. Notice that Robin wrote $6.00 in the *Income* column for each week.

Spending is the amount of income a person uses to buy goods and services. Once a week Robin buys a treat at lunch for one dollar. She decided not to buy anything else until she has enough money for her bat or the two CDs.

Savings is the amount of income that is not spent. Each week Robin's income is $6.00. Her spending is $1.00. Robin subtracted her spending from her income to find her savings.

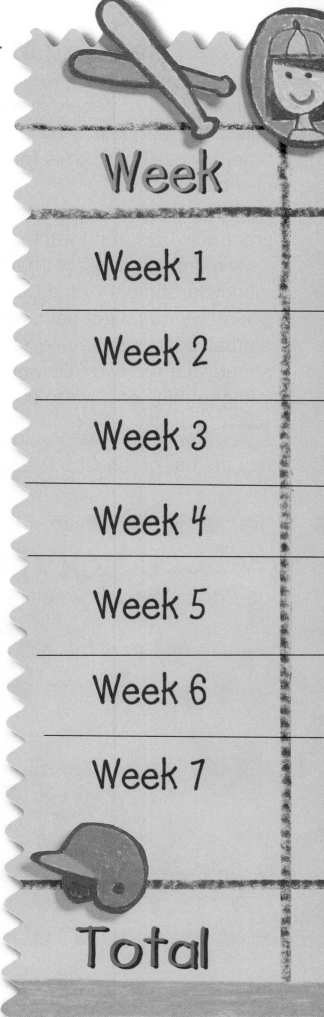

Week	
Week 1	
Week 2	
Week 3	
Week 4	
Week 5	
Week 6	
Week 7	
Total	

REVIEW Which was the last column that Robin filled in: *Income, Spending,* or *Saving?* ⟳ Sequence

292

My Budget!

Income	Spending	Saving
$6.00	$1.00	$5.00
$6.00	$1.00	$5.00
$6.00	$1.00	$5.00
$6.00	$1.00	$5.00
$6.00	$1.00	$5.00
$6.00	$1.00	$5.00
$6.00	$1.00	$5.00
$42.00	$7.00	$35.00

Saving Money

Robin showed her budget to her parents. Her dad told her he thought that the savings column is the most important. He said that no matter how much people earn, if they do not save, they will not have any money when they need it. Each week Robin saves $5.00. You save when you keep some of your money to use later.

Her parents told her that people save for things they need and want. She told her parents she needed a bat. They told her that she only wanted it.

People want softball bats. They do not need them.

Robin's dad said that a need is something that a person must have to live. He said that something a person would like to have, but can live without, is a want. Sometimes it is hard telling needs and wants apart.

People need food, clothing, and shelter.

REVIEW What do you think Robin's father believes people should do after they earn money?

⊙ **Sequence**

Summarize the Lesson

- People earn money when they work and get paid.
- People can plan to buy something if they budget their income, spending, and saving.
- Needs are things people cannot live without. Wants are things people would like to have.

LESSON 1   REVIEW

Check Facts and Main Ideas

1. ⊙ **Sequence** Copy the chart on a separate sheet of paper. Sequence some of the steps Robin used to save money.

[ ]
↓
[ ]
↓
[ ]

2. What are some things Robin can do each week to earn money?

3. How are savings and income different?

4 What are some examples of needs and wants?

5. **Critical Thinking: *Draw Conclusions*** What are some ways that Robin could save more money?

Link to 🔗 Mathematics

Make a Budget Use newspaper advertisements to find an item you want to buy. Then make a budget like Robin's to plan how you might save money to buy it.

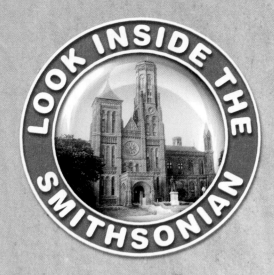

The History of Money

In ancient times, people first used a barter system to trade for goods and services. Then countries began to make coins and print paper to use as money.

Aeginan Coins
The ancient Greek island city of Aegina used this coin to buy goods and services. The sea turtle with a plain shell was used to decorate this silver coin.

Italian Coins
Charlemagne, a famous ruler, had a special way to make his initials. These initials were put on many coins.

The coins and paper bills on this page show money that was used long ago.

Athenian Coins

Athens, Greece, used an owl on their coins. The owl was for Athena, whom people believed to be the goddess of wisdom.

Ancient Roman Coins

Ancient Rome used a heavy bronze coin for money. The two-faced god, Janus, is shown here.

Byzantine Coins

This gold coin is believed to come from the Byzantine Empire. Jesus is the image on the coin.

Venetian Coins

This coin is from Venice, Italy. It was used over 500 years ago.

Early Money

The ancient civilizations of Greece, Rome, China, Iran, and other countries in Europe and Latin America used these colorful coins and bills as money.

Artifacts are from the ✸ Smithsonian Institution.

Building a Business

▶ S. Truett Cathy
started a chain of
chicken restaurants.

S. Truett Cathy was a hard-working child. He helped his mother run a small business. He earned money from a newspaper route. He started a business selling soft drinks.

BUILDING
CITIZENSHIP
Caring
Respect
★ Responsibility
Fairness
Honesty
Courage

When he was older, Mr. Cathy opened a tiny restaurant. He used money he had saved. He figured out how to cook chicken the way people liked it. His business grew into a large chain of nearly 1,000 chicken restaurants.

Many young people work for Mr. Cathy. Those who work hard may get college scholarships. Mr. Cathy has given away more than $15 million in scholarships.

> *"...we really aren't in the chicken business, we're in the people business. ..."*
> S. Truett Cathy

Mr. Cathy feels a responsibility to people and communities. He supports many programs that help communities. He helps pay for an outdoor adventure program that helps groups build trust and work as a team. He donates money to a summer camp that serves many children.

Responsibility in Action

Compare your life with Mr. Cathy's early life. How is it the same? How is it different? Why do you think Mr. Cathy feels a responsibility to help young people?

Indianapolis, Indiana

Choosing Wisely

Preview

Focus on the Main Idea
To make a decision about what to buy, people must make economic choices.

PLACES
Indianapolis, Indiana

VOCABULARY
economic choice
opportunity cost

You Are There

You have saved $35! It has been hard—very hard! You saved for something you really wanted. You saved more money than you ever have before. It has taken weeks! You've skipped treats and missed a pizza party.

You know more about how much things cost. You are going to spend your money wisely. Now, you are ready to buy something. How can you be sure you will make a wise choice?

Main Idea and Details As you read, look for the different choices Robin must make as she buys a bat.

300

People Make Choices

Everyone makes choices. You make a choice when you pick one thing instead of something else. People make an **economic choice** when they buy one thing rather than another. Robin makes an economic choice when she chooses between a softball bat and two CDs.

Think of some choices people must make when they spend money. Maybe your parents bought a microwave oven instead of a new TV. Maybe your school bought new computers instead of playground equipment. What choices have you made?

REVIEW List three examples of economic choices people make when they spend money. **Main Idea and Details**

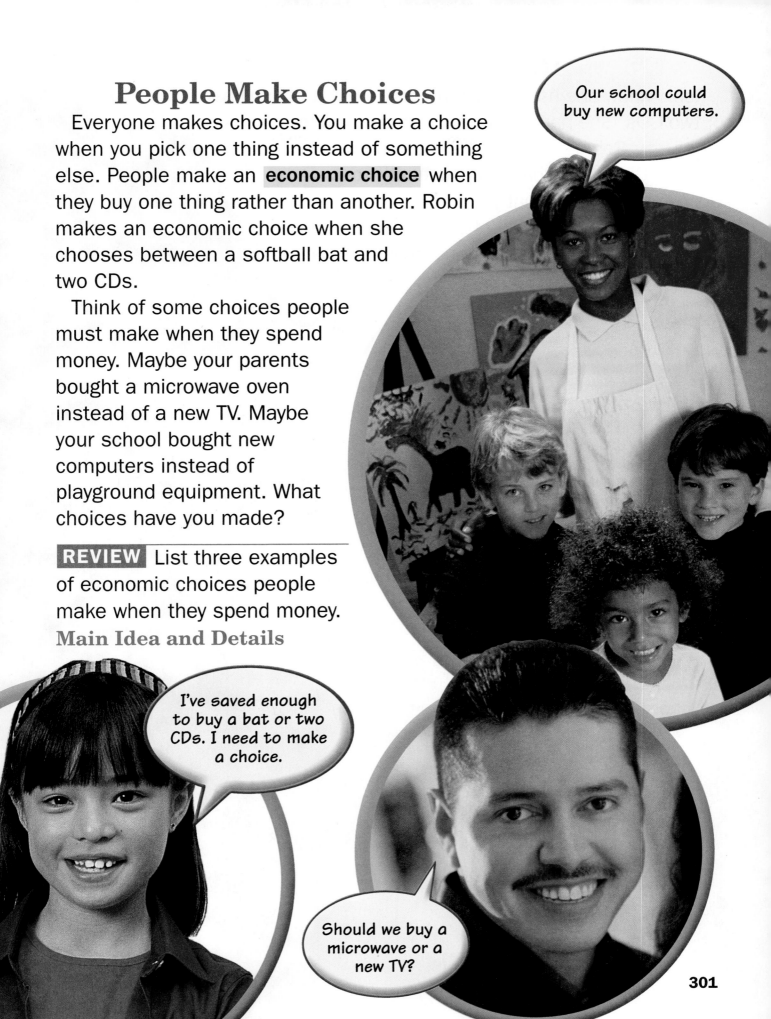

Our school could buy new computers.

I've saved enough to buy a bat or two CDs. I need to make a choice.

Should we buy a microwave or a new TV?

301

Robin's Choice

Robin knew she had enough money to buy a softball bat or two CDs. She had to choose. She decided to buy a bat.

In a way, Robin's bat cost her the two CDs. The two CDs were Robin's **opportunity cost.** Opportunity cost is what you give up when you choose one thing instead of another. Robin gave up the two CDs when she chose to buy the bat.

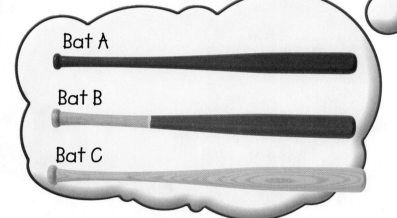

Now, Robin found she had to make another choice. Which bat should she buy? Robin used the chart below to help her choose.

Which Bat Should I Buy?

Options	Length	Weight	Color	Quality	Price
Bat A	poor	poor	best ⭐	poor	$19
Bat B	good	good	good	good	$34
Bat C	good	best ⭐	good	best ⭐	$27

She filled out the chart to show her options, or possible choices. The chart showed what was important to her as she made her choice. Then, for each option, Robin thought about what might happen if she picked it. Would the bat last? Would it be the right length and weight? Finally, she chose a bat and bought it.

REVIEW If Robin had bought two CDs, what would she have given up? **Draw Conclusions**

Summarize the Lesson

- People make economic choices when they spend money.
- Opportunity cost is what a person gives up when he or she chooses something else.
- Making a list or a chart of options can help people make decisions.

LESSON 2 REVIEW

Check Facts and Main Ideas

1. **Main Ideas and Details** Copy the chart on a separate sheet of paper. List the choices Robin must make as she chooses a bat.

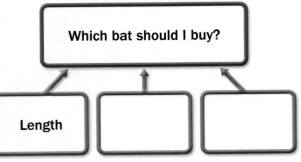

Which bat should I buy?

Length

2. Identify two examples of economic choices you have made. Tell what you picked and what you gave up.

3. What is opportunity cost? Give an example.

4. How did Robin's list help her make a choice?

5. **Critical Thinking: *Sequence*** What steps did Robin follow as she made an economic choice to buy a bat?

Link to ⟳⟳ **Art**

Make a Sign Choose one of the bats from Robin's chart. Make a sign advertising the bat you choose. Give the bat a name. Describe the features of the bat.

Make a Decision

What? You make decisions every day. Decisions are choices that you make.

Why? It is important that you make careful choices and good decisions.

How? Following a step-by-step plan can help you make a wise decision. Robin used the plan below to help her choose a softball bat.

STEP 1

Figure out what you have to decide. Robin wanted to buy a softball bat. She had to decide which bat to buy at the sporting goods store.

STEP 2

To make a good decision, you need to gather information. Robin asked her coach what made a good softball bat.

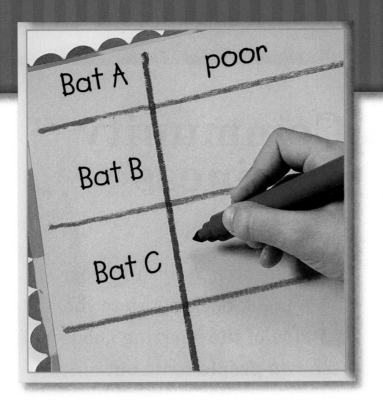

STEP 3
Before you make a decision, you need to identify, or figure out, what your choices are. Robin figured out her choices by talking to her coach and by looking at the bats at the store. She made a chart of her choices.

STEP 4
For each choice that you have, you need to think about what might happen if you make that choice. Robin looked at each bat before she decided which one to buy. She wanted to make sure that her decision was a good one.

This is the bat that I chose.

STEP 5
Finally, you are ready to make a decision. Robin decided to buy the bat that had the right length, weight, color, and quality.

Think and Apply

❶ How did Robin gather information about softball bats?

❷ What might happen if Robin chose a different bat?

❸ How could you use this step-by-step plan to make a decision?

Focus on the Main Idea
Business owners work
hard to provide goods and
services to the people in
the community.

PLACES
Indianapolis, Indiana

VOCABULARY
goods
services
products
supply
demand
profit

A Community Business

You Are There

Beep, beep, beep. You hear
a truck backing up to the
side of the sporting goods
store. You see two people come out of
the store. One signs a paper for the
driver. They begin unloading the truck.

You see a long box being unloaded.
You wonder if the box might hold the
bat you've been waiting for. Then you
see the label on the box. You can barely
read it. It says "BATS."

Cause and Effect As you read, look for
what causes prices to change.

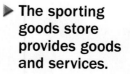

▶ The sporting
goods store
provides goods
and services.

Goods and Services

In your community, there may be large businesses and small businesses. Some businesses make things, such as softball bats. Some businesses sell things to people. All businesses provide goods, services, or both.

Goods are things that people make or grow and then sell. Softball bats, vegetables, and books are goods. Services are jobs that one person does for another. An umpire provides a service at a softball game. People who give haircuts or repair cars provide a service. Together, goods and services are called products.

The sporting goods store provides goods and services. What goods and services do you see for sale?

REVIEW How are goods and services alike? How are they different? Compare and Contrast

My store offers baseball lessons.

Shop Services
- tent repair
- bike repair
- racket repair
- baseball lessons

The Amount of a Product

The amount of a product that producers want to sell at different prices is **supply.** Usually, if supply increases, the price will go down. If a store owner has too many bats, the owner may put them on sale. If a town has too many barbers, the price of a haircut may go down.

The amount of goods or a service that people want and can pay for at different prices is the **demand.** Usually if the demand decreases, the price will go down. If few people buy bats or haircuts, the store owner may lower the price.

REVIEW How might the price of winter coats change after winter is over?

Draw Conclusions

Homer Price

by Robert McCloskey

In the story *The Doughnuts,* Homer Price has a problem. His uncle's doughnut-making machine is broken. It will not stop making doughnuts. Soon, it makes thousands of doughnuts.

A man wants to help Homer sell the doughnuts. He says, *"What you need is an advertising man. Ya know what I mean? You got the doughnuts, ya gotta create a market…Understand?…It's balancing the demand with the supply…. That sort of thing."*

They decided to lower the price of the doughnuts. But still they could not sell all the doughnuts. That was, until they discovered that a diamond bracelet was lost in the doughnut-making machine. To increase demand, Homer put a sign in the window of the store. It promised a prize to the person who found the bracelet.

"THEN…The doughnuts began to sell! Everybody wanted to buy doughnuts, dozens of doughnuts! And that's not all. Everybody bought coffee to dunk the doughnuts in too. Those that didn't buy coffee bought milk or soda."

Getting Ahead

People in a community usually work to earn an income. Businesses in a community usually try to make a profit. **Profit** is the income a business has left after all its costs are paid. Some of the costs a business may have include salaries for workers. The business also has to pay for the goods that it buys to sell to its customers.

A business makes a profit only when it can sell a product for more than it costs to provide it. Businesses try to keep the cost of producing, or making goods, down. For example, the owner of the sporting goods store tries to buy bats from a bat maker at the lowest price possible. Businesses also try to keep their cost of providing services down.

The shop owner uses charts and his computer to track profits.

A business can increase its profit if it can sell a product at a high price. Usually buyers can choose from products made by several companies. Given a choice, most people want to pay less for a product. If another store in the community sold bats for less, Robin likely would have bought her bat there.

I bought a good bat at a good price.

REVIEW Describe how the cost of making a product and the selling price can affect profits. **Cause and Effect**

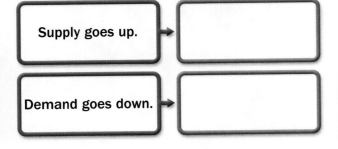

LESSON 3 REVIEW

Check Facts and Main Ideas

1. **Cause and Effect** Copy the chart on a separate sheet of paper. Describe the different ways that prices of goods and services can change.

Supply goes up. →	
Demand goes down. →	

2. What are some examples of businesses that provide goods or services?

3. Would you expect the price of a valentine to be higher or lower after Valentine's Day? Why?

4. How can a business increase its profit?

5. **Critical Thinking: *Make Inferences*** If many farmers have a lot of tomatoes to sell, would you expect the price to be higher or lower? Why?

Link to ∞ Drama

Put on a Play Pick a partner. You are a business owner. Your partner is a customer. Act out a play about supply and demand. Show how the price and then the supply may change.

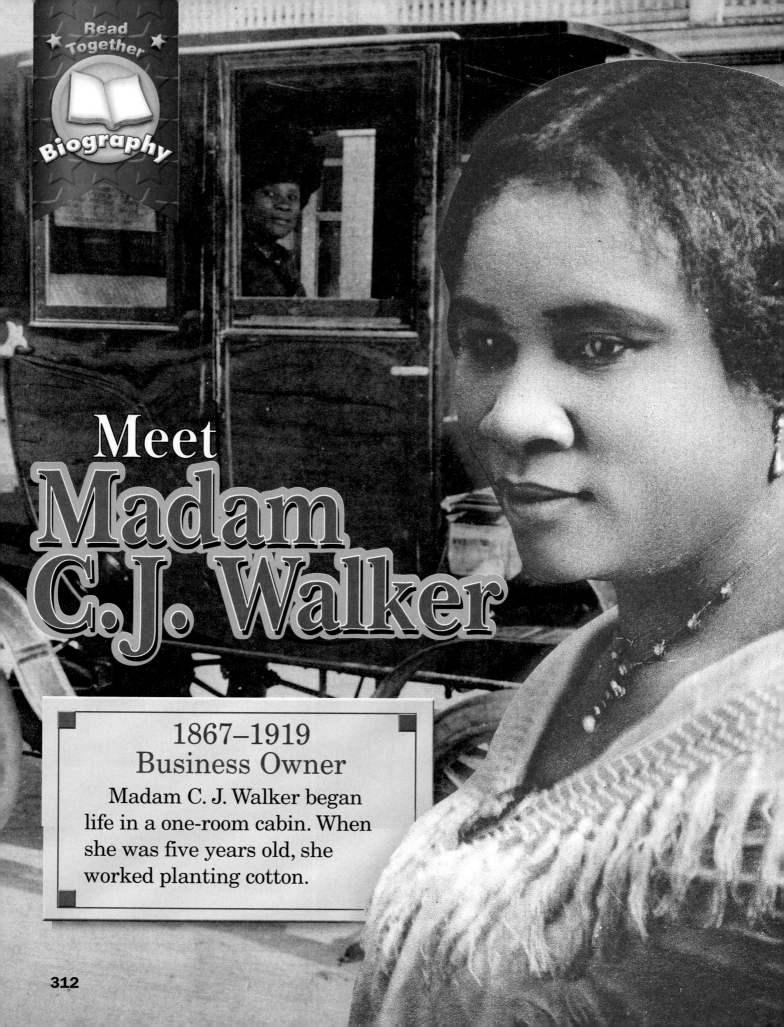

Meet Madam C.J. Walker

1867–1919
Business Owner

Madam C. J. Walker began life in a one-room cabin. When she was five years old, she worked planting cotton.

She washed people's clothes in a washtub. Later, she worked as a servant. To improve how her hair looked, she tried homemade products. With money saved from her jobs, Madam C. J. Walker made more of the products and sold them door-to-door. African American women liked the beauty products she made for them. Later, she began selling her products by mail. With the money she earned, she made her business grow. She opened beauty schools. In time, she trained thousands of people who sold her products in the United States and other countries. They were trained to make customers feel pampered [treated kindly] and valued.

Madam Walker became one of the wealthiest, self-made women of her time. She said, "I am not ashamed of my humble beginning. Don't think because you . . . [use] a washtub, you are any less a lady!"

When she died, Madam C. J. Walker owned a 34-room mansion.

BIOFACT

"I got started by giving myself a start."
—Madam C. J. Walker

Learn from Biographies

Walker learned to work very hard as a child. How do you think this habit helped her succeed?

For more information, go online to *Meet the People* at **www.sfsocialstudies.com**.

Chapter Summary

 **Sequence**

On a separate sheet of paper, fill in the steps in order that show how Madam C. J. Walker grew her business. Begin when she worked as a servant and end when she trained thousands to sell her products.

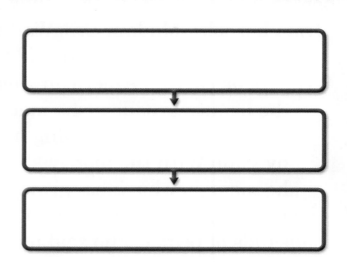

Vocabulary

Match each word with the correct definition or description.

1. budget (p. 292)
2. income (p. 292)
3. economic choice (p. 301)
4. opportunity cost (p. 302)
5. supply (p. 308)
6. demand (p. 308)
7. profit (p. 310)

a. amount of a product that is for sale at different prices

b. income a business has left after all its costs are paid

c. the amount of a product that people want and can pay for at different prices

d. all the money a person earns from a job or other places

e. a plan that shows income, spending, and savings

f. when people buy one thing rather than another

g. what you give up when you choose something else

Facts and Main Ideas

❶ Why is it important to save money?

❷ Give an example of goods and of a service.

❸ **Main Idea** What three columns are important to have on a budget?

❹ **Main Idea** Why did Robin have to choose between a bat and two CDs?

❺ **Main Idea** What do all businesses provide?

❻ **Critical Thinking:** *Draw Conclusions* What is the difference between goods and services?

Internet Activity

To help with vocabulary, people, and terms, select dictionary or encyclopedia from *Social Studies Library* at **www.socialstudies.com.**

Write About It

❶ **Write a Budget** Think of something that you would like to buy. Make a budget of the money that you could earn, spend, and save.

❷ **Write an Ad** You are a business owner. Make an advertisement for a product that is not selling very well.

❸ **Write a Glossary** of economic terms that you learned in this chapter. List the terms and their definitions in alphabetical order.

Apply Skills

Make a Decision A large new sporting goods store is moving to your town. This store will give many people jobs. It will also have many new products that you cannot get right now. This store will also take up a lot of land that was supposed to be a park. It might also put a smaller sporting goods store out of business. Should the new store come to town? Why or why not? Use the 5-step decision-making process on pages 304–305 to help you decide.

Chapter 10 Making Goods

Lesson 1

Ellicottville, New York

People use natural resources to produce goods.

1

Lesson 2

Phoenix, Arizona

People must choose how to use resources.

2

Lesson 3

New York City, New York

People around the world depend on each other for goods and services.

3

CANADA

1

3

Ellicottville

New York City

PACIFIC OCEAN

2

Phoenix

UNITED STATES

ATLANTIC
OCEAN

Gulf of Mexico

MEXICO

Why We Remember

You depend on other people for many things. Your family helps you get food and shelter. Teachers help you learn. All people depend on other people. They depend on workers in factories to build cars. They depend on farmers to grow food. In communities around the world, people depend on each other.

Ellicottville, New York

Preview

Focus on the Main Idea
Factories use natural resources, people, and machines to make products.

PLACES
Ellicottville, New York

VOCABULARY
renewable resource
nonrenewable resource
human resource
producer
specialize
capital resource

Using Resources

You Are There

Crunch, crunch, crunch. The snow crunches and squeaks under your boots as you walk through a cold, snowy forest. The forest is near Ellicottville, New York. This city is close to the border with Pennsylvania. Here, white ash trees grow tall and strong.

You are following a logger as he looks for trees to cut down. He touches the bark of one white ash tree. The logger is looking for a tree with bark that has a straight, regular pattern. You move to the side before he begins cutting. The sound of the chainsaw fills the forest. This is where softball bats begin!

Sequence As you read, look for the sequence used in how softball bats are made.

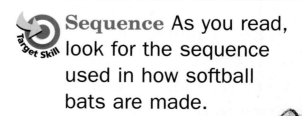

Using Natural Resources

The softball bat that Robin bought is made of wood. Trees and the wood that comes from them are a renewable resource. A **renewable resource** can be replaced within a short time.

Some natural resources are nonrenewable resources. A **nonrenewable resource** takes a very long time to replace or cannot be replaced after it is used. Nonrenewable resources include coal, oil, and natural gas.

Inside factories, people and machines change renewable and nonrenewable resources into products. The bat factory makes a piece of wood into a new bat.

REVIEW Name a nonrenewable resource.
Main Idea and Details

Literature and Social Studies

Robinson Crusoe

by Daniel Defoe

Your community uses many resources. What resources would you need if you had to start a community by yourself? Robinson Crusoe, a character in a book, had this problem. He was shipwrecked on an island.

"I had neither food, house, clothes, (or) weapon . . . and . . . saw nothing but death before me."

But Crusoe used many natural resources on the island to meet his needs. In the book, he survived for 28 years and was then rescued.

"I discovered how to make pots and plates out of clay . . . I baked my barley loaves, and became in a little time a complete pastry-cook . . . . I made me a suit of clothes wholly of skins . . . . Thus I lived mighty comfortably."

MAP ADVENTURE

Natural resources are found throughout the United States. Oil, coal, and gold are important natural resources found in different places. Look at the map. The map key tells the symbols for oil, coal, and gold.

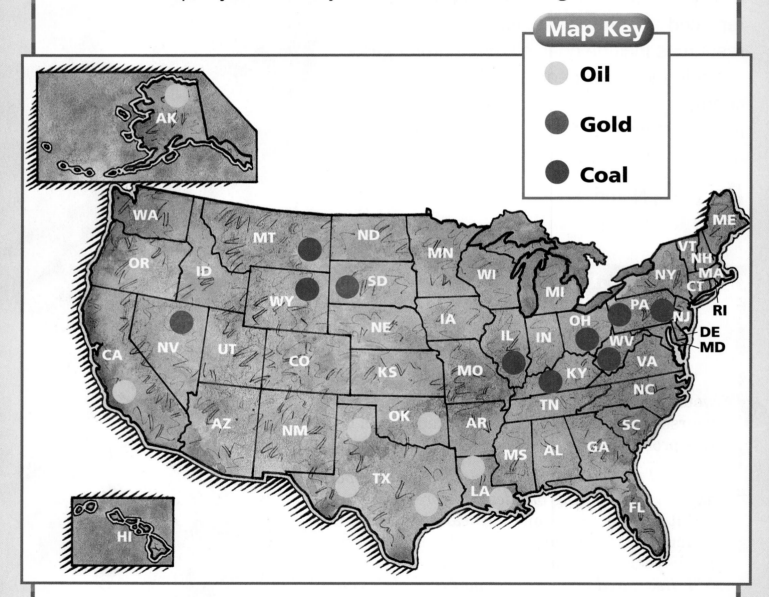

Map Key

- Oil
- Gold
- Coal

1. List the states on the map where oil is found.

2. List the states on the map where coal is found.

3. List the states on the map where gold is found.

320

People at Work

Many resources other than natural resources are needed to make goods. **Human resources** are the people who make products or provide services. The people who make products are also called **producers.**

In the past many products in factories were made by hand. Now many products in factories are made using machines.

People working in factories often specialize in one job. To **specialize** means to do one job or make one part of a product. Many specialized workers and machines are needed to make softball bats.

▶ In the past many products were made by hand. Now, many products are made using machines.

REVIEW How has the production of goods in factories changed over time?
Compare and Contrast

321

These men worked at "The World's First Bat Factory" in Louisville, Kentucky, in the 1800s.

▶ This card shows measurements of a bat made for a famous baseball player.

▶ This worker is using a hand lathe.

Machines at Work

The machines, tools, and buildings that are used to produce goods and services are called **capital resources.** Although machines are expensive, they can help make products quickly. It used to take about 15 minutes to cut and shape one bat by hand.

Today, computerized machines can cut and shape one bat in 15 to 20 seconds. Making more bats quickly can cost the company less money. The company can then sell bats at lower prices and make greater profits.

REVIEW What are some examples of capital resources? **Main Idea and Details**

▶ This bat is being turned on a computerized lathe.

Summarize the Lesson

- People make products using renewable and nonrenewable natural resources.
- People work together to provide goods and services.
- Machines are often used to produce goods and provide services.

LESSON 1 REVIEW

Check Facts and Main Ideas

1. **Sequence** Copy the chart on a separate sheet of paper. Sequence the steps needed to make a softball bat.

> Trees are cut down and split apart.

⬇

> [ ]

⬇

> [ ]

2. How is a renewable resource different from a nonrenewable resource?

3. How do specialized workers help make goods?

4. How have machines changed the amount of time needed to cut and shape one bat?

5. **Critical Thinking:** *Cause and Effect* How can machines help a company make greater profits?

Link to ∞ **Science**

Conserving Resources Find out about ways to recycle renewable and nonrenewable resources. Make a chart showing how you could recycle different resources at home and at school.

Use a Cutaway Diagram

What? Have you ever wondered what is inside a building or an object? A **cutaway diagram** shows you what is inside and outside of a building or an object. Parts of the diagram are often labeled.

Why? This diagram shows many of the steps on an assembly line on which softball bats are made. On an **assembly line**, workers and machines complete the steps in making a bat. At each step a worker or machine has a specialized job.

1 Pieces of wood called billets are dried in the warm "kiln" room.

2 Billets are cut and shaped into bat forms by automatic lathes.

3 The bat forms are then sanded.

How? To use the cutaway diagram below, find the number *1* on the diagram. It shows the first step in the sequence of making softball bats. Then find the label with the matching number and read about the picture. Continue following the numbers in order until you read about all the steps showing how softball bats are made.

Think and Apply

1 What is the first step in the sequence of making softball bats?

2 In the sequence of making a softball bat, what happens in the step before the bat forms are sanded for the first time?

3 Why do you think workers on the bat factory assembly line have specialized jobs?

4 Bats are "branded" with the company's trademark. They are then sanded again.

5 The knobs at the end of the bats are cut off and sanded down.

6 Some bats are passed through flames to darken the wood.

7 Bats are dipped in colored or clear finishes.

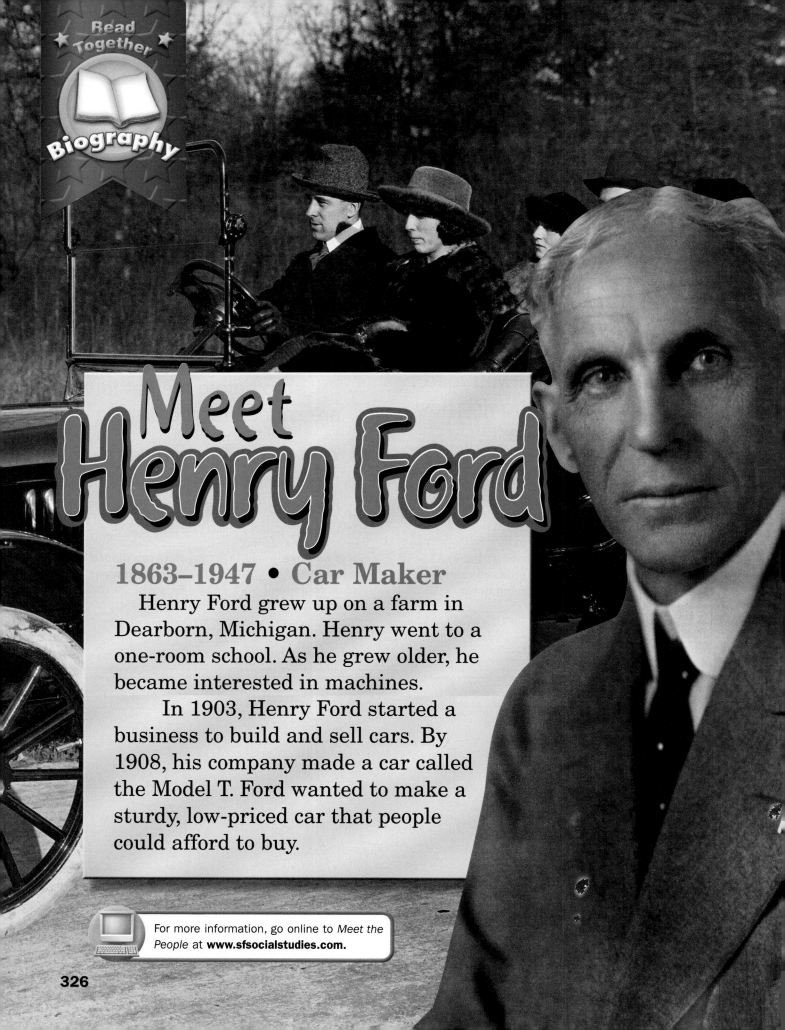

Meet Henry Ford

1863–1947 • Car Maker

Henry Ford grew up on a farm in Dearborn, Michigan. Henry went to a one-room school. As he grew older, he became interested in machines.

In 1903, Henry Ford started a business to build and sell cars. By 1908, his company made a car called the Model T. Ford wanted to make a sturdy, low-priced car that people could afford to buy.

For more information, go online to *Meet the People* at **www.sfsocialstudies.com**.

Henry Ford began to use an assembly line of workers and machines. Each worker specialized in doing a job. Ford made more cars than ever before. As cars cost less to build, Ford lowered prices for consumers. Consumers are the people who buy products. The graph below shows the drop in the price of a new Model T.

From 1914 to 1925, Ford made only black Model T's. Henry Ford said, "The customer can have any color he wants, so long as it's black."

BIOFACT

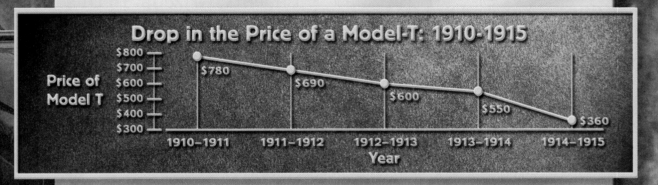

Drop in the Price of a Model-T: 1910-1915

Price of Model T

$800
$700
$600
$500
$400
$300

$780
$690
$600
$550
$360

1910–1911   1911–1912   1912–1913   1913–1914   1914–1915

Year

Although the prices of Ford's cars fell, the company still made a large profit. Ford attracted many workers by paying them high wages. He said,

"Make the best quality of goods possible at the lowest cost possible, paying the highest wages possible."

As time passed, cars allowed millions of people to live and work in different places. Cities and suburbs grew. Henry Ford changed the way cars were made. By doing so, he changed the way people lived.

Learn from Biographies

What was one effect of Henry Ford using an assembly line to make cars?

Portland, Oregon
Phoenix, Arizona

Preview

Focus on the Main Idea
People must make choices about how to use resources.

PLACES
Phoenix, Arizona
Portland, Oregon

VOCABULARY
scarcity
interdependence

Depending on Others

You Are There

You are in a car near Phoenix, Arizona. In this desert community, temperatures can be hot. You look through the car window. You see sand, rocks, and some cactuses—but not many trees.

You open the car window. Suddenly you hear the sound of hammers pounding nails. You see homes and buildings being built using wooden beams. Workers are using large piles of wood to build the homes and buildings.

Next you pass a playground. New equipment is being built using wood. Workers attach large logs together. You look around again. No trees are in sight. Where does the wood come from?

Sequence As you read, look for information about how goods travel from one community to another.

Too Few Resources

People have many wants and needs. People want homes and playground equipment. People need wood and other resources to build these goods. People want roads and bridges to be built. Even more resources are needed to build these.

There is a scarcity [SKAIR suh tee] of resources. **Scarcity** means there is not enough of something to meet all of people's wants and needs. Wood is scarce. Gasoline is scarce. All resources that people want and need are scarce.

Because of scarcity, people must make choices. We must choose how to use wood. People choose to make furniture. They decide to build homes and playground equipment. Some people choose to make paper and cardboard with wood. But wood is scarce.

REVIEW

What causes resources to be scarce?
Cause and Effect

There is not enough wood to make everything people want!

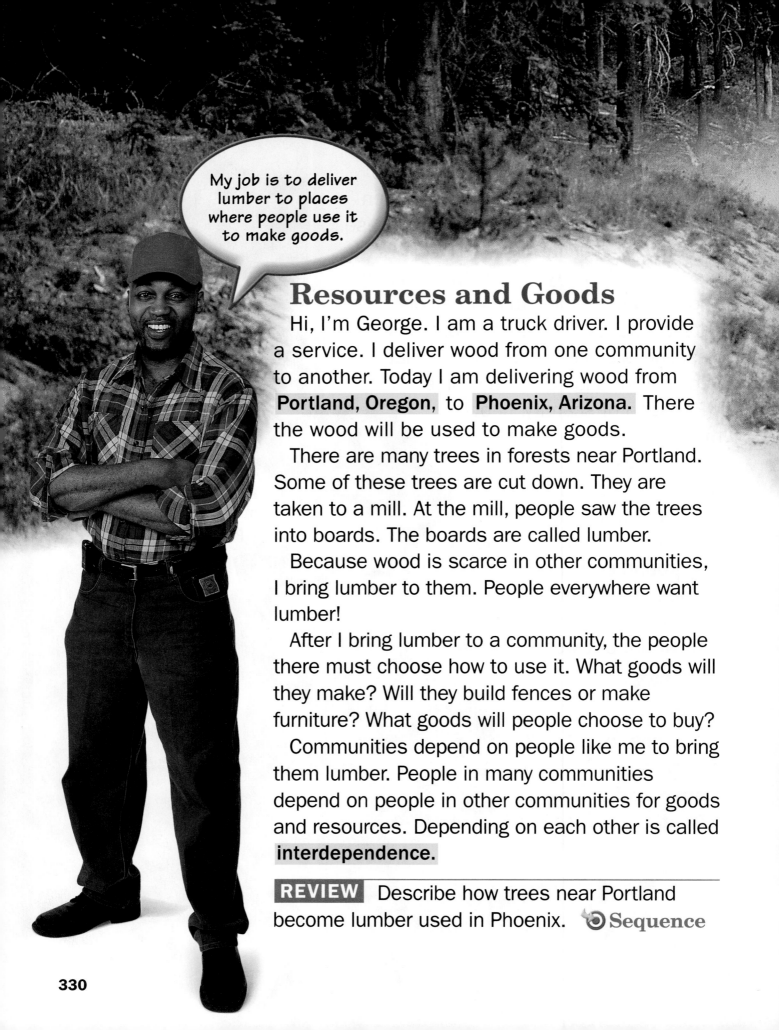

My job is to deliver lumber to places where people use it to make goods.

Resources and Goods

Hi, I'm George. I am a truck driver. I provide a service. I deliver wood from one community to another. Today I am delivering wood from **Portland, Oregon,** to **Phoenix, Arizona.** There the wood will be used to make goods.

There are many trees in forests near Portland. Some of these trees are cut down. They are taken to a mill. At the mill, people saw the trees into boards. The boards are called lumber.

Because wood is scarce in other communities, I bring lumber to them. People everywhere want lumber!

After I bring lumber to a community, the people there must choose how to use it. What goods will they make? Will they build fences or make furniture? What goods will people choose to buy?

Communities depend on people like me to bring them lumber. People in many communities depend on people in other communities for goods and resources. Depending on each other is called **interdependence.**

REVIEW Describe how trees near Portland become lumber used in Phoenix. ⊙ Sequence

The All-American Girls Professional Baseball League

In 1941, the United States entered World War II. Many men went to fight in the war. Because of this, male baseball players were scarce. In 1943, a new baseball league was formed. The All-American Girls Professional Baseball League had teams in several cities.

After the war, men returned to play professional baseball. The All-American Girls Baseball League ended in 1954. Many people enjoyed women's baseball. Now, women's softball is a popular Olympic sport.

▶ Kenosha Comets in 1943

▶ Julie Smith batting in the Olympics

People Helping People

Land is another scarce resource. In Robin's community, some people wanted a field for softball and baseball. Other people in the community wanted to build a community swimming pool. The community owned a piece of land. The land was in a good place, and it was the right size. The people in Robin's community chose to build a softball and baseball field there.

Money was needed to pay for the fences, the grass, and other things for the field. Because money was scarce, Robin and other children helped raise money. People volunteered to build the field. People donated money. Others gave goods and services.

Finally enough money was raised. Work began on the field.

Places for people to sit and watch the games were built.

Some people built the dugouts.

Other people planted grass.

A scoreboard was built.

People in Robin's community depended on each other. Land was scarce. Money was scarce. But people worked together to build beautiful fields. Play ball!

REVIEW How did people in Robin's community depend on each other?
Main Idea and Details

We worked together!

LESSON 2   REVIEW

Check Facts and Main Ideas

1. **Sequence** Copy the chart on a separate sheet of paper. Sequence the path wood takes from forests near Portland to Phoenix.

Trees are cut in forests near Portland.
↓
↓
↓

2. What are some scarce resources that people use?

3. How does wood get from the community where it is produced to the community where it is used?

4. How does scarcity cause people to depend on each other for goods and services?

5. **Critical Thinking:** *Cause and Effect* How did World War II lead to the formation of the All-American Girls Professional Baseball League?

Link to ⟡⟡ Writing

Scarcity Story Write a story about another way a community could choose to use a scarce resource, such as land. Include examples of how people depend on each other. Use the problem-solving process on pages 270–271.

New York City, New York

Preview

Focus on the Main Idea
People in communities around the world depend on each other for goods and services.

PLACES
New York City, New York
Rome
Greece

VOCABULARY
trade
communication
international trade
import
export
free market

A World of Trade

You Are There
You are in a supermarket in New York City. You look at your shopping list. You are making fruit salad for dinner. The first item is bananas. You choose a bunch and place them in your basket. There is a sticker on the bananas. It shows they are from the country of Costa Rica.

Next on your list is kiwi fruit. The label on the kiwi fruit shows that it is from New Zealand. The last item is grapes. On the bag it shows they are from the country of Chile.

As you stand in line to pay, you begin to wonder. How do these foods travel thousands of miles to reach your supermarket?

Compare and Contrast As you read, look for ways that trade long ago was similar to and different from trade now.

Depending on Others

Communities in the United States and other parts of the world depend on each other. These communities trade with one another. When people **trade,** they buy or sell goods and services.

One reason people around the world can depend on each other is transportation. People can now move goods from one country to another very quickly. Kiwi fruit, grapes, and other foods can be sent thousands of miles in only a few days. People use airplanes, trains, ships, and trucks to move goods.

Another reason people can depend on each other is communication. **Communication** is the sharing of information or news. People now use phones, computers, and the Internet to communicate around the world. If a grocery store needs goods quickly, it can call or email producers. As more goods are traded, people depend on each other more and more.

REVIEW What are some goods that people might want to transport very quickly? **Make Inferences**

▶ These people are traders at the New York Stock Exchange.

Trade Then and Now

Long ago, people also depended on each other. People in one place often made few kinds of goods. They would trade with people in other places for goods that they did not produce. Sometimes people used the goods they received to make other goods.

Now, people may trade goods and services for money. One person may get a good or a service. The other person may get money. People choose to trade with each other because they both benefit.

New York City is an important place for trade in the United States. It is home to the New York Stock Exchange. New York City's banks are some of the largest in the world.

REVIEW Why did people long ago trade with each other? **Main Idea and Details**

Ancient Greece

In ancient **Greece**, farmers grew olives and grapes. People made beautiful pottery. Greeks traded these items for goods they needed, such as cotton, fruits, rice, wheat, and animals. The Greeks specialized in building ships. They traded with Egypt and other nearby communities. Cotton was used to make cloth. Wheat was used to make bread.

Ancient Rome

In ancient times, people in the city of **Rome** also specialized in road-building, trade, and building ships. Romans traded for many goods with Egypt and other nearby Mediterranean communities. They also traded farm goods such as olive oil for silk cloth from China and gems from India. The silk cloth was used to make clothing. Gems were used to make jewelry.

Oil-Exporting Countries of the World

NORWAY

CANADA

UNITED
KINGDOM

UNITED
STATES

IRAQ

SAUDI
ARABIA

MEXICO

VENEZUELA

COLOMBIA

NIGERIA

ANGOLA

N

Map Key

Major countries
exporting oil

0   1,500   3,000 Miles

0   1,500   3,000 Kilometers

▶ Major oil-exporting countries are colored orange on this map.

MAP SKILL Places and people change each other: *What effect do you think the discovery of oil had on these countries?*

KEIΠ ΜΑΣΤΑΝΓΧ
ΠΕΙΡΑΙΕΥΣ

Trade Between Countries

Today, people buy and sell goods and services from communities around the world. Trade between different countries is called international trade.

People and companies import products from other countries. Import means to bring resources and other products from one country into another country.

People export products to other countries. Export means to send products to other countries. Computers and airplanes are exported from the United States to other countries.

REVIEW How are importing and exporting similar? How are they different? **Compare and Contrast**

Free Markets

In the United States, people and companies are part of a free market. In a **free market,** people choose what to produce and what to buy.

In a free market, farmers decide which crops to plant. Factories decide which goods to produce. Store owners decide which products to sell to consumers.

In some countries, the government controls what is bought and sold. In the United States, producers and consumers decide what is bought and sold.

REVIEW Why do you think free markets are called "free"? **Draw Conclusions**

Summarize the Lesson

- Communities around the world depend on one another for goods and services.
- Now, as in the past, communities trade for goods.
- In a free market, producers and consumers decide what is bought and sold.

LESSON 3 ⟩ REVIEW

Check Facts and Main Ideas

1. Compare and Contrast
Copy the chart on a separate sheet of paper. Compare and contrast trade long ago with trade now.

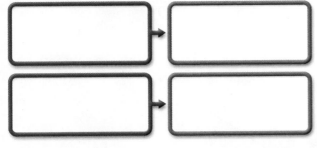

2. How have modern transportation and communication changed trade?

3. What is the reason people choose to trade?

4. How did people in ancient Greece and Rome use the goods for which they traded?

5. Critical Thinking: *Fact and Opinion*
Which of the following are statements of fact, and which are statements of opinions?

a. World trade has made the world a better place.

b. The United States has a free market.

c. In a free market, people and companies decide what is bought and sold.

Link to ⟨⟩ Science

Time Line Research inventions in communication. Find out how they have changed over time. Make a time line to show inventions in communication.

339

HERE AND THERE

Around the World

Countries around the world have different natural resources and human resources. These resources are used to produce goods. Many of these goods are exported.

United States: airplanes

Brazil: orange juice

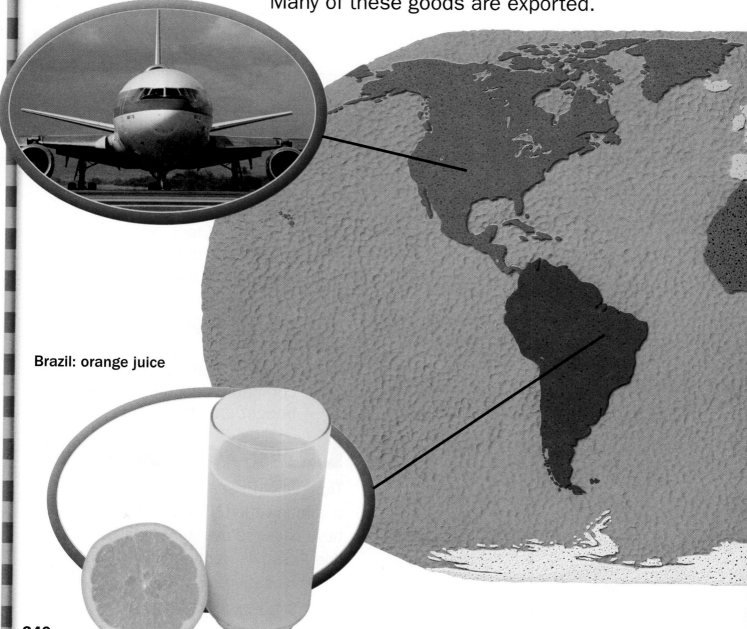

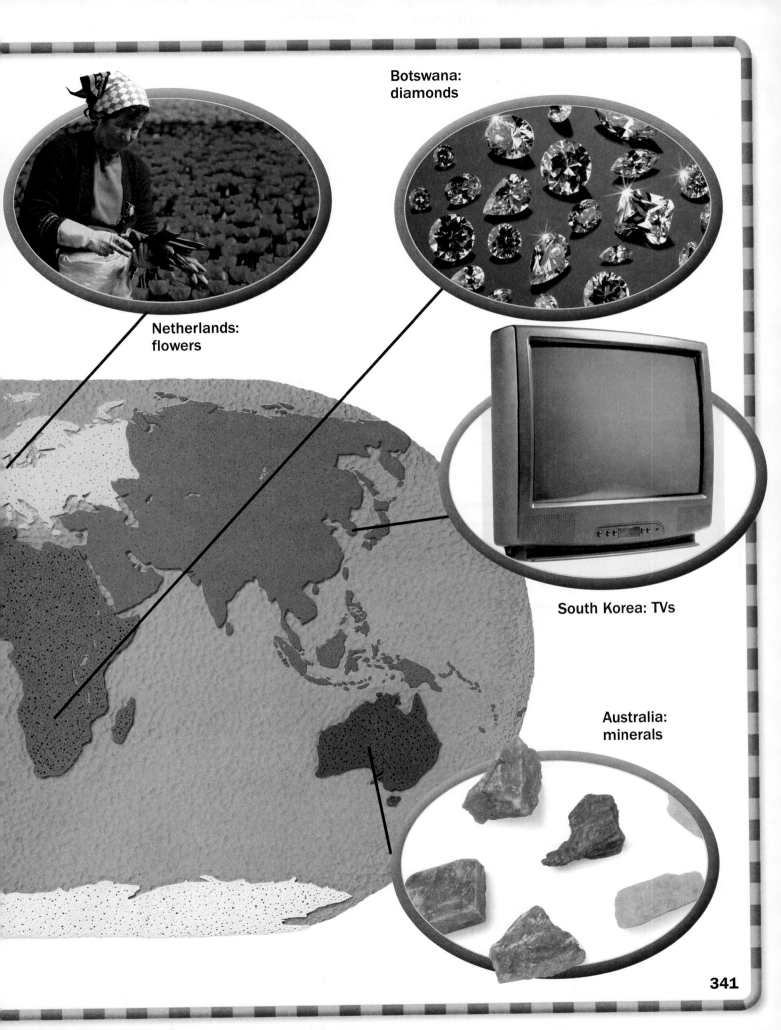

Netherlands:
flowers

Botswana:
diamonds

South Korea: TVs

Australia:
minerals

341

Chapter Summary

 Sequence

On a separate sheet of paper, list the seven steps that it takes to make a softball bat.

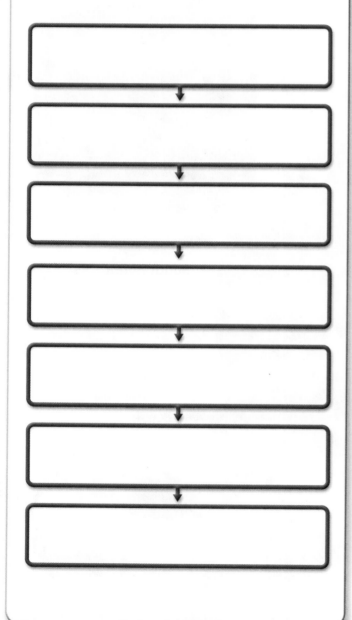

Vocabulary

Fill in the blank with the correct word.

❶ To _____ means to do one job or make one part of a product.

❷ _____ means that there is not enough of something to meet people's wants and needs.

❸ When people _____, they buy or sell goods and services.

❹ You _____ when you bring products into a country from another country.

❺ You _____ when you send products out of a country.

a. trade (p. 335)

b. export (p. 338)

c. specialize (p. 321)

d. import (p. 338)

e. scarcity (p. 329)

Facts and Main Ideas

1 How does an assembly line work?

2 Give an example of a human resource and a capital resource.

3 **Main Idea** What do factories need to make products?

4 **Main Idea** Why do people need to make choices about how to use natural resources?

5 **Main Idea** Why do people depend on trade with other people around the world?

6 **Critical Thinking:** *Draw Conclusions* What is the difference between a renewable resource and a nonrenewable resource?

Write About It

1 **Make a list** Think about something that you do many times, like make your favorite kind of sandwich. List the steps that you take to do this. Show these steps to a friend. Does your friend follow these same steps when he or she does this?

2 **Make a map** of your state. Title it. Research the products that your state sends to other states or countries. Draw symbols for these products on your state map. Make a map key. Add a compass rose.

3 **Write a letter** to a local factory. Find out what they manufacture. Ask if they give factory tours.

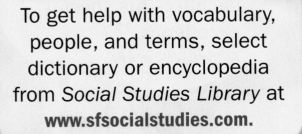

Internet Activity

To get help with vocabulary, people, and terms, select dictionary or encyclopedia from *Social Studies Library* at **www.sfsocialstudies.com.**

Apply Skills

Use a Cutaway Diagram
Look at the cutaway diagram. Tell what a baseball is made of from the center to the outside.

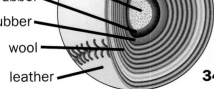

cork and rubber

black rubber

red rubber

wool

leather

343

"I've always believed that if you put in the work, results will come."

Michael Jordan, from I Can't Accept Not Trying

"There is no substitute for hard work."

Thomas A. Edison

"Remember that time is money."

Benjamin Franklin

"Whatever your life's work is, do it well."

Dr. Martin Luther King, Jr.

"The same man cannot be skilled in everything, each has his special excellence."

Euripides, c. 485-406 B.C.

"A penny saved is a penny earned."

Benjamin Franklin, from Poor Richard's Almanac

"Laziness may *look* inviting, but only work gives you *true* satisfaction."

Anne Frank, from Anne Frank: The Diary of a Young Girl, July 6, 1944

Main Ideas and Vocabulary

TEST PREP

Read the passage. Then answer the questions.

Every day people make choices about how they will earn, spend, and save their money. People earn money in many ways. You might walk your neighbor's dog or weed a garden.

Your can keep track of money by making a budget. A budget shows all the money that you earn, how much you want to spend, and how much you will have left to save.

When you decide to spend your money, you want to make a good choice. Businesses provide goods and services. You can decide how to spend your money.

Natural resources, people, and machines are needed to make products. People around the world depend on each other for goods and services.

❶ According to the passage, people make choices about

A earning money
B saving money
C spending money
D all of the above

❷ According to the passage, you can keep track of what you earn, spend, and save by

A making a chart
B making a graph
C making a budget
D making a table

❸ What is the main idea of the passage?

A People make choices about what goods and services to buy.
B People make choices about earning, spending, and saving their money.
C People and machines are needed to make products.
D Businesses provide goods and services.

Vocabulary

Write a letter to a friend telling him or her about how a business works. Use five of these vocabulary words.

1 supply (p. 308)

2 demand (p. 308)

3 profit (p. 310)

4 import (p. 338)

5 export (p. 338)

6 producers (p. 321)

7 capital resources (p. 322)

8 human resources (p. 321)

Apply Skills

Sequence
Every morning you get ready for school. Based on your experience, you know that one thing that you should do is brush your teeth. List the steps, in order, that you take to brush your teeth. Write complete sentences. Use standard grammar, spelling, sentence structure, and punctuation.

Write and Share

Make an Options Chart You have outgrown your bicycle. You have permission to look for a new bike. What will you look for before you decide to buy a certain bike? List the options that you will want your bicycle to have. Share your chart with the class. Explain how you decided which bike you want to buy. Describe the decision-making process you used.

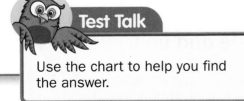

Test Talk

Use the chart to help you find the answer.

Read on Your Own

Look for books like these in the library.

IF YOU MADE A MILLION
by David M. Schwartz
pictures by Steven Kellogg

BILL COSBY
Money Troubles
Illustrated by Varnette P. Honeywood

BUNNY MONEY
MAX
ROSEMARY WELLS

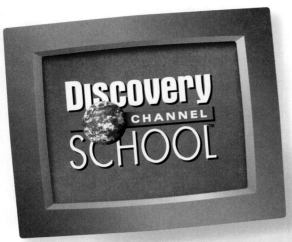

5 Project

On the Market

Create an advertisement for goods or a service that you think is important.

1 **Choose** goods or a service to advertise.

2 **Draw** pictures of the goods or service.

3 **Make** your advertisement complete by including the name of the goods or service, the price, and why people should buy or use it.

4 **Present** your advertisement to the class.

Internet Activity

Learn more about goods and services on the Internet. Go to www.sfsocialstudies.com/activities and select your grade and unit.

Community Government

What is a good citizen?

The Pledge of Allegiance

I pledge allegiance to the flag
of the United States of America
and to the Republic for which it
stands, one nation under God,
indivisible, with liberty and
justice for all.

Governments

▶ The Parthenon, shown here, is one of the most famous buildings in Greece. It is on the Acropolis, the highest point in Athens. In ancient Athens, citizens gathered there to make laws and choose their leaders. The columns of the Parthenon have been copied by architects around the world.

▶ The Plimoth (Plymouth) Plantation is the site where the Pilgrim leaders and families first made their home. Today you can visit there to learn more about how these settlers lived.

▶ The rulers of England at one time lived in the Tower of London. Today it is a museum. People visit the Tower of London to learn more about the government and history of England.

Today the government of the United States is located in Washington, D.C. The United States Capitol is where the laws for our country are made. Notice the columns on the building.

Government Services

Summarize

- A summary is a short statement that tells the main idea of an article or tells what happened in a story.

- When you summarize a paragraph, look at the details. Then figure out the main idea. Sometimes the topic sentence of a paragraph makes a good summary.

- Most articles have more than one paragraph. To summarize an article, figure out the main idea of each paragraph. Then tell in a sentence or two what the whole article is about.

Lawmakers work in Jefferson City.	The state government is located there.	There are many historic buildings to visit.

Jefferson City is an important community in Missouri.

Read the paragraph. The first sentence tells the main idea. It is a good summary of this paragraph. The other sentences tell important details.

Jefferson City is an important community in Missouri. The state government is located there. The governor and the men and women who make the laws come to Jefferson City to do their work. Downtown Jefferson City has many historic buildings for people to visit.

Services from Local Governments

Your community government provides you with many services. Your local government makes sure that you can get a good education. Your town probably has a school and a library. Maybe there is a local museum.

Your government makes sure that your community is safe. It may have a police department and a fire department.

Your community government wants you to have a good place to play. It may provide parks or bike paths.

Your community government cannot provide these services for free. It must collect money from its citizens to pay for these services. You and your family pay taxes. Taxes help pay for services that you need.

Use the reading strategy of summarizing to answer these questions.

1 What is the main idea of the first paragraph?

2 What is the main idea of the last paragraph?

3 Which statement is the better summary of the article?

  a. Services such as education and police protection are important to a community. Parks are important too.

  b. Your community government provides important services. Citizens pay taxes to help pay for these services.

Chapter 11 — Rights and Responsibilities

Lesson 1

Plymouth, Massachusetts

The Mayflower Compact is written.

1

Lesson 2

Washington, D.C.

Washington, D.C., is the home of our national government.

2

Lesson 3

Jefferson City, Missouri

Citizens have responsibilities.

3

CANADA

1

2

3

Plymouth

Washington, D.C.

Jefferson City

UNITED STATES

PACIFIC OCEAN

ATLANTIC OCEAN

Gulf of Mexico

MEXICO

Why We Remember

Each citizen has many rights and responsibilities. People have formed governments to protect their rights and property. People are expected to obey the laws that their governments set up. As a citizen of our country, it is important to remember that you have rights recognized by our government, but you also have responsibilities to our country.

Plymouth, Massachusetts   Athens, Greece

Preview

Focus on the Main Idea
Governments of the past influenced the founders of our country.

PLACES
Athens, Greece
England
Plymouth, Massachusetts

VOCABULARY
direct democracy
republic

TERMS
Magna Carta
Mayflower Compact

Governments in the Past

You Are There

The year is 439 B.C. Your family lives in Athens, in ancient Greece. Today your father is heading up the hill called the Pnyx. Other citizens are walking with him. They are all part of the Assembly. The Assembly makes important decisions about Athens. Each citizen has the right to give a speech about any of the topics in the Assembly. Only citizens have the right to vote. The citizens vote by raising their hands.

You cannot wait for your father to get home. You want to know what happened at the Assembly. You want to know what decisions were made there.

Statue of a Greek youth wearing a hat.

Summarize As you read, think of a one-sentence summary for each paragraph.

Ancient Greece

People long ago formed communities for the same reasons we form communities today. People wanted a safe place to live, work, and play. People also wanted a place where they could live under laws that were fair.

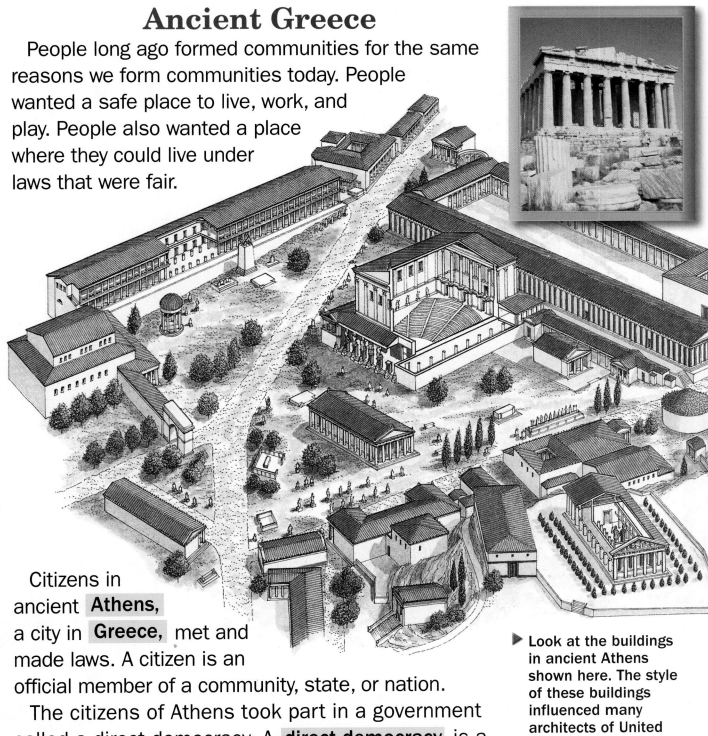

Citizens in ancient **Athens,** a city in **Greece,** met and made laws. A citizen is an official member of a community, state, or nation.

The citizens of Athens took part in a government called a direct democracy. A **direct democracy** is a government that is run by the citizens who live under it. The government we have today in the United States is a republic. A **republic** is a government in which citizens elect representatives to speak for them.

▶ Look at the buildings in ancient Athens shown here. The style of these buildings influenced many architects of United States government buildings. Sometimes mosaics, sculpture, or paintings were displayed on buildings.

REVIEW Describe the government of ancient Athens. ⟳ **Summarize**

The Magna Carta and the U.S. Constitution

Citizens who lived in England before 1215 had few rights. The king had most of the power. Noblemen became angry and forced King John to sign a paper called the Magna Carta. The Magna Carta limited the king's power. It said that the king must obey the law and consult citizens when he made decisions.

The Magna Carta helped make England's government better for its citizens. In time English laws were made by people who were elected by others to act as their representatives in the government. Rights won then are still rights English citizens have today. Colonists from England took these ideas with them to the Americas. Today, many of these ideas about government are found in the U.S. Constitution.

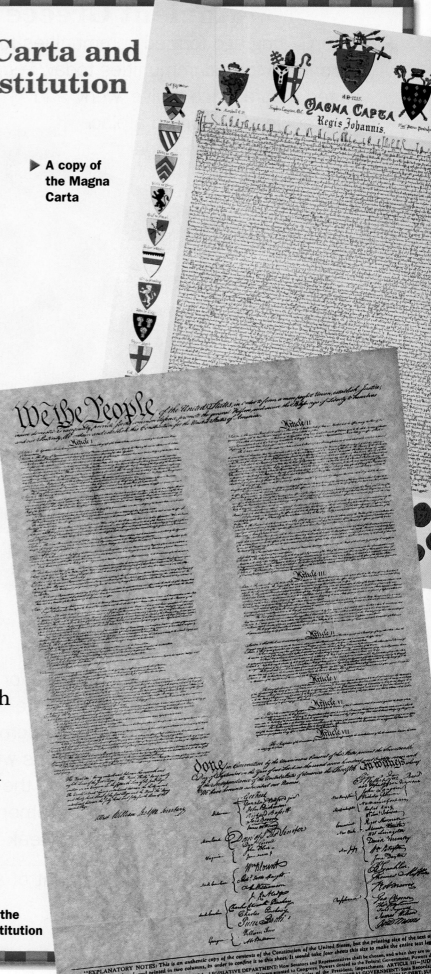

▶ A copy of the Magna Carta

▶ A copy of the U.S. Constitution

Mayflower Compact

In 1620, the *Mayflower* landed with a group of English colonists in **Plymouth, Massachusetts.** They had come to be free to practice their religion. They formed a community. People form a community to be secure and form a government to make laws. The Mayflower leaders wrote a plan of government called the **Mayflower Compact.**

The Mayflower Compact said that the colonists themselves would make laws for the good of the community. Everyone agreed to obey these laws. This was the first time European colonists in America had made a plan to make laws for themselves. The belief that people could govern themselves influenced the founders of our country.

REVIEW What was the Mayflower Compact?
Summarize

Summarize the Lesson

- The government of ancient Athens was a direct democracy.
- The Magna Carta said the King of England must obey the law.
- The Mayflower Compact was a plan made by colonists to govern themselves.
- The Magna Carta and the Mayflower Compact influenced the founders of the United States.

LESSON 1 REVIEW

Check Facts and Main Ideas

1. **Summarize** On a separate sheet of paper, fill in details that support the lesson summary.

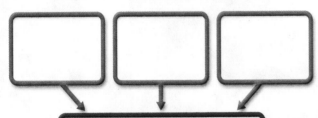

The government of the United States was influenced by governments of the past.

2. Why do people form communities?

3. Why did the English colonists create a plan of government?

4. Why was the Mayflower Compact an important plan?

5. **Critical Thinking: *Draw Conclusions*** Why do you think that the Magna Carta was an important document?

Link to ∞ Writing

Make a List If you were a colonist aboard the *Mayflower,* you would face many problems in North America. List the ways your life would change as you leave the safety of the *Mayflower.* Share this list with a friend.

361

Identify Point of View

What? A point of view is the way a person feels about an issue. In the 1200s, King John of England wanted to increase taxes. The barons, powerful noblemen who would pay the taxes, did not agree. The king and the barons had different points of view about taxes.

Why? Identifying different points of view can help you understand why people disagree. The king wanted to increase taxes because he wanted more money. The king also wanted to show he was powerful. The barons did not want to pay higher taxes. They also worried that if the king could raise taxes, he might try to take away some of their other rights.

In 1215, the barons captured King John and forced him to sign the Magna Carta. The Magna Carta limited the king's power. The king could not raise taxes on his own. He had to work with the barons to raise taxes. Today, in England, these same ideas described in the Magna Carta are part of the government. The king or queen must still obey the same laws as everyone else does.

How? To identify a person's point of view, ask yourself, "How does the issue affect the person?" With the taxes, it helped to know how the king and the barons felt about raising taxes.

Sometimes you can identify a person's point of view by reading things the person has written. People show their point of view when they use the words "I think," "I feel," and "in my opinion."

Think and Apply

1 Why did the king want to raise taxes?

2 Why did the barons think raising taxes was wrong?

3 Think about taxes people pay today. What is your point of view about taxes?

Meet
William Bradford

1590–1657 • Governor

"It was granted the dangers were great, but not desperate. The difficulties were many, but not invincible [impossible]."

William Bradford was born in a small rural village in England. As a young boy, William helped out on the farm. He looked after the cattle and plowed his family's fields.

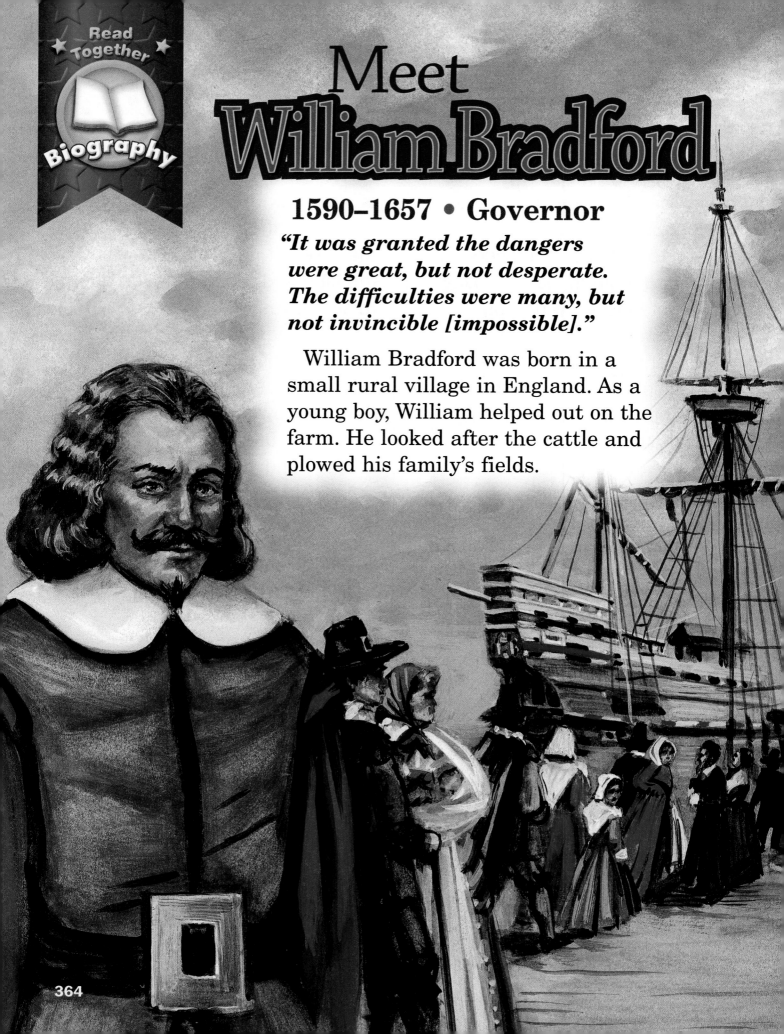

William got very sick. He could no longer work on the farm. His family decided that William should learn how to read and write. Very few people in England could read and write at this time. Soon he was reading the Bible.

You can visit the Mayflower II, a replica of the ship, at Water Street and State Pier in Plymouth.

BIOFACT

Because of his studies, Bradford's beliefs grew to be very different from those of the Church of England. Bradford, and many others who believed as he did, were punished for their beliefs. They wanted to go to a place where they could worship without fear.

In 1620, Bradford led a group of Pilgrims on board the *Mayflower.* Sixty-six days later, they landed on the coast of present-day Massachusetts.

The Pilgrims built a new colony at Plymouth. Bradford became governor of the colony. He was a good leader. He made peace with the Wampanoag Indians. This made it possible for the Pilgrims and Wampanoag communities to begin trading food and other goods.

In November 1621, the Pilgrims and the Wampanoag sat down to a feast. The holiday we celebrate today as Thanksgiving had begun.

Learn from Biographies

William Bradford and the people he led believed that they should be able to worship as they wished. How is this belief still important to us today?

For more information, go online to *Meet the People* at **www.sfsocialstudies.com.**

Philadelphia,
Pennsylvania

Washington, D.C.

United States Government

Preview

Focus on the Main Idea
The government of the United States protects the rights of the people.

PLACES
Philadelphia, Pennsylvania
Washington, D.C.

PEOPLE
Thomas Jefferson
George Washington
Benjamin Franklin
James Madison
Rosa Parks
Thurgood Marshall

VOCABULARY
amendment

TERMS
Declaration of
  Independence
United States Constitution
Bill of Rights

You Are There
Today is a very important day. It's July 8, 1776, and the Declaration of Independence is about to be read from the State House steps in Philadelphia, Pennsylvania. The crowd around you is very noisy. Everyone wants to know what Thomas Jefferson and other leaders have written.

Suddenly, the crowd grows still. The Declaration of Independence is being read aloud. After the Declaration is read, you hear church bells ringing. You wonder, "What will become of this new nation?"

Summarize As you read, look for details and main ideas to help you summarize.

Declaring Independence

The government of England and the governments in the colonies did not always agree. Many colonists believed that England was taking away the rights that the Magna Carta said were theirs. The American colonies declared independence. **Thomas Jefferson** helped write the Declaration of Independence. The **Declaration of Independence** can be broken up into three parts. The first part says that people have rights the government must protect. The second part lists the complaints the colonies had against the king. The third part tells the world the colonies are declaring their independence. It said that the colonies were now free and independent states and no longer part of England.

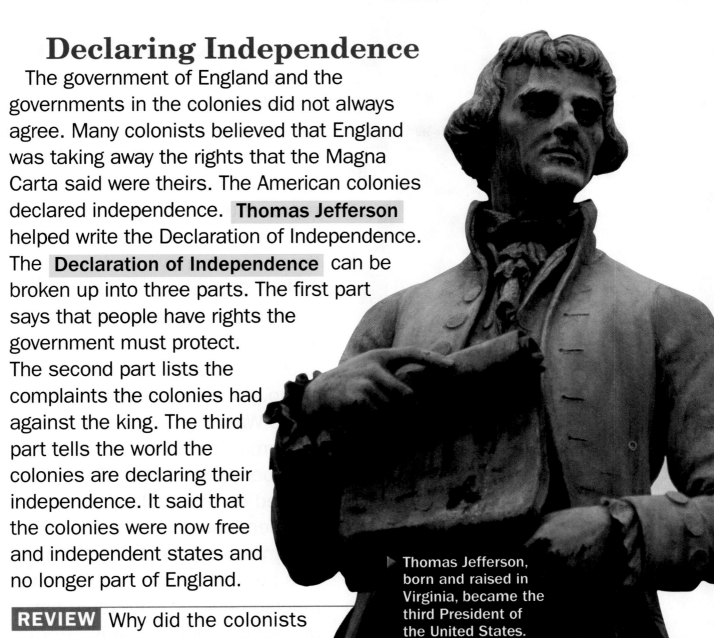

Thomas Jefferson, born and raised in Virginia, became the third President of the United States.

REVIEW Why did the colonists declare their independence?

Summarize

Literature and Social Studies

The Declaration of Independence

The Declaration of Independence said that there are rights that every person has. One part of this declaration is written below.

. . . .

"We hold these truths to be self-evident, that all men are created equal, that they are endowed by their Creator with certain unalienable Rights, that among these are Life, Liberty and the pursuit of Happiness."

George Washington led the United States in their war with England. He was chosen as the first President of the United States. Because of his leadership skills, George Washington is called the "Father of Our Country."

George Washington

Benjamin Franklin wrote books and was an inventor. People remember him for his famous experiment with a kite and electricity.

Benjamin Franklin

The meetings about the Constitution were held in secret. Much of what we know about the meetings comes from notes written by James Madison. He became the fourth President of the United States.

James Madison

The U.S. Constitution

In May 1787, 55 people met in Philadelphia, Pennsylvania, to write a new plan of government for the United States. Twelve of the thirteen states sent a representative. Only Rhode Island did not. During the hot summer, these members wrote the **United States Constitution.**

George Washington and **Benjamin Franklin** were two well-known and respected men in this group. All 55 delegates voted to make Washington the leader. Benjamin Franklin was the oldest member of the group. He had also worked on the Declaration of Independence.

James Madison from Virginia was also a member of this group. Madison helped write large parts of the constitution. He is often called the "Father of Our Constitution."

On September 17, 1787, the members completed their work. A new plan of government for the United States was written. The people, not a king, had the power to govern.

REVIEW In the United States who has the power to govern?
Main Idea and Details

MAP ADVENTURE

You want to visit our nation's capital, Washington, D.C. It is named after our first President, George Washington. Pierre Charles L'Enfant was chosen to make plans for the city. He had many ideas about how the capital should look. His ideas helped shape the way our nation's capital looks today.

Use the cardinal and intermediate directions on the compass rose to find your way to three important places in Washington, D.C.

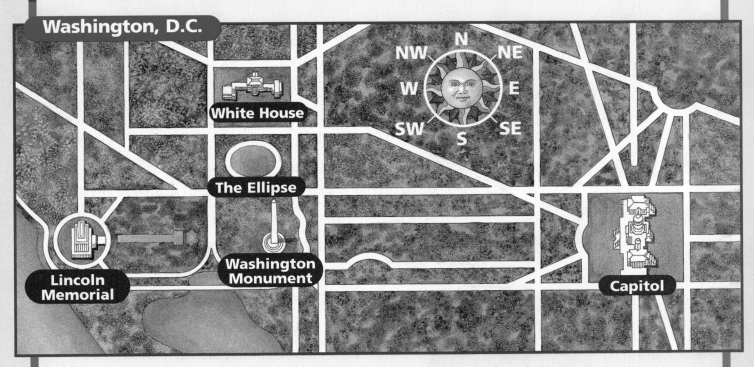

Washington, D.C.

1. Identify the building that is directly north of The Ellipse.

2. Identify the monument that is directly south of The Ellipse.

3. Identify the building that is southeast of the White House.

▶ Rosa Parks

The Bill of Rights: Protecting Freedom

Not everyone thought the U.S. Constitution protected their rights. Before some states would vote to accept the Constitution, they demanded that a Bill of Rights be added to the document. In 1791, ten **amendments,** or changes, to the Constitution were added. These ten amendments are called the **Bill of Rights.**

The Bill of Rights protects some of the rights of the people. Among the freedoms promised in the Bill of Rights are freedom of speech, of religion, and the right to gather together.

Even after the Bill of Rights was included in the Constitution, not everyone felt that their rights were protected. African Americans were sometimes treated differently from other Americans.

Rosa Parks, an African American woman from Montgomery, Alabama, thought that her rights were not protected. Simply because she was African American, she was asked to give up her seat on a bus to a white person. She would not. Other African Americans decided they would not ride buses until their rights were protected. In time, because of people like Rosa Parks and others, laws were passed to help protect people's rights.

Thurgood Marshall was the first African American to serve on the U.S. Supreme Court. He worked to make sure that our laws treated all people the same. Marshall served on the Supreme Court for 24 years. He often used the Bill of Rights to protect the rights of people.

People throughout our history have shown a belief in equality and justice—two characteristics of good citizenship. Good citizens are important to a community. Learning about your national, state, and local governments is an important first step in becoming a good citizen.

REVIEW Identify two characteristics of good citizenship. **Main Idea and Details**

Summarize the Lesson

- The Declaration of Independence said the colonies were free and independent states.
- The Constitution is the plan of government for the United States.
- The Bill of Rights lists the ten basic rights that every American has.
- Rosa Parks and Thurgood Marshall both fought for equality and justice.

LESSON 2 REVIEW

Check Facts and Main Ideas

1. **Summarize** On a separate sheet of paper, fill in details to complete the lesson summary.

Three important men helped write the United States Constitution.

2. What three rights does the Declaration of Independence say that people have?

3. Why was the Bill of Rights added to the Constitution?

4. How did Rosa Parks's community change because of her actions?

5. **Critical Thinking: Compare and Contrast** How are the Declaration of Independence and the Bill of Rights alike and different?

Link to ∞ **Writing**

Write a Biography Use the library or the Internet to find more information about a person in this lesson. Write two paragraphs. Share your biography with your class.

HERE AND THERE

Ancient Rome and Washington, D.C.

▶ Ancient Roman buildings influenced the way architects built some U.S. government buildings.

The heart of ancient Rome was an open area called the Roman Forum. The Roman Forum had many monuments and public buildings. Buildings and monuments are human characteristics of a place or region.

You learned that Pierre Charles L'Enfant designed our nation's capital, Washington, D.C. The heart of our capital is also a large open area. It is known as the National Mall. Like the Roman Forum, it has monuments and public buildings around it. Architecture from ancient Greece and Rome influenced the way many of these buildings were designed.

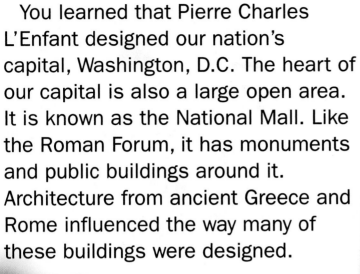

Ruins from ancient buildings still stand in the Roman Forum today.

The Capitol in Washington, where our lawmakers meet, has a dome. Domes were common on buildings in ancient Rome.

Roman government also influenced the founders of our country. The early government of ancient Rome was a republic. A republic is a representative form of government. Our founders used some ideas from ancient Rome when they wrote the U.S. Constitution.

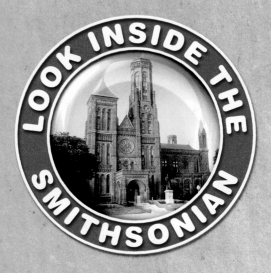

LOOK INSIDE THE SMITHSONIAN

Abraham Lincoln

Abraham Lincoln became President of the United States in 1861. He served until his death on April 15, 1865.

Lincoln Portrait
The line across this famous picture was an accident that happened when the picture was made. The picture, taken on February 5, 1865, was one of the last formal portraits that Lincoln posed for.

Abraham Lincoln was our 16th President!

Lincoln Axe, 1860
Many of the people who wanted Lincoln to be President may have carried wooden axes like this in parades to show their support for him.

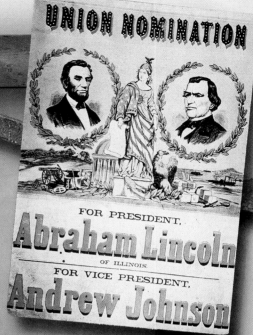

UNION NOMINATION

FOR PRESIDENT.
Abraham Lincoln
OF ILLINOIS.
FOR VICE PRESIDENT,
Andrew Johnson

Lincoln-Johnson Campaign Poster, 1864
People put this poster in the windows of their stores.

Lincoln's Second Inaugural Address
Lincoln was reelected President in 1864. He told the American people that he wanted the North and the South to become one nation again.

Bugle
This was used to play final taps at Lincoln's funeral.

Lincoln's Last Party
This party, to honor Civil War heroes, was the last one that Lincoln held in the White House. He was killed several weeks later.

THE FUNERAL OF PRESIDENT LINCOLN, NEW YORK, APRIL 25TH 1865.

Funeral for Lincoln
The wagon carrying Lincoln's body moved through the streets of New York City.

Artifacts are from the Smithsonian Institution.

375

Jefferson City, Missouri

Preview

Focus on the Main Idea
Citizens have rights and responsibilities to their community, state, and country.

PLACE
Jefferson City, Missouri

VOCABULARY
responsibility

Being a Good Citizen

You Are There Your teacher has just asked you to think about how you can be a better citizen of your community. She asked you the difference between having rights and having responsibilities.

You remember that your parents explained what it meant to be part of a family. They take care of you because you are special to them. But they expect you to help out because you are part of the family.

You think that a family is like a small community.

 Summarize As you read, think of a one-sentence summary for each part of this lesson.

Respect the rights and property of others. Do not take things that do not belong to you.

Ways to Be a Good Citizen

Hi! My name is Sabrina. I am from the capital of **Missouri, Jefferson City.** As a citizen, I have many rights and many freedoms. I also have responsibilities. A **responsibility** is a duty, or something you should do. For example, I have a responsibility to obey the laws of my country and my community.

Think of some other important responsibilities you have. Compare your ideas with these ideas.

Obey laws or community rules. Follow the laws that your community and your country have made.

Pay taxes. A tax is money you pay to the government for services that you use.

Help improve the community and country. You can help improve your school too.

Vote in elections. By voting in school elections, you help decide who runs your student government.

REVIEW Explain how you can be a good citizen. ⟳ **Summarize**

Taking Responsibility

Voting is an important responsibility. Citizens vote to elect leaders. In the United States we elect the leaders who run our country's government and speak for us on important issues. We also elect our state and local leaders. After we vote our leaders into office, we all work together. It does not matter if the candidate we wanted won or lost. We accept the results. Our leaders work for the common good.

In a school election, you vote for your school leaders. They run the student government.

1 First, you listen to the people who want to be elected.

2 Next you decide which person you think would be the best person for the job.

3 Then you vote.

4 Then you support your views and ideas by participating.

Many people, either as groups or individuals, improve their community by volunteering to help others. They feel they have a responsibility to help. Volunteers in your community might help people who are hungry or need clothing. Communities become special places when people just like you give their time and talent to help others. What ways can you think of to help make your community a better place to live?

REVIEW What is one way groups or individuals improve their community? **Main Idea and Details**

Summarize the Lesson

- Citizens have rights and responsibilities to their community, state, and country.
- Responsibilities are to obey laws, vote, pay taxes, improve your community, and respect the rights and property of others.
- Volunteering is a way to improve your community and to help others.

LESSON 3 ⟩ **REVIEW**

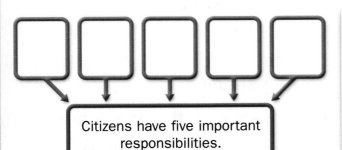

Check Facts and Main Ideas

1. ☉ **Summarize** On a separate sheet of paper, fill in the details to complete the summary of this lesson.

Citizens have five important responsibilities.

2. What is a responsibility?
3. Who speaks for the people of the United States on important issues?

4. What is one way to help improve your community?
5. **Critical Thinking: *Sequence*** What are three steps in voting for leaders?

Link to ⸺∞∞⸺ **Art**

Make a Poster Think of a job that you would like to do in your school or community. Make a poster that tells why you would be the best person for the job. Hang your poster in the classroom.

379

Chapter Summary

 **Summarize**

Look over Chapter 11. On a separate sheet of paper, write a summary sentence to complete the chart.

| People over time have had different kinds of governments. | Citizens of the United States have rights. | Citizens of the United States have responsibilities. |

Vocabulary

Match each word with the correct definition or description.

❶ direct democracy (p. 359)

❷ Mayflower Compact (p. 361)

❸ Bill of Rights (p. 370)

❹ amendment (p. 370)

❺ responsibility (p. 377)

❻ United States Constitution (p. 368)

❼ Declaration of Independence (p. 367)

a. a change to the U.S. Constitution

b. plan of government for the *Mayflower* colonists

c. a duty; something that you should do

d. the first ten changes to the Constitution

e. government that is run by the people who live under it

f. document stating that the colonies were free and independent from England

g. plan for the government of the United States

Facts and Main Ideas

1 How did the Magna Carta change the power of the English king?

2 What is a republic?

3 **Main Idea** What governments from the past influenced the United States government?

4 **Main Idea** Explain the importance of the Declaration of Independence and the U.S. Constitution.

5 **Main Idea** What are the responsibilities of a good citizen?

6 **Critical Thinking:** *Draw Conclusions* Why are the steps you take before voting important?

Internet Activity

To get help with vocabulary, people, and terms, select the dictionary or encyclopedia from *Social Studies Library* at **www.sfsocialstudies.com.**

Write About It

1 **Write a "You Are There"** for your class describing what you think it was like to come ashore from the *Mayflower* to the new land.

2 **Write directions** from the White House to a place that you would like to go in Washington, D.C. Use the map on page 369 to help you. Use both cardinal and intermediate directions.

3 **Write an introduction** for one of the people you read about in this chapter. Identify the person and the reason he or she became famous.

Apply Skills

Identify the Point of View
Read a letter to the editor from a local newspaper or from a news magazine. Explain the point of view of the writer to a classmate.

Lesson 1

St. Louis, Missouri

Local governments provide services to communities.

1

Lesson 2

Traverse City, Michigan

Community leaders help a community meet its needs.

2

Lesson 3

Toms River, New Jersey

Individuals and groups help change communities.

3

Why We Remember

Today, as in the past, people around the world form communities to meet their needs. Some of these needs include the need for safety, education, communication, transportation, recreation, and a way to earn a living. People organize governments to provide services to meet people's needs and to improve communities.

St. Louis, Missouri

Preview

Focus on the Main Idea
Local governments provide community services.

PLACE
St. Louis, Missouri

VOCABULARY
recreation

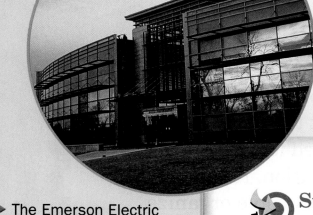

▶ The Emerson Electric Center is part of the Missouri History Museum in **St. Louis, Missouri.**

Community Services

 **You Are There**
You can't wait to get started. Today your class is going on a field trip to the public museum!

You get to school, line up, and get on the bus. You ride for just a short time and then you are there.

Your city's public museum has all kinds of great things to see. You go first to the history section. You want to know more about people from long ago.

You look around and think about how lucky you are that your community has such a great place where you can learn more about our country's history.

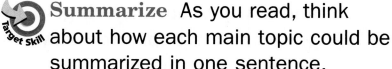 **Summarize** As you read, think about how each main topic could be summarized in one sentence.

Services People Want

People in communities want services that provide safety, education, transportation, and recreation. People choose to live in communities that have these services.

Local governments provide the services that people want. These services make your community a better place to live. What kinds of services does your community provide?

REVIEW Identify the four types of services people in communities usually want. **Main Idea and Details**

Community Services

- Education
- Safety and Security
- Transportation
- Recreation

Services Local Governments Provide

Education, recreation, transportation, and safety are important to the adults in your community. Your local government provides these services.

Safety and Security

Because safety and security are important to people, local governments have police and fire departments. Police officers and firefighters protect people and property.

Education

Because people care about education, your local government has a school you can attend and a library with many books to read. Some communities have students from other countries live with families in the community. You can learn all about another culture this way.

Recreation

Recreation is a way of enjoying yourself. Recreation is important to many people. Local governments offer many different things to do. Your community might have parks, swimming pools, senior centers, and sports leagues.

Transportation

Local governments meet the need for transportation by building and fixing roads. Some governments run buses and subways, trains that run below ground. Some governments build sidewalks and bike paths.

The services provided by local government cost money. People in your community pay for them.

REVIEW Compare and contrast the types of recreation in your community with those shown on this page. **Compare and Contrast**

Paying for Local Government

People in your community pay taxes to your local government. Your local government uses this money to pay for the services it provides.

Your community government also charges fees for some services. You may pay to swim at the community pool or to play on a sports team. Your family may pay a fee for trash pickup.

Finally, your local government gets money from the state and national governments. Money from the state might have paid for a traffic signal near your school. The national government may have helped pay to connect your school to the Internet.

REVIEW Describe three ways a local government pays for the services it provides.
Summarize

Summarize the Lesson

- Communities help people meet their needs for safety, education, transportation, and recreation.
- Local governments provide the services that people want.
- Local governments get money from taxes, fees, and state and national governments.

LESSON 1 REVIEW

Check Facts and Main Ideas

1. **Summarize** On a separate sheet of paper, fill in details that support the lesson summary.

Local governments provide services to the people in the community.

2. Why do local governments provide services the people want?

3. What services help meet a community's need for safety and security?

4. Name one way that local governments get money for the services that they provide.

5. **Critical Thinking: *Summarize*** Identify the four types of services usually provided by local governments.

Link to ⊶ Writing

Make a list of activities that you would like your park district to offer. List reasons why you think each activity is important. Explain how each activity will make the people of your community healthier.

Understand Grid Systems

What? Look at the map below. Notice the lines on the map. A globe also has lines. To help people find places on a map or globe, mapmakers use a grid system. A grid system is made of two sets of lines that cross. One set of lines extends from east to west. One set of lines extends from north to south.

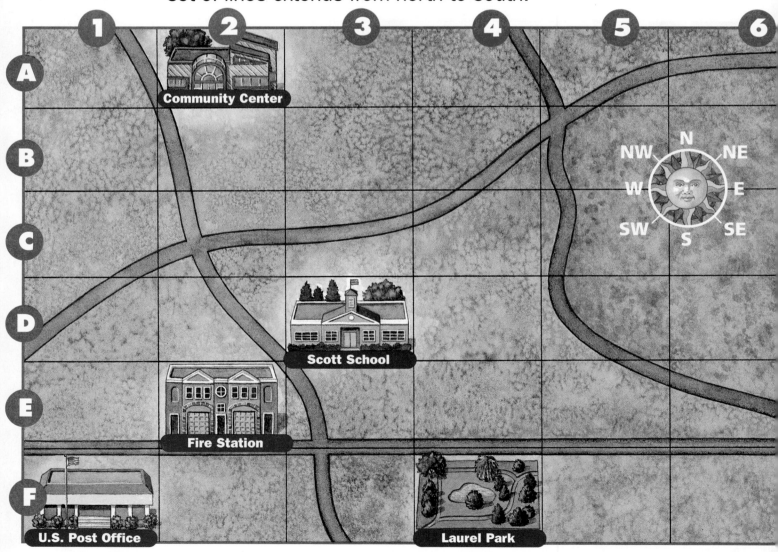

Look at the squares formed by the lines. Find the school. Slide your finger to the left edge of the map. You come to the letter **D**. Put your finger back on the school. Slide your finger to the top edge of the map. You come to the number **3**. Mapmakers give the school's location as D-3.

Why? People use grid systems to tell others where to find schools, parks, and other places.

How? Suppose a friend called you to find the location of the community center. You could tell your friend it was at A-2 on the town map. Your friend would find A-2 on the town map and know the location of the community center.

Geographers use a grid system that covers the world. One set of imaginary lines circles the Earth from east to west. These are called lines of **latitude**. The equator is a line of latitude. Another set of imaginary lines circles the Earth from north to south. These lines pass through the poles. They are called lines of **longitude**. The prime meridian is a line of longitude.

As on other map grids, lines of latitude and longitude can help you locate places on a globe or map. Lines of longitude are numbered east and west from the prime meridian. Lines of latitude are numbered north and south of the equator. Ship captains, airline pilots, and others use lines of latitude and longitude to describe exactly where they are and where they are going.

Think and Apply

1. Identify what the system of lines on this map is called.

2. What is at F-4?

3. Where is the post office?

Internet Activity

For more information, go online to the *Atlas* at **www.sfsocialstudies.com**.

Traverse City, Michigan

Preview

Focus on the Main Idea
Community leaders help a community meet its needs.

PLACE
Traverse City, Michigan

VOCABULARY
council
mayor
candidate
consent

Community Leaders

You Are There It's the Fourth of July. You are in **Traverse City, Michigan,** and you are sitting in the same spot where you and your family always sit. Your friends are sitting nearby too. You all can't wait for the parade to begin.

Suddenly you hear the fire engines blasting their horns! A police motorcycle is leading the big red engines. Here comes the mayor in the car without a top. Who are all those people with the mayor?

Summarize As you read, think of a one-sentence summary for each main topic.

Custodians

Teachers

Schools

Government Officials

The adults in your community pick local leaders by voting. They elect a town or city council. A town or city **council** is a group of people who make laws and rules for a community.

Town or City Council

Mayor

The adults in your community may also elect a mayor. A **mayor** is the leader of the community. In some places, the council chooses the mayor.

Subways

Public Transportation

Buses

Local Government

Police and Fire Departments

Parks and Recreation Department

Police Chief

Fire Chief

The mayor and the council decide what the local government should do. They pick people to provide services. The mayor might choose the police chief and the fire chief. The police chief will run the police department. The fire chief will run the fire department.

REVIEW Describe some parts of a local government. **Main Idea and Details**

391

FACT FILE

Community Leaders

Every community is a little different. Many communities have government leaders like these.

Members of the City/Town Council

- Make local laws.
- Hold meetings to listen to citizens.
- Elected by the citizens of the community.

Mayor

- In some communities, the mayor is powerful. The mayor can make important decisions without asking the council. The mayor chooses the fire chief, police chief, and other government officials.
- In other communities, the mayor is less powerful. Running council meetings might be the mayor's most important job.
- Usually elected by the citizens of the community.

Members of the Park District Board

- Make most decisions about parks and recreation programs.
- Can ask voters to approve new taxes.
- Usually elected by the citizens of a community.
- Help the community meet its needs for recreation.
- Usually choose the head of the Parks and Recreation Department.

Police Chief/ Fire Chief

- Runs the police or fire department.
- Hires police officers or firefighters.
- Depending on the community, may be chosen by the mayor or by the town/city council.
- Helps a community meet its needs for safety.
- Enforces and applies the laws of the community.

Superintendent of Schools

- Carries out rules made by the school board.
- Helps the community meet its needs for education.
- Usually chosen by the school board.
- Usually hires principals.
- May hire teachers and other staff.

Members of the School Board

- Make rules for the school district.
- Can ask voters to approve new taxes.
- Elected by citizens of the community.
- Help the community meet its needs for education.

If you elect me, I would work to improve the...

As your candidate, I promise you that I will always listen to...

Electing Leaders

Before members of a town or city council were elected, they had to run for office. A person who runs for office is a **candidate.**

Candidates talk to people in the community. They explain what they would do to help the community.

People in a community listen to the candidates. People also read about the candidates in newspapers. Finally, they compare the candidates. On Election Day, people vote for the candidates they think will be best for the community.

Voting is an important responsibility. People can help change and improve communities by voting.

REVIEW Identify the important responsibility that citizens have on Election Day. Explain why it is important. **Summarize**

Consent of the People

People living in a community vote for the candidates they want. People want the leaders they elected to make and carry out laws. People give their **consent,** or permission, to the elected leaders to do this. People agree to follow these laws. Leaders and citizens who obey the laws help the local community and its government work smoothly.

If a leader does not do a good job, the people may decide that they will not vote for this person in the next election. Then this leader will not have their consent to speak for them.

REVIEW How do voters give their consent to their leaders? ◎ **Summarize**

Summarize the Lesson

- Local government officials include a mayor, city or town council, police chief, fire chief, and others.
- Some local officials are elected by the people.
- Some local officials are chosen by the mayor or town/city council.
- People give their consent by electing leaders to positions in their local government.

LESSON 2 REVIEW

Check Facts and Main Ideas

1. ◎ **Summarize** On a separate sheet of paper, fill in a sentence to summarize this lesson.

```
┌──────────────┐   ┌──────────────┐   ┌──────────────┐
│ Mayor and    │   │ Police and   │   │ School Board │
│ City or Town │   │ Fire Chief   │   │ and Park     │
│ Council      │   │              │   │ District Board│
└──────┬───────┘   └──────┬───────┘   └──────┬───────┘
       │                  ▼                  │
       └────────► ┌───────────────┐ ◄────────┘
                  │               │
                  │               │
                  └───────────────┘
```

2. Identify six local officials and explain how they are chosen.

3. What happens if a leader does not do a good job?

4. Whose job is it to carry out the rules made by the school board?

5. **Critical Thinking:** *Compare and Contrast* How is government as described in this lesson the same or different from your local government?

Link to ⊷⊶ Reading

Go to the library or get a copy of your local newspaper. Have an adult read to you articles about the people who run your local government. Share the main ideas of the articles in an oral report to your class.

An Honest Man

▶ Charles Curtis

"Curtis's word is as good as gold."

—George Norris, a senator who often disagreed with Senator Curtis

Charles "Charley" Curtis was born in 1860. As a young boy, he lived with his grandparents on the Kaw Reservation in Kansas. He learned to speak the Kaw language before he learned English. He was proud to be a Native American.

When Charley finished high school, he decided to become a lawyer. He worked as a janitor while he studied law.

▶ Charles Curtis and others watch Herbert Hoover sign a farm relief bill.

BUILDING CITIZENSHIP
Caring
Respect
Responsibility
Fairness
★ Honesty
Courage

After he became a lawyer, Curtis ran for the office of county attorney of Shawnee County, Kansas. The county attorney helps enforce and apply laws. He told people, "If you don't want the laws enforced, don't vote for me." Voters liked his honesty. They elected him county attorney.

Later, voters elected Curtis to the U.S. House of Representatives. Next, he was elected to the U.S. Senate. As a senator, he led the fight to give women equal voting rights. He worked to give U.S. citizenship to all Native Americans living in the country.

Curtis was known as a leader who always kept his word. By his actions, Curtis showed a belief in honesty, a characteristic of good citizenship. One senator who often disagreed with Curtis said he never knew Curtis to break his word or to fail to carry out an agreement.

In 1928, voters picked Charles Curtis to be the 31st Vice-President of the United States. He was Vice-President from 1929 to 1933 when Herbert Hoover was President.

► Campaign sheet music

Honesty in Action

Identify the characteristic of good citizenship shown by Charles Curtis. Why is this an important quality?

Toms River,
New Jersey

Preview

Focus on the Main Idea
Individuals and groups
help change and improve
communities.

PLACE
Toms River, New Jersey

VOCABULARY
marsh

People Change Communities

You Are There

What is the principal doing sitting in the dunk tank? Today is the school fair. Every year your school holds a fair to earn money to help people with cancer. The beanbag toss, face-painting, and the dunking machine are your favorite parts of the fair.

You have $8. You've been saving this money to go to the movies. You decide to give your money to help others who are sick by spending your money at the school fair instead. The woman collecting the money thanks you. She tells you that you have made a difference in your community.

 Summarize As you read, think of a one-sentence summary for each main topic.

Individuals Improve Communities

Across the country, people work to improve their communities. For example, Martha was concerned that biking on busy streets was not safe. She knew that children in her community would be safer if bike lanes were built.

Martha decided to write her city council a letter asking the city to build bike lanes. Others wrote too. Her city decided to build bike lanes. Because of people like Martha, bike lanes are being built in communities across the country.

What are some ways individuals help improve your community? How could you make your community a better place to live?

REVIEW What action did Martha decide to take to improve her community? How did her community improve?

Summarize

Bike riding is a lot safer in my cousin's city since the city built bike lanes!

Groups Improve Communities

Students at Silver Bay School in Toms River, New Jersey, live near the Toms River. The river and its marshes are important to the community. A marsh is an area of land sometimes covered by water.

On a field trip, students visited a marsh not far from their school. They saw trash such as bottles and an old mattress in the marsh.

The group of students made a decision to clean up the marsh. They collected trash in large trash bags. They worked hard. As a result, the marsh was cleaner.

The group made a decision to get their community involved in cleaning up other areas near the river. Others agreed to clean up the river too. They started a project called "Save Our Bays and Waterways." They helped make their community a better place to live.

What groups help improve your community? Suppose you started a group. What would you want the group to do to improve your community?

REVIEW Summarize the decisions and the actions taken by the group of students to change and improve their community.
↻ **Summarize**

LESSON 3 REVIEW

Check Facts and Main Ideas

1. ↻ **Summarize** On a separate sheet of paper, fill in details to complete the lesson summary.

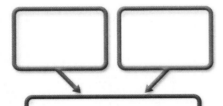

People can change their communities.

2. What is one way that people can try to change their community?

3. What decision did a group of students make?

4. How did Silver Bay School students change their community?

5. **Critical Thinking: *Cause and Effect*** The students from Toms River saw that the marsh was littered. What effect did the students' actions have on the marsh?

Link to ⚭ **Writing**

Write a letter to your city or town council. Describe a project that you can do to help make your community a better place to live.

Meet Emily Bissell

1861–1948
Red Cross Volunteer

Emily Bissell was born in Wilmington, Delaware. Bissell knew that she wanted to help needy people.

For more information, go online to *Meet the People* at **www.sfsocialstudies.com**.

In 1905 Bissell helped to start the Delaware chapter of the American Red Cross. She was its first secretary. The American Red Cross is an organization that serves the common good—it helps people and their communities. During and after disasters, volunteers for the American Red Cross provide food and shelter for those in need. This organization also helps train people in first aid, swimming, and safety.

In the early 1900s, many people were dying from a lung disease called tuberculosis, or TB. Emily Bissell's cousin, Dr. Joseph Wales, needed Emily's help. He needed money to keep a TB hospital open. He knew that Emily worked for the American Red Cross. He wrote to her, "Unless $300 can be raised somehow, the poor patients will have to be sent home to die. . . ."

Emily Bissell designed the first American Christmas Seal. The national Red Cross agreed that she could use its symbol, the red cross, on the seal. Bissell borrowed money to print the seals. She worked hard to sell them. The first year the Christmas Seal sales raised more than $3,000. It was a big success.

"Put this stamp with message bright
On every Christmas letter;
Help the tuberculosis fight,
And make the New Year better."

Learn From Biographies

Emily Bissell and Dr. Joseph Wales both wanted to help people with TB. How did each help? How does the American Red Cross help people today?

The first Christmas seal was a red cross surrounded by holly. It had the words "Merry Christmas" printed below.

BIOFACT

Chapter Summary

 Summarize

On a separate sheet of paper, fill in a sentence to summarize these details about Chapter 12.

| Community services are provided. | Community leaders have the consent of the people. | People can change and improve communities. |

Vocabulary

Fill in the blank with the correct word.

a. candidate (p. 394)

b. consent (p. 395)

c. council (p. 391)

d. mayor (p. 391)

e. recreation (p. 386)

❶ _____ is a way of enjoying yourself.

❷ People give their _____ to their leaders to speak for them.

❸ A town or city _____ is a group of people who make the rules and laws for a community.

❹ A _____ is the leader of the community.

❺ A person who runs for office is a _____.

Facts and Main Ideas

1 What needs do the police chief and the fire chief help a community meet?

2 What should citizens do on a day that elections are held?

3 **Main Idea** What are four kinds of services that local governments provide?

4 **Main Idea** What group of people are always elected in a local government?

5 **Main Idea** How did the students from Toms River improve their community?

6 **Critical Thinking:** *Sequence* List the steps voters take to choose an elected official.

Write About It

1 **Write a letter** to a government official. Look at the Fact File on pages 392–393. Choose one local official that you want to know more about. Write to the person who has this job in your community. Ask questions that you have about his or her job.

2 **Make a list** of the educational services that your community provides. Write one paragraph about the service that you think is most important. Be sure to tell why you feel this way.

3 **Write a newspaper article** telling about someone who volunteers in your school or community.

Internet Activity

To get help with vocabulary, people, and terms, select the dictionary or encyclopedia from *Social Studies Library* at **www.sfsocialstudies.com.**

Apply Skills

Understand Grid Systems

Look at the map on pages 388–389. Use the following grid numbers to locate places on the map. Tell what you found in each place.

A-2	**D-3**
E-2	**F-4**

Greek and Roman myths are stories involving gods, goddesses, or heroes and their deeds. Usually there are many versions.

The Founding of Athens

People in one part of ancient Greece gathered to form a new city. Athena, the goddess of wisdom, was there. She gave the new city a gift to help them get started— the first olive tree.

The people were thankful for the gift. They knew they could grow more olive trees. They could eat the olives. From the olives, they could make the oil they need for cooking and lighting lamps. They knew they could trade the olives and the olive oil.

The people decided to name their city for Athena. Athena was pleased. She promised always to watch over the new city of Athens.

The Founding of Rome

Romulus and Remus were twin boys. Their grandfather once had been a king, but had been overthrown. When Romulus and Remus were born, they were placed in a basket. The new king worried that someday these two boys might try to overthrow him. He had the basket carrying the baby twins thrown into a river.

Luckily, the basket floated to the edge of the river. A wolf found the babies. The wolf took care of the babies as if they were her own wolf pups. Later, a shepherd and his wife raised the boys.

When the boys grew up, they learned about their history. They overthrew the king. They made their grandfather king again.

They decided to start a city of their own. They chose the place where the wolf had found them. Romulus became the first leader of the new city. The city was named Rome in his honor.

Review

Main Ideas and Vocabulary

Read the passage. Then answer the questions.

You are a citizen of your local community, your state, and of the United States of America. As a citizen, you have many rights and responsibilities. Being a good citizen is an important responsibility.

In ancient times, the city-state of Athens created a government called a direct democracy. The people ran the government. Citizens voted on everything.

In England, the king was in charge. He decided everything. In time though, even the king had to obey the laws.

In the United States, our government is called a <u>republic</u>. Citizens elect others to speak for them and to run the government. We elect leaders for our nation, our state, and our community.

It is a citizen's responsibility to vote on election day. In local communities, citizens elect members of a town or city council to run the government. These people then choose others to provide services.

❶ According to the passage, the government of Athens was

A a republic
B ruled by a king
C a direct democracy
D run by a city council

❷ According to the passage, the government of England was

A a republic
B ruled by a king
C a direct democracy
D run by a city council

❸ In the passage the word *republic* means a government

A ruled by a king
B run by the people
C run by elected officials
D none of the above

Vocabulary

Use the following words in a paragraph: *direct democracy, republic*. Tell the difference between the two forms of government. Remember to:

- use standard grammar
- use standard spelling
- use standard sentence structure
- use standard sentence punctuation

Read On Your Own

Look for books like these in the library.

Write and Share

Write and send an email to a relative who lives in another city. Tell this person about your local government. Ask your relative to answer with a letter describing his or her local government. Compare and contrast the two types of government.

Apply Skills

Understand a Grid System
Draw a map of your room at home. Use a scale of 1/4" to one foot. Show the scale on the map. Make a grid system on the map. Then draw important things in your room on it. Give your map a title. Put a compass rose on the map. Explain symbols you used in a map key. Write three questions about your map. Trade maps with a classmate. Answer each other's questions.

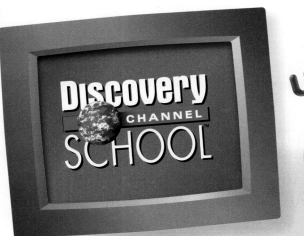

Discovery
CHANNEL
SCHOOL

UNIT 6 Project

Next Question!

Ask questions of a local government leader at a press conference.

1 Choose students to play the roles of local government leaders and news reporters at a press conference in your community.

2 Prepare a variety of questions to ask local government leaders about your community. Write answers to the questions.

3 Make press passes for the news reporters and official name tags for the government leaders.

4 Hold your press conference during class.

Press Pass
Daily World
Andy Tyler

Sheriff
Maria Lopez

Internet Activity

Learn more about government on the Internet. Go to www.sfsocialstudies.com/activities and select your grade and unit.

Table of Contents

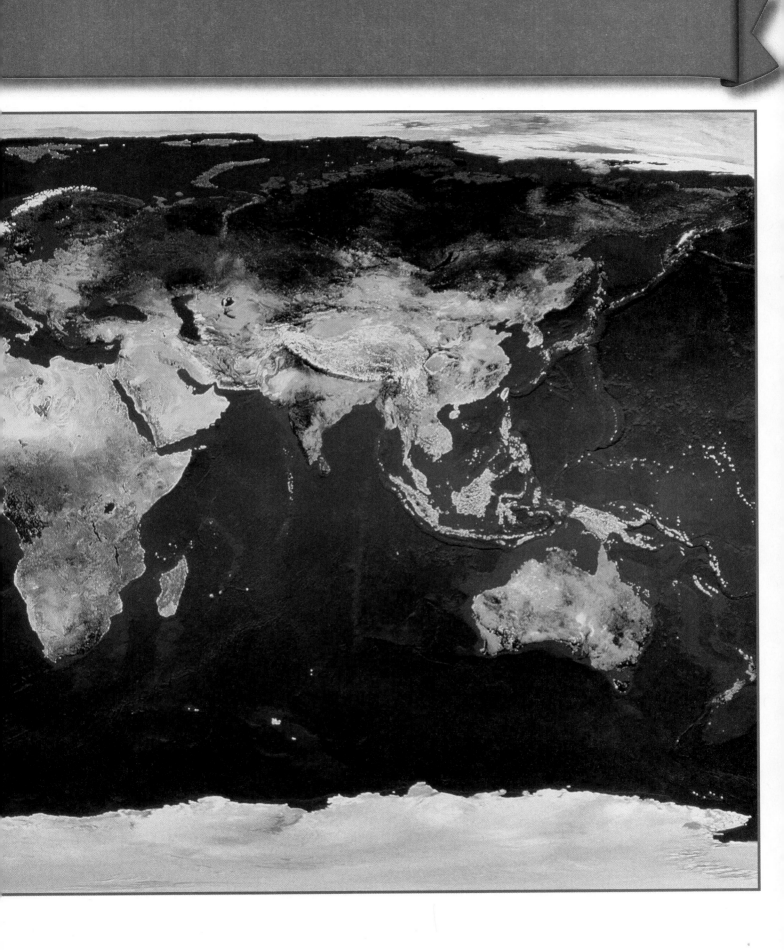

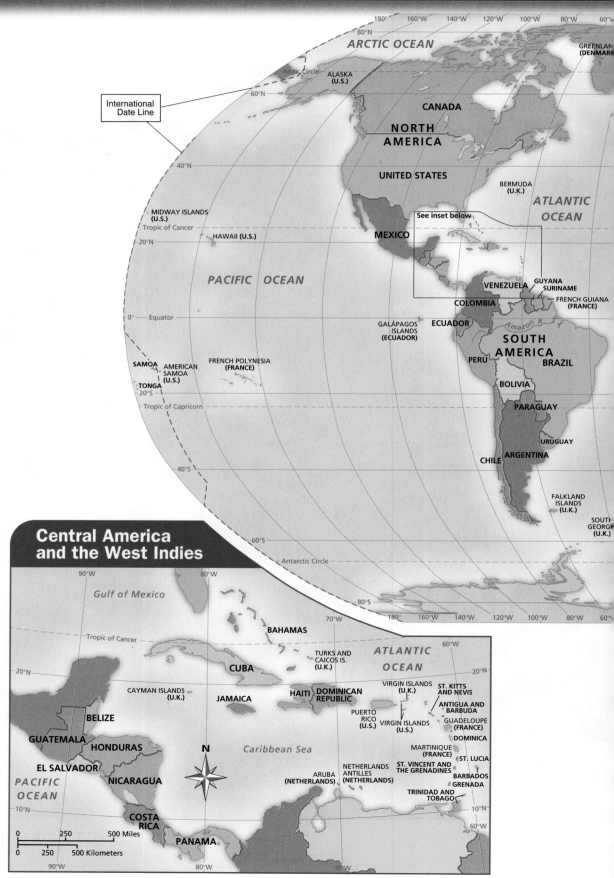

Central America and the West Indies

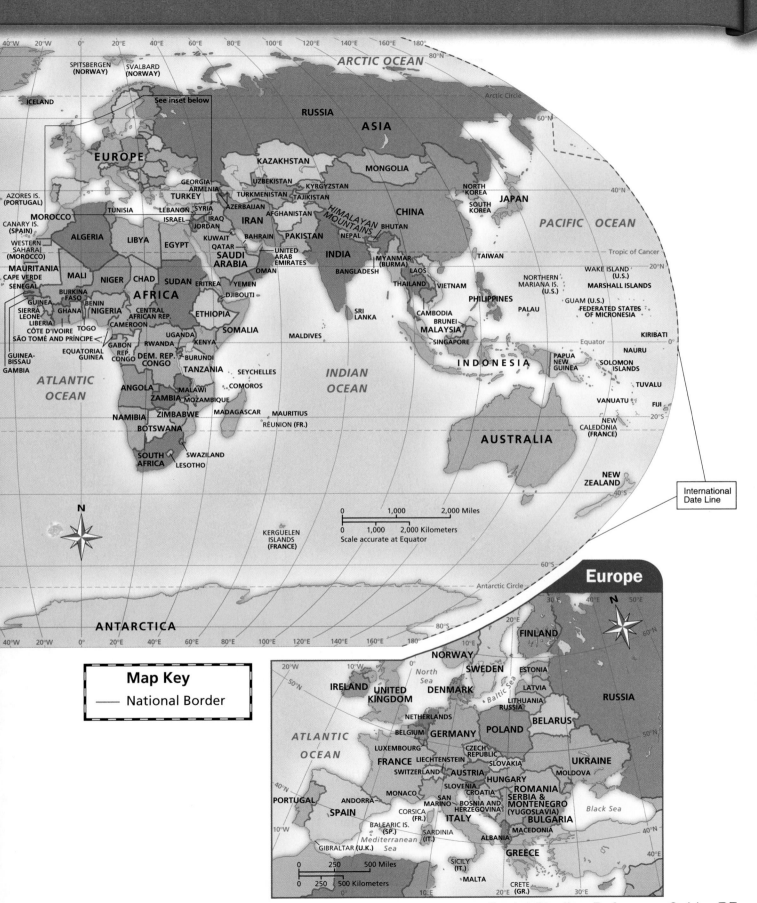

Map Key

— National Border

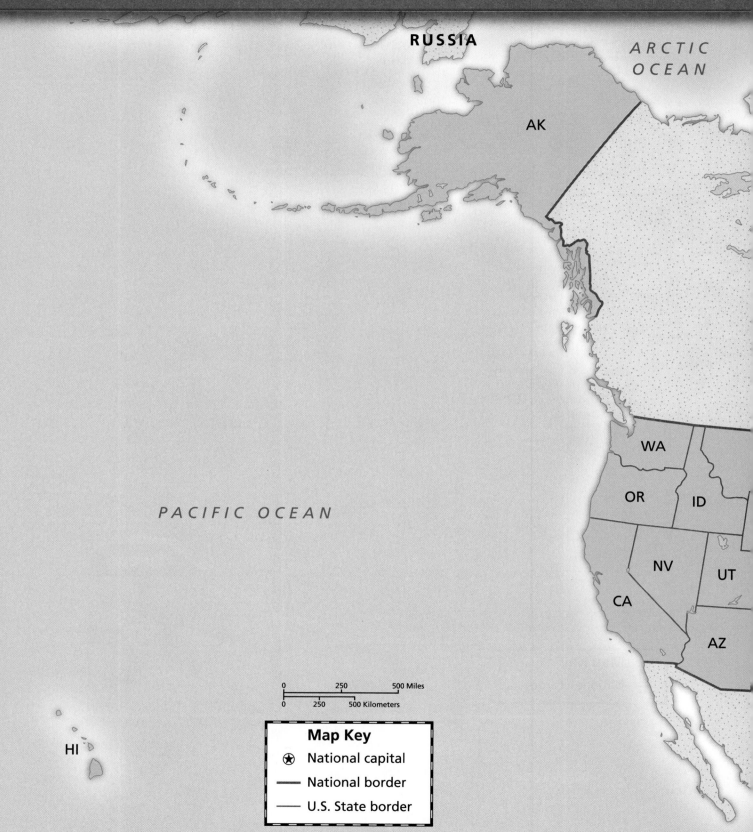

RUSSIA

ARCTIC OCEAN

AK

PACIFIC OCEAN

WA

OR

ID

NV

UT

CA

AZ

HI

0   250   500 Miles
0   250   500 Kilometers

Map Key

⊛ National capital

— National border

— U.S. State border

State or area	Abbreviation
Alabama	AL
Alaska	AK
Arizona	AZ
Arkansas	AR
California	CA
Colorado	CO
Connecticut	CT
Delaware	DE
District of Columbia	DC
Florida	FL
Georgia	GA
Hawaii	HI
Idaho	ID
Illinois	IL
Indiana	IN
Iowa	IA
Kansas	KS
Kentucky	KY
Louisiana	LA
Maine	ME
Maryland	MD
Massachusetts	MA
Michigan	MI
Minnesota	MN
Mississippi	MS
Missouri	MO
Montana	MT
Nebraska	NE
Nevada	NV
New Hampshire	NH
New Jersey	NJ
New Mexico	NM
New York	NY
North Carolina	NC
North Dakota	ND
Ohio	OH
Oklahoma	OK
Oregon	OR
Pennsylvania	PA
Rhode Island	RI
South Carolina	SC
South Dakota	SD
Tennessee	TN
Texas	TX
Utah	UT
Vermont	VT
Virginia	VA
Washington	WA
West Virginia	WV
Wisconsin	WI
Wyoming	WY

Atlas
Map of Our Fifty States: Political

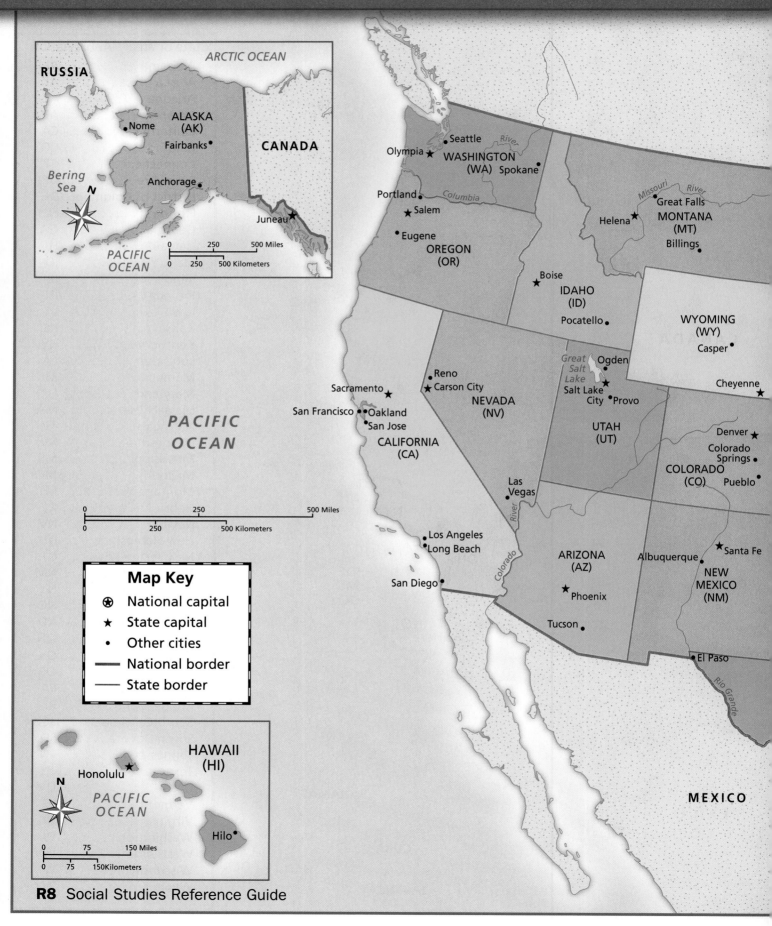

Map Key

⊛ National capital
★ State capital
• Other cities
— National border
— State border

RUSSIA
ARCTIC OCEAN
ALASKA (AK)
Nome
Fairbanks
CANADA
Bering Sea
Anchorage
Juneau
PACIFIC OCEAN
0   250   500 Miles
0   250   500 Kilometers

HAWAII (HI)
Honolulu
PACIFIC OCEAN
Hilo
0   75   150 Miles
0   75   150 Kilometers

PACIFIC OCEAN

Seattle
Olympia ★ WASHINGTON (WA)
Spokane
Portland
Columbia
★ Salem
Eugene
OREGON (OR)
Boise
IDAHO (ID)
Pocatello

Helena ★
Great Falls
MONTANA (MT)
Billings
Missouri River

WYOMING (WY)
Casper
Cheyenne ★

Great Salt Lake
Ogden
Salt Lake City ★
Provo
UTAH (UT)

Reno
Carson City ★
NEVADA (NV)

Sacramento ★
San Francisco
Oakland
San Jose
CALIFORNIA (CA)

Las Vegas

Denver ★
Colorado Springs
COLORADO (CO)
Pueblo

Los Angeles
Long Beach

San Diego

Colorado River

ARIZONA (AZ)
Phoenix ★
Tucson

Albuquerque
Santa Fe ★
NEW MEXICO (NM)

El Paso

Rio Grande

MEXICO

0   250   500 Miles
0   250   500 Kilometers

R8 Social Studies Reference Guide

CANADA

NORTH DAKOTA (ND)
• Bismarck
Grand Forks
• Fargo

SOUTH DAKOTA (SD)
★ Pierre

Sioux Falls

MINNESOTA (MN)
• Duluth
Minneapolis • ★ St. Paul

NEBRASKA (NE)
★ Lincoln
Omaha •

IOWA (IA)
Cedar Rapids •
Des Moines ★
Davenport •

Missouri River

WISCONSIN (WI)
Green Bay •
Madison ★
Milwaukee •

Rockford •
Chicago •

Lake Superior

MICHIGAN (MI)
Grand Rapids •
Lansing ★
Detroit •

Lake Michigan

Lake Huron

KANSAS (KS)
Kansas City •
Topeka ★
Wichita •

Kansas City •

Jefferson City ★

MISSOURI (MO)
St. Louis •

ILLINOIS (IL)
Peoria •
Springfield •

Mississippi River

INDIANA (IN)
Fort Wayne •
Gary •
Indianapolis ★

OHIO (OH)
Toledo •
Columbus ★
Cincinnati •

Cleveland •

Lake Erie

Lake Ontario

NEW HAMPSHIRE (NH)
VERMONT (VT)
Burlington •
Montpelier ★

MAINE (ME)
★ Augusta
• Portland
★ Concord

NEW YORK (NY)
Albany ★
Buffalo •

MASSACHUSETTS (MA)
Boston ★
• Providence

Hartford ★
RHODE ISLAND (RI)
CONNECTICUT (CT)

PENNSYLVANIA (PA)
Harrisburg ★
Pittsburgh •
Wheeling •

Newark •
New York •
Trenton ★
NEW JERSEY (NJ)
Philadelphia •

Dover ★
DELAWARE (DE)

Baltimore •
⊗ Annapolis
Washington, D.C.

MARYLAND (MD)

WEST VIRGINIA (WV)
Charleston ★

Ohio River

VIRGINIA (VA)
Richmond ★
• Norfolk

KENTUCKY (KY)
Louisville •
Frankfort ★
Evansville •

OKLAHOMA (OK)
• Tulsa
★ Oklahoma City

KANSAS (KS)

ARKANSAS (AR)
Fort Smith •
Little Rock ★

Memphis •

TENNESSEE (TN)
Nashville ★
Knoxville •

NORTH CAROLINA (NC)
Raleigh ★
Charlotte •

SOUTH CAROLINA (SC)
Columbia ★
Charleston •

TEXAS (TX)
Fort Worth •
Dallas •
Austin ★
Houston •
San Antonio •
Laredo •
Corpus Christi •

LOUISIANA (LA)
Shreveport •
Baton Rouge ★
New Orleans •

MISSISSIPPI (MS)
Jackson ★

Biloxi •

ALABAMA (AL)
Birmingham •
Montgomery ★
Mobile •

GEORGIA (GA)
Atlanta ★
Columbus •
Savannah •

Tallahassee ★

FLORIDA (FL)
Jacksonville •
Tampa •
Miami •

ATLANTIC OCEAN

Gulf of Mexico

N

BAHAMAS

CUBA

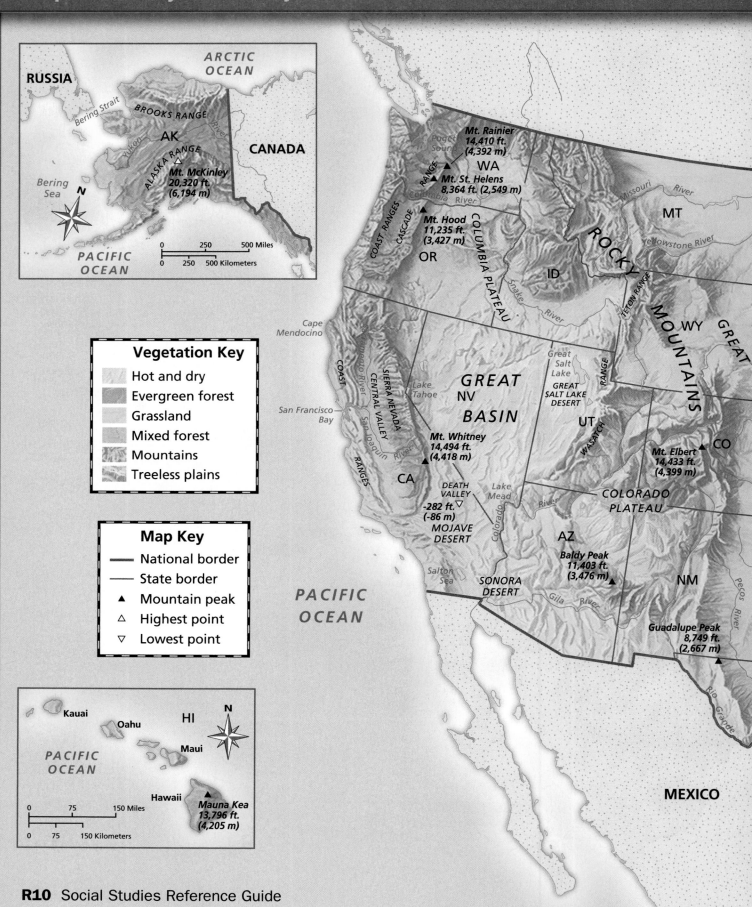

ARCTIC OCEAN

RUSSIA

Bering Strait

BROOKS RANGE

Yukon River

AK

CANADA

ALASKA RANGE

Mt. McKinley
20,320 ft.
(6,194 m)

Bering Sea

N

PACIFIC OCEAN

0   250   500 Miles
0   250   500 Kilometers

Vegetation Key

Hot and dry
Evergreen forest
Grassland
Mixed forest
Mountains
Treeless plains

Map Key

— National border
— State border
▲ Mountain peak
△ Highest point
▽ Lowest point

Puget Sound

Mt. Rainier
14,410 ft.
(4,392 m)

Mt. St. Helens
8,364 ft. (2,549 m)

WA

RANGE

Columbia River

Mt. Hood
11,235 ft.
(3,427 m)

COAST RANGES

CASCADE

OR

COLUMBIA PLATEAU

MT

Missouri River

ROCKY

Yellowstone River

ID

Snake River

TETON RANGE

MOUNTAINS

WY   GREAT

Cape Mendocino

COAST

Sacramento River

SIERRA NEVADA

CENTRAL VALLEY

Lake Tahoe

San Francisco Bay

San Joaquin River

GREAT

NV

BASIN

Great Salt Lake

GREAT SALT LAKE DESERT

RANGE

WASATCH

UT

Mt. Whitney
14,494 ft.
(4,418 m)

RANGES

CA

DEATH VALLEY

-282 ft. ▽
(-86 m)
MOJAVE DESERT

Lake Mead

Colorado River

Mt. Elbert
14,433 ft.
(4,399 m)

CO

COLORADO PLATEAU

Salton Sea

PACIFIC OCEAN

SONORA DESERT

AZ

Baldy Peak
11,403 ft.
(3,476 m)

Gila River

NM

Pecos River

Guadalupe Peak
8,749 ft.
(2,667 m)

Rio Grande

MEXICO

Kauai

Oahu

HI

N

Maui

PACIFIC OCEAN

Hawaii

Mauna Kea
13,796 ft.
(4,205 m)

0   75   150 Miles
0   75   150 Kilometers

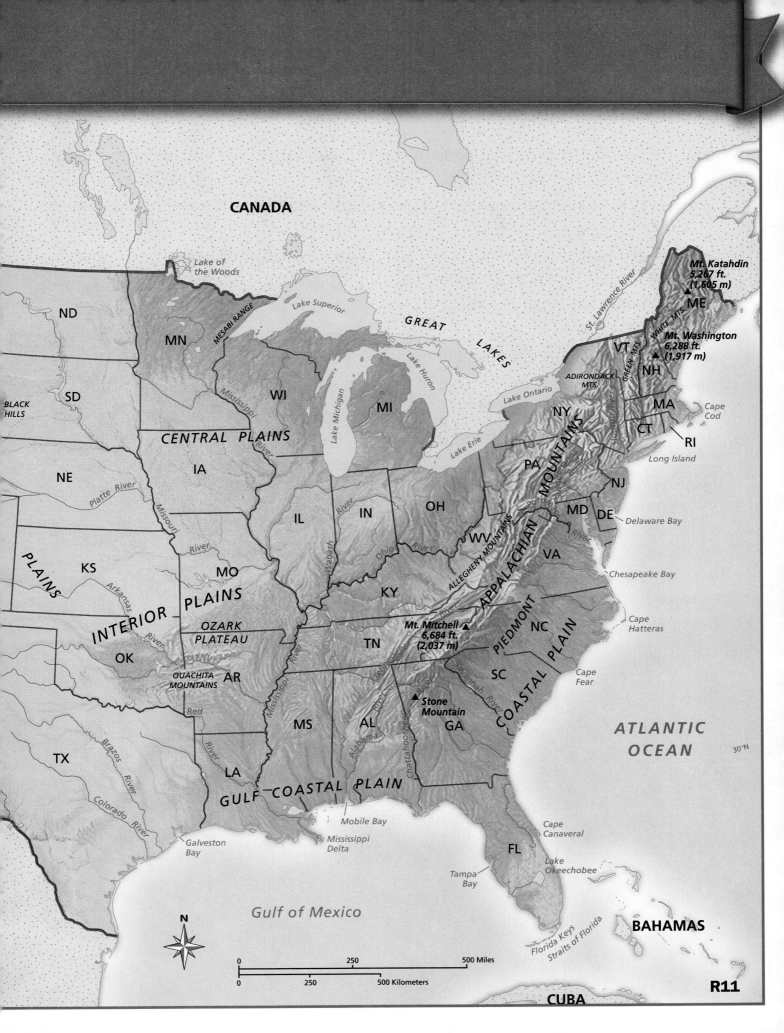

CANADA

ND

MN

Lake of the Woods

MESABI RANGE

Lake Superior

GREAT

LAKES

St. Lawrence River

Mt. Katahdin
5,267 ft.
(1,605 m)
▲ ME

BLACK
HILLS

SD

WI

MI

Lake Huron

Lake Michigan

Lake Ontario

Lake Erie

GREEN MTS.

WHITE MTS.

Mt. Washington
6,288 ft.
(1,917 m) ▲

VT

NH

ADIRONDACK
MTS.

CENTRAL PLAINS

NE

IA

Mississippi River

Platte River

IL

IN

OH

NY

PA

APPALACHIAN MOUNTAINS

ALLEGHENY MOUNTAINS

MA

CT

RI

Cape Cod

Long Island

NJ

MD DE

Delaware Bay

WV

VA

Chesapeake Bay

Missouri River

PLAINS

KS

Arkansas River

MO

INTERIOR

PLAINS

OZARK
PLATEAU

KY

TN

Mt. Mitchell ▲
6,684 ft.
(2,037 m)

Ohio River

Wabash River

PIEDMONT

NC

Cape Hatteras

OK

OUACHITA
MOUNTAINS

AR

Mississippi River

Red River

MS

AL

▲ Stone
Mountain

GA

SC

COASTAL PLAIN

Savannah River

Cape Fear

TX

Brazos River

Colorado River

Galveston Bay

LA

GULF COASTAL PLAIN

Mobile Bay

*Mississippi
Delta*

Alabama River

Chattahoochee River

Tennessee River

ATLANTIC
OCEAN

30°N

FL

Cape Canaveral

Lake Okeechobee

Tampa Bay

Florida Keys

Straits of Florida

BAHAMAS

N

Gulf of Mexico

0   250   500 Miles

0   250   500 Kilometers

CUBA

Geography Terms

bay narrower part of a large body of water that cuts into land

canyon steep, narrow valley with high sides

cliff steep wall of rock or earth, sometimes called a bluff

coast land at the edge of a large body of water such as an ocean

desert very dry land with few plants

foothills hilly land at the bottom of a mountain

forest large area of land where many trees grow

gulf body of water, smaller than a sea, with land around part of it

harbor sheltered body of water where ships safely tie up to land

hill rounded land higher than the land around it

island land with water all around it

lake large body of water with land all or nearly all around it

mesa hard-to-climb flat-topped hill, with steep sides

mountain highest land on Earth

mountain range long row of mountains

ocean any of four largest bodies of water on Earth

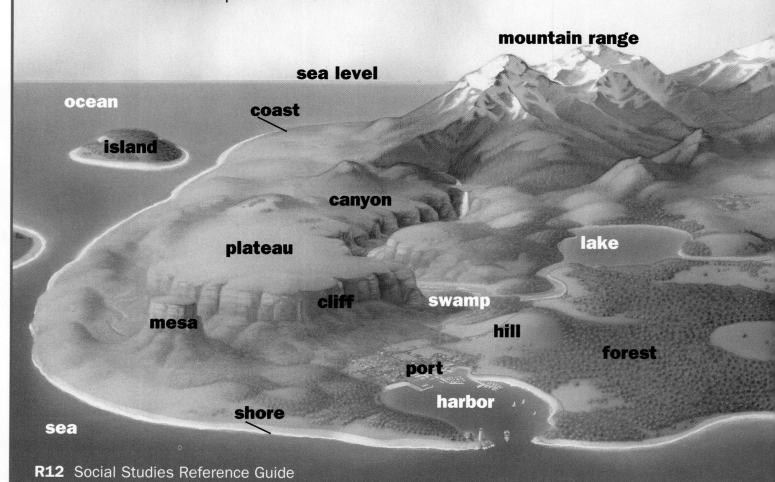

peak pointed top of a mountain

peninsula land with water on
three sides

plain very large area of flat land

plateau high, wide area of flat land,
with steep sides

port place, usually in a harbor, where
ships safely load and unload goods
and people

river large stream of water leading to a
lake, other river, or ocean

sea large body of water somewhat
smaller than an ocean

sea level an ocean's surface, compared
to which land can be measured
either above or below

shore land along a river, lake, sea,
or ocean

swamp very shallow water covering low
land filled with trees and other plants

valley low land between mountains
or hills

volcano mountain with opening at the
top formed by violent bursts of steam
and hot rock

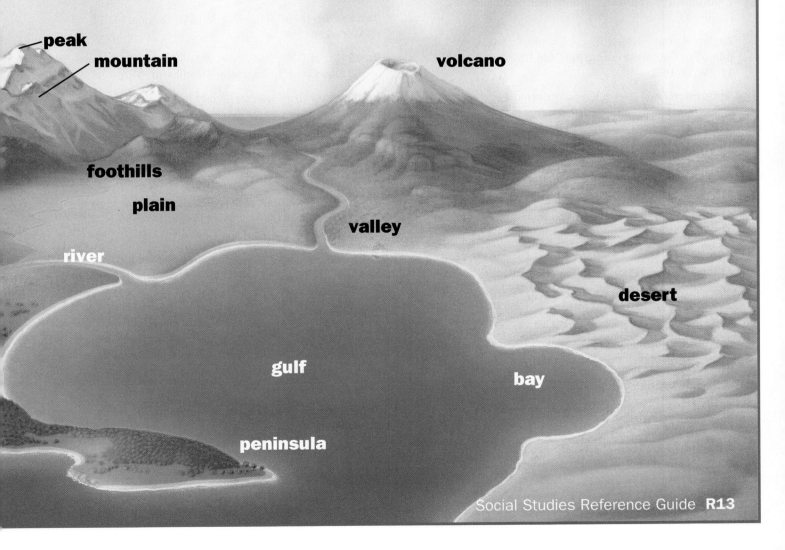

peak

mountain

volcano

foothills

plain

valley

river

desert

gulf

bay

peninsula

Gazetteer

This Gazetteer is a geographic dictionary that will help you locate and pronounce the names of places in this book. Latitude and longitude are given for cities. The page numbers tell you where each place appears on a map (m) or in the text (t).

★ A ★

Africa (af′ rə kə) A continent south of Europe and east of the Atlantic Ocean. It is the second largest continent. (m. 111, t. 87)

Alexandria, Egypt (al′ig zan′ drē ə) This city is an important seaport in Egypt. It is located in the delta area of Northern Egypt: 31°N, 30° E. (m. 33)

Angel Island (ān′ jel ī′ lənd) It is an island off the coast of California. It was a site of former immigration entry. (t. 86–87)

Angels Camp (ān′ jelz kamp) This was a site of gold mining in California during the Gold Rush in 1849: 38°N, 120°W. (t. 162)

Antarctica (ant′ ärk′ tə kə) Southernmost of the seven continents. The South Pole is here. (m. 111)

Arizona (âr′ ə zō′ nə) A state in the southwestern part of the United States. The capital is Phoenix. (t. 128, 215)

Asia (ā′ zhə) It is the largest of the seven continents. It is east of Europe and west of the Pacific Ocean. (m. 111, t. 86)

Astoria (ə stôr′ ē ə) Seaport in northwestern Oregon near the mouth of the Columbia River: 46°N, 123°W. (m. 9, t. 5,19,20)

Athens (ath′ ənz) Capital of Greece located in the southeastern area of the country: 37°N, 23°E. (t. 352, 358–359, 406)

Atlanta (at lan′ tə) It is a city in the northern part of Georgia. It is the capital of the state: 33°N, 84°W. (m. 149)

Atlantic Ocean (at lan′ tik) It is bordered by North America and South America, Europe, and Africa. (m. 73, 103)

Austin (ȯ′ stən) Capital of the state of Texas: 30°N, 97°W. (t. 57)

Australia (ȯ strā′ lyə) The smallest continent located in the South Pacific area. The nation of Australia covers the entire continent. (m. 111, m. 341)

★ B ★

Baltimore (bȯl′ tə môr) A city in the northern part of Maryland: 39°N, 76°W. (t. 250)

Barrow (bâr′ ō) A city at the northern tip of Alaska: 71°N, 7°W. (t. 137, 150–151)

Beaumont (bō′ mont) A city in southeastern Texas: 30°N, 94°W. (m. 141, t. 137, 163)

Benin (be nēn′) A former kingdom in West Africa but now a part of Nigeria. (t. 87)

Boston (bȯ′stən) A seaport and capital of the state of Massachusetts: 42°N, 71°W. (m. 73, t. 68, 72, 75–76, 78–79)

Botswana (bot swä′ nə) This is a nation in South Africa. Its capital is Gaborone. (m. 341)

Bozeman (bōz′ man) A city in southern Montana: 45°N, 111°S. (m. 141, t. 136)

Brattleboro (brat′ əl ber ō) A town in Vermont: 42°N, 72°W. (t. 158–159)

Brazil (brə zil′) Largest nation in South America, located on the East Coast. Its capital is Brasilia. (m. 340)

Bridgewater (brij′ wȯ′ tər) A city in Virginia. It is in the Shenandoah Valley on the North River: 38°N, 79°W. (m. 37, t. 4, 38–41)

★ C ★

Cádiz (kə diz′) A seaport in southwestern Spain. Most of Columbus' trips to the New World began here: 36°N, 6°W. (t. 220–221)

California (kal′ ə fôr′ nyə) A western state of the United States on the Pacific Coast. The capital is Sacramento. (m. 245, 320)

Cameroon (kam′ ə rün′) A republic in West Africa. Its capital is Yaounde. (t. 87)

Canada (kan′ ə də) The North American nation to the north of the United States. The capital of this nation is Ottawa. (m. 73, 103, t. 87, 211)

Cape Cod (cāp kod) Located in Massachusetts: 41°N, 70°W. (m. 153)

Carson City (kär′ sən sit′ ē) The capital of the state of Nevada. It is located in the western part of Nevada: 39°N, 119°W. (m. 252)

Cascade Mountains (ka skād) A mountain range in the northwestern part of the United States. (t. 178)

Central America (sen′ trəl ə mer′ ə kə) A part of North America. It includes a total of seven nations. (t. 111)

Charleston (chärlz′ tən) A seaport in the eastern part of South Carolina: 32°N, 80°W. (t. 144)

Chicago (shə kȯ′ gō) Seaport and largest city in Illinois, located on Lake Michigan: 41°N°, 87W°. (m. 37, t. 2, 5, 48–53, 83, 90, 186)

Chicago River (shə kȯ′ gō) This river flows through the city of Chicago and empties into Lake Michigan. (t. 49)

Chile (chil′ ē) A nation on the west coast of South America. Its capital is Santiago. (t. 334)

China (chī′ nə) The largest country in eastern Asia. The capital is Beijing. (t. 210)

Columbia River (kə lum′ bē ə) This river flows through the state of Washington to the Pacific Ocean. (m. 20)

Costa Rica (kos′ tə rē kə) This nation is found in Central America on the West Coast. Its capital is San Jose. (t. 334)

Council Bluffs (koun′ səl blufs) A city in Iowa across the river from Omaha, Nebraska: 41°N, 95°W. (m. 245)

Cuba (kyü′ bə) A republic in the Caribbean. Its capital is Havana. (t. 87)

Dearborn (dir′ bôrn) This city is located in the southeastern part of the state of Michigan: 42°N, 83°W. (t. 326)

Delaware River (del′ ə wer) This river flows from north to south through the state of Delaware. (t. 88)

Denmark (den′ märk) A country in northern Europe on the Baltic Sea. Its capital is Copenhagen. (t. 20)

Denver (den′ vər) Capital of the state of Colorado: 39°N, 105°W. (t. 22)

Detroit (di troit′) A city on the Detroit River in the southeastern part of Michigan: 42°N, 83°W. (t. 246)

El Paso (el pas′ ō) A city in west Texas, on the Rio Grande. It is across the river from Juarez, Mexico: 31°N, 106°W. (m. 9, t. 2,4,11–15)

Ellicottville (el ə kȯt′ vil) A town near the Pennsylvania border in Allegany county. It is noted for the wood from the white ash tree that is used to make softball bats: 42°N, 78°W. (t. 285, 318)

Ellis Island (el′ is ī′ lənd) An island in New York Bay. It is the site of former immigration entry. (t. 86–87)

England (ing′ glənd) The southern part of Great Britain. Today it is combined with Northern Ireland, Wales, and Scotland to form the United Kingdom. (m. 210, t. 209, 360, 362, 364, 367, 408)

Europe (yur′ əp) This continent lies west of Asia. It includes a total of 43 nations that are entirely in that continent. (m. 111, t. 84–85)

Finland (fin′ lənd) A country in northern Europe. Its capital is Helsinki. (t. 20)

Fort Bridger (fôrt brij′ ər) An important station on the Oregon Trail. (m. 252)

Fort Kearny (fôrt kär nē) An important post on the Oregon Trail. It was located in what is today the state of Nebraska. (m. 245)

Fort Laramie (fôrt lar′ ə mē) Located in the southeastern part of Wyoming on the Oregon Trail. (m. 252)

Fort Myers (fôrt mī′ ərz) A city on the West Coast of Florida: 26°N, 81°W. (m. 222)

Fort Wayne (fôrt wān′) This is a city in northeast Indiana: 41°N, 85°W. (m. 73, t. 72, 74, 75)

France (frans) A country in western Europe. Its capital is Paris. (m. 210, t. 209, 211)

Pronunciation Key

a in hat	ō in open	sh in she
ā in age	ȯ in all	th in thin
â in care	ô in order	ᴛʜ in then
ä in far	oi in oil	zh in measure
e in let	ou in out	ə = a in about
ē in equal	u in cup	ə = e in taken
ėr in term	ù in put	ə = i in pencil
i in it	ü in rule	ə = o in lemon
ī in ice	ch in child	ə = u in circus
o in hot	ng in long	

Gazetteer

G

Gainesville (gānz′ vil) A city in the northern part of Florida: 29°N, 82°W. (m. 222)

Galveston (gal′ vən stən) An island seaport in southeast Texas: 29°N, 94°W. (t. 86)

Germany (jer′ mə nē) A large country in central Europe. Its capital is Berlin. (t. 87–88)

Ghana (gä′ nə) A republic in West Africa. Its capital is Accra. (t. 87)

Glenwood Springs (glen′ wủd springz) It was originally named Fort Defiance. This city in Colorado has rich coal mines. It also is famous for its hot springs: 30° N, 107° W. (t. 172–173)

Great Britain (grāt brit′ n) This is an island nation in Europe and it includes England, Scotland, and Wales. The capital is London. (See *United Kingdom*)

Great Salt Lake (grāt sȯlt lāk) Located in the northwestern part of Utah. It covers from 1,000 to 1,500 square miles. It is saltier than sea water. (m. 252)

Greece (grēs) This nation in eastern Europe is at the southern tip of the Balkan Peninsula. Its capital is Athens. (t. 337)

Gulf of Mexico (gulf of mek′ sə kō) This is a body of water between Florida and Mexico. (m. 73, 103)

H

Haiti (hā′ tē) A small Caribbean nation on the west end of the Island of Hispanola. Its capital is Port-au-Prince. (t. 78–80)

Hutchinson (huch′ in sən) This city is in central Kansas, on the Arkansas River: 38°N, 98°W. (t. 116)

I

Iceland (īs′ lənd) An island country in northern Europe. Its capital is Reykjavik. (t. 20)

Illinois (il′ ə noi′) One of the states in the Midwest section of the United States. Its capital is Springfield. (m. 320, t. 49)

Independence (in′ di pen′ dəns) City in Missouri, at the east end of the Santa Fe Trail: 39°N, 94°W. (m. 245)

India (in′dē ə) A nation in South Asia. The capital is New Delhi. (t. 210)

Indianapolis (in′dē ə nap′ ə lis) Capital of the state of Indiana: 39°W, 86°W. (m. 171, t. 137, 186–189)

Ireland (īr′ lənd) A large island west of England. The capital of the republic is Dublin. (t. 87, 109)

Italy (it′l ē) This nation is in southern Europe. The capital is Rome. (t. 87)

J

Jacksonville (jak′ sən vil) A city in northeastern Florida: 30°N, 8°W. (m. 222)

James River (jāmz) This river is in the state of Virginia. Jamestown was founded on it. It empties into the Chesapeake Bay. (t. 230–231)

Jamestown (jāmz′ toun) Site of the first permanent English settlement in 1607, in North America: (m. 207, t. 206, 231–232, 237)

Japan (jə pan′) A Pacific island nation located in Asia. Its capital is Tokyo. (t. 54)

Jefferson City (jef′ ər sən sit′ ē) Capital of Missouri on the Missouri River: 38° N, 92° W. (m. 357, t. 354, 356–357, 377)

Joplin (jop′ len) City in southwest Missouri: 37°N, 94°W. (t. 96)

Juarez (hwär′ es) A city in Mexico across the Rio Grande from El Paso, Texas: 31°N, 106°W. (t. 4,13)

K

Kansas (kan′ zəs) One of the western states within the United States. The capital is Topeka. (t. 69, 96)

Kauai (kä wī′) An island of the state of Hawaii. (m. 141, 152, t. 136)

Kentucky (kən tuk′ ē) A Midwest state in the United States. The capital is Frankfort. (t. 177, 319)

Kentucky River (kən tuk′ ē) The river flows from east Kentucky to the Ohio River. (t. 177)

Key West (kē west) An island off the southwest coast of Florida. It is a part of Florida. (m. 222)

Kitty Hawk (kit′ ē hȯk) A town in North Carolina. This is where Orville and Wilbur Wright first successfully tested an airplane: (m. 241, t. 240, 247)

Korea (kō rē′ ə) Today it is a nation divided into North and South. The capital of South Korea is Seoul. The capital of North Korea is Pyongyang. These nations are in Asia. (t. 87)

Lake Michigan (mish′ ə gən) One of the largest of the five Great Lakes of North America. It forms a boundary between the United States and Canada. At its southern part, it is surrounded by Wisconsin, Illinois, Indiana and Michigan. (t. 49)

Lawrence (lôr′ əns) City in eastern Kansas, on the Kansas River: 39°N, 95°W. (t. 97)

Levittown (lev′ it toun′) It is a planned community of affordable housing. It was built on Long Island after World War II: 40°N, 73°W. (m. 37, t. 4, 43–45, 47)

London (lun′ dən) Seaport and capital of England on the Thames River: 51° N, 0° W. (t. 353)

Long Island (long ī′ lənd) This island is a part of the state of New York. (t. 43)

Louisiana (lü ē zē an′ ə) One of the southern states in the United States. The capital is Baton Rouge. (t. 215)

Marrekesh (mä rə′ kesh) A city in the west part of Morocco: 31°N, 8° W. (m. 33)

Maryland (mer′ ə lənd) One of the Northeast states in the United States. The capital is Annapolis. (t. 190)

Menlo Park (men′ lō pärk) City in New Jersey, famous as the home of Thomas A. Edison: 37°N, 122°W. (m. 241, t. 203, 240, 258)

Mexico (mek′ sə kō) The nation to the south of the United States. The capital of this nation is Mexico City. (t. 87, 215)

Miami (mī am′ ē) A city in southeastern Florida: 25°N, 80°W. (m. 222)

Mississippi River (mis′ ə sip′ ē) This river begins in northern Minnesota. It flows into the Gulf of Mexico. It is the longest river in the United States. (t. 243)

Missouri River (mə zùr′ ē) A river that flows from the southwestern part of Montana into the Mississippi River. (t. 242)

Montana (mon tan′ ə) One of the states in the western part of the United States. Its capital is Helena. (m. 320)

Montgomery (mont gum′ ər ē) Capital of Alabama on the Alabama River: 32°N, 86°W. (t. 370)

Montreal (mon′ trē ol′) A large city and important seaport. It is in the southern part of the province of Quebec: 47°N, 73°W. (t. 225)

Mount Rainier (mount rə nir′) The highest mountain in the Cascade Mountains, at 14,408 feet. It is in the state of Washington: 47°N, 121°W. (t. 178)

Nashville (nash′ vil) City in the central part of Tennessee. It is the capital of the state: 36°N, 86°W. (t.121, 186)

Netherlands (ne ′ ᴛʜər ləndz) This nation is on the west coast of Europe. Sometimes it is called Holland. Its capital is Amsterdam. (m. 341)

Nevada (nə vad′ ə) One of the states in the western part of the United States. Its capital is Carson City. (m. 320)

New Mexico (nü mek′ sə kō) One of the states in the southwestern part of the United States. Its capital is Santa Fe. (t. 215)

New Orleans (nü ôr′ lē ənz) Seaport in southeast Louisiana, on the Mississippi River: 29°N, 90°W, (m. 103, t. 68, 102, 114–115)

New York City (nü yôrk) Largest city in the United States. It is located in the southeastern part of the state of New York. 40°N, 74°W. (m. 73, t. 24, 72, 84, 284, 336)

New Zealand (nü zē′ lənd) This island nation is located in the South Pacific. Its capital is Wellington. (t. 334)

Pronunciation Key

a in hat	ō in open	sh in she
ā in age	ȯ in all	th in thin
â in care	ô in order	ᴛʜ in then
ä in far	oi in oil	zh in measure
e in let	ou in out	ə = a in about
ē in equal	u in cup	ə = e in taken
ėr in term	u̇ in put	ə = i in pencil
i in it	ü in rule	ə = o in lemon
ī in ice	ch in child	ə = u in circus
o in hot	ng in long	

Gazetteer

Newfoundland (nü′ fənd lənd) It is a province of Canada that is an island. It is off the northeastern coast of Nova Scotia. The capital is St. John's. (t. 225)

Nigeria (nī jir′ ē ə) A republic in West Africa. Its capital is Lagos. (t. 87)

North America (nôrth ə mer′ kə) A continent that includes Canada, the United States, Mexico and all of Central America. (t. 228)

North Carolina (nôrth kar′ ə lī nə) One of the southeastern states. The capital is Raleigh. (t. 177, 184)

North Platte (nôrth plat) This river flows from the central part of Nebraska into the Missouri River. (m. 245)

Norway (nôr′ wā) A country in northern Europe. Its capital is Oslo. (t. 20, 87)

 O

Oaxaca (wä hä′ kä) A state in the country of Mexico. It is also the name of the state capital. (t. 13)

Ohio (ō hī′ ō) One of the states in the Midwest section of the United States. Its capital is Columbus. (m. 320)

Oklahoma (ō′ klə hō′ mə) One of the southwestern states in the United States. The capital is Oklahoma City. (t. 194)

Omaha (ō′ mə hô) A city in eastern Nebraska: 41°N, 96°W. (m. 153, 245, t. 145, 244)

Oneida County (ō nī′ də) It is a county in New York State. It was the home of many Native Americans who were Iroquois. (t. 209)

Oregon Trail (ôr′ ə gon trāl) This route began in Independence, Missouri. It continued into Oregon. It was important for settlers going westward in the nineteenth century. (m. 245, t. 243)

Orlando (ôr lan′ dō) A city in east Florida: 28°N, 81°W. (m. 222)

 P

Pacific Ocean (pə sif′ ik) The largest ocean in the world. It is bordered by Asia, Australia, and North and South America. (m. 73, 103)

Paris (pâr′ is) Capital of France on the Seine River: 48°N, 2°E. (m. 241, t. 240)

Pecos River (pā′ kos) It flows through New Mexico to the Rio Grande. (t. 194)

Pennsylvania (pen′ səl vā′ nyə) One of the eastern states in the United States. The capital is Harrisburg. (t. 101, 318)

Pensacola (pen′ sə kō lə) A seaport in northwestern Florida: 30°N, 87°W. (m. 222)

Philadelphia (fil′ ə del′ fē ə) Largest city in southeastern Pennsylvania. Capital of the state from 1790–1800: 40°N, 75°W. (t. 88, 186)

Philippines (fil′ ə pēnz′) A nation in Asia composed of many islands. The capital is Manila. (t .87)

Phoenix (fē′ niks) This is the capital of the state of Arizona: 33°N, 112°W. (t. 285)

Pittsburgh (pits′ bėrg) City in Pennsylvania where two rivers meet. They are the Monongahela and Allegheny rivers: 40°N, 79°W. (t. 90, 94)

Plymouth (plim′ əth) City in Massachusetts. It is the site of the 1620 English settlement by Puritans: 42° N, 70° W. (m. 357, t. 68, 122, 353, 356, 365)

Poland (pō′ lənd) A country in central Europe on the eastern border of Germany. The capital is Warsaw. (t. 84)

Portland (pôrt′ lənd) A seaport in the northwestern part of Oregon: 45°N, 122°W. (t. 285)

Portugal (pôr′ chə gəl) A republic in southwestern Europe on the Iberian Peninsula. Its capital is Lisbon. (m. 210, t. 211)

Promontory Point (prom′ ən tôr′ ē point) This is in Utah. Here the two railroads came together to form the first transcontinental railroad in 1869. (t. 244)

Puerto Rico (pwer′ tō rē kō) It is an island in the West Indies. It is under the protection of the United States. The capital is San Juan. (t. 215)

Puget Sound (pyü′ jit sound) A long narrow bay of the Pacific in northwest Washington. (t. 178–180)

 Q

Quebec (kwi bek′) The French-speaking province of Canada. (t. 209)

Quebec City (kwi bek′ sit′ ē) It is a Canadian seaport. It is also the capital of Quebec Province, on the St. Lawrence River: 46°N, 71°W. (m. 207, t. 202, 206, 224–226)

Reading (red′ ing) A city in southeastern Pennsylvania: 40°N, 76°W. (t. 177)

Rio Grande (rē′ ō grand) Boundary river between the United States and Mexico. (t. 13)

Rocky Mountains (rok′ ē moun′ tənz) This is the highest mountain range in North America. It goes from Alaska to New Mexico. (t. 172–173, 242)

Rome (rōm) It is the capital of Italy. It is located in southern Europe: 41°N, 12°E. (t. 372, 407)

Russia (rush′ ə) A nation that lies in both Europe and Asia. The capital is Moscow. (t. 87)

Sacramento (sak′ rə men′ tō) The capital of California, in the north central area: 38°N, 121°W. (m. 252, t. 244)

Sahara (sə her′ ə) It is the world's largest desert. It stretches across Africa from Senegal in the west to Ethiopia in the east. (m. 32, t. 26–27)

San Antonio (san an tō′ nē ō) City in southern Texas, site of the Battle of the Alamo: 29°N, 98°W. (t. 117, 119)

San Francisco (san fran sis′ kō) Seaport on the western coast of California: 37°N, 122°W. (m. 103, t. 86, 93, 102, 104, 108, 250)

San Ildefonso (san il də fon′ sō) This pueblo in central New Mexico is on the Rio Grande. (t. 156–157)

Santa Fe (san′ tə fā′) Capital of the state of New Mexico: 35° N, 106°W. (t. 154)

Scandinavia (skan′ də nā′ vē ə) A region of northern Europe including Norway, Sweden, Denmark, and Iceland. (t. 20)

Seattle (sē at′ l) A seaport in western Washington on Puget Sound: 47°N, 122°W. (m. 171, t. 170, 178–179)

Shawnee County (shə nē′) County in eastern Kansas. (t. 397)

Snake River (snāk) This river begins in the northwestern part of Wyoming. It flows through Idaho to the Columbia River in the state of Washington. (m. 245)

South America (south ə mer′ ə kə) A continent in the Southern hemisphere, west of the Atlantic Ocean. It contains thirteen nations. (t. 111)

South Dakota (south də kō′ tə) One of the states in the Midwest section of the United States. Its capital is Pierre. (m. 320)

Spain (spān) A country in southwestern Europe on the Iberian Peninsula. The capital is Madrid. (m. 210, t. 209, 211)

St. Augustine (sānt ȯ′ gə stēn′) A city in Florida. It is the oldest settlement in the United States: 29°N, 81°W. (m. 207, 222, t. 203, 215, 217–219)

St. Joseph (sānt jō′ zəf) A city in the northwestern part of Missouri. It is on the Missouri River: 39°N, 94°W. (m. 241, 245, 252, t. 240)

St. Lawrence River (sānt lôr′ əns) A river in the southeastern part of Canada. It flows from Lake Ontario to the Gulf of St. Lawrence. (t. 226)

St. Louis (sānt lü′ is) A city in eastern Missouri. It is on the Mississippi River: 38°N, 90°W. (t. 186)

Stadacona (sta də kō′ nə) A former Native American village on the St. Lawrence River. (t. 225)

Stamford (stam′ fərd) City in the southwestern part of Connecticut: 41°N, 73°W. (t. 144)

Sweden (swēd′ n) A country in northern Europe. Its capital is Stockholm. (t. 20, 87)

Tallahassee (tal′ ə has′ ē) The capital of Florida: 30°N, 84°W. (m. 222)

Tampa (tam′ pə) A seaport in west Florida: 28°N, 82°W. (m. 222)

Taos (tous) A resort city in northern New Mexico: 36°N, 105°W. (t. 154)

Pronunciation Key

a in hat	ō in open	sh in she
ā in age	ȯ in all	th in thin
â in care	ô in order	ŦH in then
ä in far	oi in oil	zh in measure
e in let	ou in out	ə = a in about
ē in equal	u in cup	ə = e in taken
ėr in term	u̇ in put	ə = i in pencil
i in it	ü in rule	ə = o in lemon
ī in ice	ch in child	ə = u in circus
o in hot	ng in long	

Gazetteer

Tennessee (ten′ ə sē′) A state in the southeast part of the United States. Its capital is Nashville. (t. 117–119)

Texas (tek′ səs) The largest southwestern state in the United States. The capital is Austin. (m. 320, t. 119, 215)

Timbuktu (tim buk′ tü) A city and cultural center in Mali, West Africa. It is also famous for its gold: 16°N, 3°W. (m. 9, 32, t. 27–29)

Togo (tō′ gō) A republic in West Africa. Its capital is Lome. (t. 87)

Tokyo (tō′ kē ō) It is a seaport and the largest city in Japan. It is also the capital of Japan: 35°N, 139°E. (t. 54–55)

Toms River (tomz) Town in eastern New Jersey: 36° N, 74° W. (m. 383, t. 382)

Traverse City (tra′ vėrs sit ē) City in northwestern Michigan: 44°N, 85°W. (m. 383, t. 382, 390)

Tripoli (trip′ ə lē) This city is the capital of Libya. It is also an important seaport: 32°N, 13°E. (m. 33)

Tucson (tü′son) A city in southern Arizona: 32°N, 111°W. (t. 145)

United Kingdom (yü nī′ tid king′ dəm) This European nation today includes England, Wales, Scotland, and a part of Ireland. (t. 87)

United States (yü nī′ tid stāts) This usually refers to the United States of America. It is a large English-speaking nation. It is south of Canada and north of Mexico. The capital is Washington, D.C. (m. 73, 103, t. 68, 69, 76–77, 79, 81, 83, 408)

Virginia (vər jin′ yə) One of the southern states. Its capital is Richmond. (t. 118, 236)

Washington (wäsh′ ing tən) A state in the Pacific Northwest. The capital is Olympia. (t. 178)

Washington, D.C. (wäsh′ ing tən) Capital of the United States: 39°N, 77°W. (m. 357, t. 12, 353, 356, 357, 369, 372)

West Virginia (west vər jin′ yə) One of the southern states in the United States. Its capital is Charleston. (t. 319)

Wichita (wich′ ə tȯ) City in south Kansas on the Arkansas River: 37°N, 97°W. (t. 139)

Wilmington (wil′ ming tən) Seaport in southeastern North Carolina on Cape Fear River: 34°N, 77°W. (t. 21)

Wilmington (wil′ ming tən) Seaport in the state of Delaware on the Delaware River: 39°N, 75°W. (t. 402)

Wyoming (wī ō′ ming) One of the states in the western part of the United States. Its capital is Cheyenne. (m. 320)

Zambia (zam′ bē ə) A republic in South Africa. Its capital is Lusaka. (t. 124)

Biographical Dictionary

This Biographical Dictionary tells you about the people in this book and how to pronounce their names. The page numbers tell you where the person first appears in the text.

Addams, Jane (ad′ əmz), 1860–1935 She was an American social worker. She made Hull House in Chicago a good example for other centers helping new immigrants. (pp. 82–83)

Antin, Mary (an′ tin), 1881–1949 She was born in Russia. In the 1890s, she came to the United States. She wrote a book about her life and living in America. The name of the book was *The Promised Land*. (p. 87)

Bates, Katharine Lee (bāts), 1859–1929 She was a poet and teacher at Wellesley College. She wrote the words for the song, "America, the Beautiful." (p. 60)

Bell, Alexander Graham (bel), 1847–1922 He was born in Scotland. He came to America and taught the deaf to speak. He invented the telephone in 1876. (p. 253)

Benz, Karl (benz), 1844–1929 He was a German engineer. He invented a car ignition system, a water cooled engine, and a system for shifting gears in 1885. (p. 246)

Bissell, Emily (bis′ əl), 1861–1948 She was an American woman who had an idea to raise money to fight tuberculosis. She sold Christmas seals or stamps. This is still done today. Her idea raised millions of dollars to fight the disease. (pp. 402–403)

Boone, Daniel (bün), 1734–1820 He was an American frontiersman. He helped create the Wilderness Road. This encouraged the settlement of Kentucky. (pp. 176–177)

Bradford, William (brad′ fərd), 1590–1657 He was born in England. He was the second governor in the Plymouth colony. He organized the first Thanksgiving. (pp. 364–365)

Cabot, John (kab′ ət), 1450–1498? He was an Italian navigator who sailed for England. He landed on the North American mainland, and claimed it for England in 1497. (pp. 210–211)

Cathy, S. Truett (kath′ ē), 1921– He is an American businessman. He created hundreds of restaurants. With his profits, he gave scholarships to students. He also developed outdoor programs and summer camps for children. (pp. 298–299)

Clark, William (klärk), 1770–1838) He was a U.S. soldier who explored the Louisiana Territory in 1804–1806 with Meriwether Lewis. He kept the records and made maps. (p. 243)

Cartier, Jacques (kär tyā′), 1491–1557 He was a French navigator and explorer of Canada. He discovered the St. Lawrence River in 1535. He gave the French a claim to North America. (pp. 210–211, 225)

Champlain, Samuel de (sham plän′), 1567–1636 He was a French explorer in Canada. He founded Quebec. It was the first permanent French settlement in North America. (pp. 210–211, 225)

Pronunciation Key

a in hat	ō in open	sh in she
ā in age	ȯ in all	th in thin
â in care	ô in order	ᴛʜ in then
ä in far	oi in oil	zh in measure
e in let	ou in out	ə = a in about
ē in equal	u in cup	ə = e in taken
ėr in term	u̇ in put	ə = i in pencil
i in it	ü in rule	ə = o in lemon
ī in ice	ch in child	ə = u in circus
o in hot	ng in long	

Biographical Dictionary

Columbus, Christopher (kə lum′ bəs), 1451–1506 He was an Italian navigator who sailed for Spain. He discovered America in 1492. He claimed the land for Spain. (pp. 210, 220, 229)

Cooper, Isaac (kü′ pər), 1814–1887 In 1881 he helped set up the town of Ft. Defiance in Colorado which was later named Glenwood Springs. (p. 173)

Crockett, David (krok′ it), 1786–1836 He was an American scout and Congressman. He moved to Texas and was probably killed at the Battle of the Alamo. (p. 118)

Curtis, Charles (kėr′ tis), 1860–1936 He was part Native American and was raised on the Kaw Reservation. He became a member of the House of Representatives and then a Senator. He was Vice President from 1929 to 1933. (pp. 396–397)

Daguerre, Louis (də ger′), 1789–1851 He was a French painter and inventor. He developed a form of early photography in 1839. (p. 261)

Daimler, Gottlieb (dim′ lər) , 1834–1900 He was a German engineer. He invented a light internal combustion engine. He and Karl Benz produced the first Mercedes-Benz car in 1926. (p. 246)

Defoe, Daniel (di fō′), 1660–1731 He was an English journalist and novelist. His most famous novel was *Robinson Crusoe*. (p. 319)

Du Sable, Jean (dü sä′ bəl), 1745–1818 He was a Black American pioneer. He opened a trading post that would develop into the city of Chicago. He was probably born in Haiti. (p. 49)

Eastman, George (ēst′ mən), 1854–1932 He invented the Kodak camera and film rolls. This made it easy for everyone to take photographs. (p. 261)

Edison, Thomas (ed′ ə sən), 1847–1931 He was an American who invented the electric light and the phonograph. He also developed one of the first modern research laboratories at Menlo Park, New Jersey. (pp. 203, 258)

Elion, Gertrude (el′ ē on), 1918–1999 She was an American scientist. She won the Nobel Prize in medicine. She worked to find cures for many diseases. She improved medical treatment for malaria, gout, and some viral diseases. (p. 268)

Esteban (e stā bän′), 1500?–1539 He was an African servant or slave from Morocco. He accompanied Cabeza de Vaca in his exploration through Texas, Arizona, and New Mexico. (p. 215)

Ford, Henry (fôrd), 1863–1947 He developed the assembly line. This lowered costs for Ford cars. He paid high wages and produced a car that could be bought by millions of people. (pp. 326–327)

Frank, Anne (frangk), 1929–1945 She was a German-Jewish girl. She kept a diary during the time she and her family were in hiding in Holland. Eventually, she was killed by the Nazis. (p. 345)

Franklin, Benjamin (frang′ klən) 1706–1790 He was an American statesman, diplomat, author, scientist, inventor and printer. He invented an efficient heating stove and bifocals. He wrote *Poor Richard's Almanac* and organized the first hospital in the United States. He helped set up much of the postal system. (pp. 251, 368)

H

Hudson, Henry (hud′ sən), (15?–1611) He was an English navigator and explorer. He sailed for England and Holland. He gave England a claim to the entire Hudson Bay area. (pp. 210–211)

Hughes, Langston (hyüz), 1902–1967 He was an African American poet and writer. He experimented with new rhythms in his poetry. He founded a theater in New York City. (pp. 96–97)

J

James I of England (jämz), 1566–1625 He was the first Stuart King of England. He encouraged settlement in the New World. Jamestown was named after him. (p. 231)

Jefferson, Thomas (jef′ ər sən), 1743–1826 He was born and raised in Virginia. He was an architect and a diplomat. He became the third President of the United States. He also wrote much of the Declaration of Independence. (pp. 366–367)

Jenner, Edward (jen′ ər), 1749–1823 He was an English physician who developed a way to prevent smallpox. This process is called vaccination. (p. 267)

John I (jon), 1167?–1216 He was King of England from 1199-1216. The nobles of England forced him to sign the Magna Carta. (pp. 360, 362–363)

K

Keller, Helen (kel′ ər), 1880–1968 She was an American. She was blind and deaf from early youth. However, she became a lecturer, author, and educator. She was taught to speak by Anne Sullivan. (pp. 272–273)

King, Dr. Martin Luther, Jr. (king), 1929–1968 He was an African American civil rights leader. He led nonviolent protest marches. He was noted for his "I Have a Dream" speech. He also helped to get the Civil Rights Act of 1964 passed. He received the Nobel Peace Prize in 1964. (p. 121)

L

Latimer, Lewis (lat′ ə mər), 1848–1928 He was an African American. He was an inventor and engineer. He helped improve the light bulb and drafted plans for the telephone for Alexander Graham Bell. (p. 259)

L'Enfant, Pierre Charles (län fän′), 1754–1825 He was an architect. He helped design much of the public areas and buildings of Washington, D.C. (pp. 369, 373)

Leutze, Emanuel Gottlieb (lütz), 1816–1868 He was an artist. He was born in Germany but came to America when he was young. His most famous painting was *Washington Crossing the Delaware*. (pp. 88–89)

Levitt, William (lev′ it), 1907–1994 He was a pioneer in building affordable housing following World War II. Levittown was built on Long Island. (pp. 44–47)

Lewis, Meriwether (lü′ is), 1774–1809 He was private secretary to Thomas Jefferson. He later explored the Louisiana Territory from 1804 to 1806 with William Clark. (p. 243)

Pronunciation Key

a in hat	ō in open	sh in she
ā in age	ȯ in all	th in thin
â in care	ô in order	ŦH in then
ä in far	oi in oil	zh in measure
e in let	ou in out	ə = a in about
ē in equal	u in cup	ə = e in taken
ėr in term	ù in put	ə = i in pencil
i in it	ü in rule	ə = o in lemon
ī in ice	ch in child	ə = u in circus
o in hot	ng in long	

Biographical Dictionary

Longfellow, Henry Wadsworth (lȯng′ fel′ ō), 1807–1882 He was professor of languages at Harvard University. He wrote many poems, including *Hiawatha* and *The Courtship of Miles Standish*. (p. 209)

Madison, James (mad′ ə sən), 1751–1836 He helped write the Constitution. He was Secretary of State for Thomas Jefferson. Later he became the fourth President of the United States. (p. 368)

Manzano, Sonia (män sä′ nō), She is an American writer and actress. Her most famous role is as Maria on *Sesame Street*, a television show. (p. 24)

Marconi, Guglielmo (mär kō′ nē, gü lyel′ mō)1874–1937 He invented the wireless telegraph and the radio in 1896. He also experimented with short waves and microwaves. He won a Nobel Prize in physics in 1909. (p. 254)

Marshall, Thurgood (mär′ shəl), 1908–1993 He was the first African American judge appointed to the United States Supreme Court. He served for 24 years. (p. 371)

Martinez, Maria (mär tē′ nez), 1887–1980 She was known as the Potter of San Ildefonso Pueblo, New Mexico. Her designs and colors made the pottery beautiful. (pp. 156–157)

McCormick, Cyrus Hall (mə kôr′ mik), 1809–1884 He was a U.S. inventor of farm machinery. His most famous invention was the reaper. It harvested wheat. (p. 260)

Menéndez de Avilés, Pedro (mə nen′ dez dā a vē lāz′), 1519–1574 He was a Spanish admiral and colonizer. He founded St. Augustine, Florida, in 1565. (p. 216)

Morse, Samuel (môrs), 1791–1872 He was a U.S. artist and inventor. He developed the first telegraph system in the U.S. He also created the Morse code system. (p. 253)

Newport, Christopher (nü′ pôrt), c. 1525–1617 He was an English navigator. He brought colonists to Virginia in 1607. They founded Jamestown. In 1608 and 1610, he brought them more supplies. (p. 231)

Parks, Rosa (pärks), 1913– An African American woman, she refused to give her seat on a bus to a white person in Montgomery, Alabama. Others refused to ride the bus until all people were treated equally. (p. 370)

Pasteur, Louis (pas tėr′), 1822–1895 He was a professor of chemistry and physics in France. He developed a process that heated liquids to kill germs harmful to the people who drank the liquids. This process is called pasteurization. (p. 267)

Pocahontas (pō′ kə hȯn′ təs), 1595?–1617 She was the daughter of Powhatan, an Algonquin chief. John Smith of Jamestown said she saved his life. She married John Rolfe, moved to England, and died there. (pp. 231, 236)

Ponce de Leon, Juan (pons′ də lē′ ən), 1460?–1521 He was a Spanish nobleman and explorer. He claimed Florida for Spain. He named it Florida because of all the flowers there. (pp. 210, 211, 215)

Powhatan (pou′ ə tan′), 1550?–1618 He was an Algonquin chief in Virginia. He was the father of Pocahontas. He helped unify many Algonquin settlements. (p. 231)

Rolfe, John (rolf), 1585–1622 He was an English colonist in Virginia and married Pocahontas. (p. 237)

Sacagawea (sak′ ə jə wē′ ə), 1787?–1812? She was a Shoshone woman. She acted as guide to the explorers Lewis and Clark. She helped them through the Louisiana Territory. (p. 243)

Salk, Jonas (sȯlk), 1914–1995 He was an American scientist. He helped develop the polio vaccine to prevent the disease. (p. 268)

Smith, John (smith), 1580–1631 He was an English colonist in Virginia. He led the colony at Jamestown. It was the first permanent English settlement in North America. Jamestown was established in 1607. (pp. 231–232)

Sullivan, Anne (sùl′ ə vən), 1866–1936 She was the teacher of Helen Keller. She gave hope to others who were blind or deaf. (p. 273)

Swinton, A.A. Campbell (swin′ tən), 1863–1930 In 1908, he developed a simple type of television by using a special tube. (p. 254)

Tubman, Harriet (tub′ mən), 1820–1913 She was a slave who escaped and helped others to escape also. The road they took to freedom was called "The Underground Railroad." (pp. 190–191)

Walker, Madame C. J. (wȯ′ kər), 1867–1919 This African-American woman became a millionaire early in the twentieth century. She produced hair care goods, marketed them, and established hair salons. (pp. 312–313)

Washington, George (wäsh′ ing tən), 1732–1799 He was called the Father of his Country by many Americans. He became a general in the Revolutionary War and first President of the United States. (pp. 368, 369)

Watt, James (wät), 1736–1819 He was a Scottish engineer who invented the modern steam engine and manufactured the engines in England. (p. 244)

Wright, Orville and Wilbur (rīt) 1871–1948 and 1867–1912 These brothers were American inventors. They built gliders, invented the first airplane, and flew it at Kitty Hawk, North Carolina. (p. 247)

Pronunciation Key

a in hat	ō in open	sh in she
ā in age	ȯ in all	th in thin
â in care	ô in order	ŦH in then
ä in far	oi in oil	zh in measure
e in let	ou in out	ə = a in about
ē in equal	u in cup	ə = e in taken
ėr in term	ù in put	ə = i in pencil
i in it	ü in rule	ə = o in lemon
ī in ice	ch in child	ə = u in circus
o in hot	ng in long	

Glossary

This Glossary will help you understand the meanings and pronounce the vocabulary words in this book. The page number tells you where the word first appears.

adapt (ə dapt´) to change the way you do something (p. 146)

adobe (ə dō´ bē) a mixture of earth, straw, and water that is formed into bricks and dried (p. 155)

amendment (ə mend´ mənt) change to the U.S. Constitution (p. 370)

ancestor (an´ ses tər) relative who lived long ago (p. 85)

assembly line (ə sem´ blē līn) a row of workers and machines that complete the steps to produce something (p. 324)

bastion (bas´ chən) a part built out from the corner of a fort (p. 217)

Bill of Rights (bil uv rīts) an addition to the United States Constitution that lists ten basic freedoms that every American has (p. 370)

broadcast (brȯd´ kast) to send out information over a wide area (p. 254)

budget (buj´ it) a plan that shows income, spending, and saving (p. 292)

candidate (kan´ də dāt) a person who runs for office (p. 394)

capital resource (kap´ ə təl ri sôrs´) a machine, tool, or building used to produce goods and services (p. 322)

cardinal directions (kärd´ n əl də rek´ shənz) on a map — north, south, east, and west (p. 98)

cause (kȯz) something that makes something else happen (p. 204)

century (sen´ chər ē) a period of 100 years (p. 248)

citizen (sit´ ə zen) an official member of a community (p. 91)

city (sit´ ē) a town with a large population (p. 49)

Civil Rights Movement (siv´ əl rīts müv´ mənt) a drive for equal treatment of all people (p. 121)

classify (klas´ ə fī) to place things that have similar features together in a group (p. 56)

climate (klī´ mit) the kind of weather a place has from year to year (p. 143)

communication (kə myü´ nə kā´ shən) the sharing of information or news (p. 335)

community (kə myü´ nə tē) a place where people live, work, and have fun together (p. 11)

compass rose (kum´ pəs rōz) a symbol on a map that shows directions (p. 98)

consent (kən sent´) permission (p. 395)

conserve (kən sėrv´) to use resources carefully (p. 164)

council (koun səl´) a group of people who make laws and rules for a community (p. 391)

crossroads (krȯs´ rōdz) a place where many different roads meet one another (p. 187)

culture (kul´ chər) the way a group of people live (p. 28)

curtain (kėrt´ n) a wall in a fort that connects two bastions (p. 217)

custom (kus´ təm) a way of doing things (p. 79)

cutaway diagram (kut´ ə wā dī´ ə gram) a drawing or picture that shows what is inside of a building or object (p. 324)

★ D ★

daguerreotype (də ger´ ə tīp) the first photographs, developed on a piece of metal with a silver surface (p. 261)

decade (dek´ ād) a period of 10 years (p. 248)

Declaration of Independence (dek lə rā´ shən uv in di pen´ dəns) the document written in 1776 that said that the American colonies were free and independent states and no longer part of England (p. 367)

Pronunciation Key

a in hat	ō in open	sh in she
ā in age	ȯ in all	th in thin
â in care	ô in order	ᴛʜ in then
ä in far	oi in oil	zh in measure
e in let	ou in out	ə = a in about
ē in equal	u in cup	ə = e in taken
ėr in term	ù in put	ə = i in pencil
i in it	ü in rule	ə = o in lemon
ī in ice	ch in child	ə = u in circus
o in hot	ng in long	

Glossary

demand (di mand´) the amount of goods or a service that people want and can pay for at different prices (p. 308)

direct democracy (də rekt´ di mok´ rə sē) government run by the people who live under it (p. 359)

drawbridge (drȯ´ brij) a bridge in a fort that can be raised to keep people out and lowered to allow people to cross a moat (p. 217)

earn (ern) to get something, such as money, after working (p. 291)

economic choice (ē kə nom´ ik chois) a decision to buy one thing instead of another (p. 301)

ecosystem (ē´ kō sis təm) the physical environment and living things in it (p. 145)

effect (ə fekt´) the outcome or result of a cause (p. 204)

equator (i kwā´ tər) a line drawn around the middle of a globe (p. 110)

ethnic group (eth´ nik grüp) a group of people who have the same culture (p. 81)

explorer (ek splôr´ ər) a person who travels looking for new lands and discoveries (p. 209)

export (ek spôrt´) to send products and resources from one country to another (p. 338)

fleet (flēt) a large group of ships (p. 217)

fortification (fôr tə fə kā´ shən) things, such as walls, around an object or building that protect it from invasion (p. 226)

free market (frē mär´ kit) trade in which people choose what to produce and what to buy (p. 339)

fuel (fyü´ əl) a resource that can be used to produce light, heat, or other forms of energy (p. 161)

geography (jē og´ rə fē) the study of Earth, how people live on it, and the land around a place (p. 11)

goods (gu̇dz) things that are made or grown and then sold (p. 307)

Great Migration (grāt mī grā´ shən) the movement of African Americans from the South to the North in the early 1900s (p. 94)

★ H ★

hemisphere (hem´ ə sfir) one half of the earth (p. 110)

holiday (hol´ ə dā) a special day to remember an important person or event (p. 105)

human resource (hyü mən´ ri sôrs´) a person who makes products or provides a service (p. 321)

★ I ★

immigrant (im´ ə grənt) a person who moves into a country to live there (p. 79)

import (im pôrt´) to bring products and resources into one country from another (p. 338)

income (in´ kum) all the money a person gets from a job or other source (p. 292)

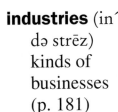

industries (in´ də strēz) kinds of businesses (p. 181)

interdependence (in´ tər di pen´ dens) depending on each other (p. 330)

intermediate direction (in tər mē´ dē it də rek´ shən) a direction in the middle of two cardinal directions such as northeast or southwest (p. 98)

international trade (in tər nash´ ə nəl trād) trade between different countries (p. 338)

internet search (in´ tər net sėrch) a way to look for information on the Internet (p. 212)

invention (in ven´ shən) something made up for the first time (p. 253)

★ K ★

keyword search (kē´ wėrd sėrch) a way of looking for information on the Internet using the most important word or words in a request (p. 213)

★ L ★

landform (land´ fôrm) a shape or part of the Earth's surface, such as a mountain or a desert (p. 143)

livestock (līv´ stok) farm animals (p. 116)

location (lō kā´ shən) where something can be found (p. 19)

Pronunciation Key

a	in hat	ō	in open	sh	in she
ā	in age	ȯ	in all	th	in thin
â	in care	ô	in order	ŦH	in then
ä	in far	oi	in oil	zh	in measure
e	in let	ou	in out	ə	= a in about
ē	in equal	u	in cup	ə	= e in taken
ėr	in term	u̇	in put	ə	= i in pencil
i	in it	ü	in rule	ə	= o in lemon
ī	in ice	ch	in child	ə	= u in circus
o	in hot	ng	in long		

Glossary

locator map (lō kā′ tər map) a small map, usually on a large one, that shows the general location of a place (p. 222)

logging (lò′ ging) the cutting down of trees (p. 180)

lumber (lum′ bər) wood that is cut into boards for building (p. 180)

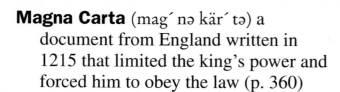

Magna Carta (mag′ nə kär′ tə) a document from England written in 1215 that limited the king's power and forced him to obey the law (p. 360)

marsh (märsh) an area of land sometimes covered by water (p. 400)

Mayflower Compact (mā′ flou ər kom′ pakt) a plan of government written by the colonists aboard the ship the *Mayflower* in 1620 before they landed in North America (p. 361)

mayor (mā′ ər) a leader of a community (p. 391)

migration (mī grā′ shən) moving from one part of the country to live in another part (p. 94)

miner (mī′ nər) someone who digs materials from the Earth (p. 173)

mineral (min′ ər əl) a natural resource that has never been alive (p. 161)

moat (mōt) a wide, deep ditch dug around a fort or castle (p. 217)

Morse code (môrs cōd) a series of dots and dashes that represent letters and numbers (p. 253)

natural resources (nach′ ər əl ri sôrs′ əz) useful materials that come from the earth (p. 161)

nonrenewable resource (non ri nü′ əbl ri sôrs′) a resource that cannot be replaced after it is used (p. 319)

Northern Hemisphere (nôr′ ᴛʜərn hem′ ə sfir) the half of the earth north of the equator (p. 110)

★ O ★

opportunity (op ər tü´ nə tē) a chance for something better to happen (p. 76)

opportunity cost (op ər tü´ nə tē kȯst) what you give up when you choose to buy one thing over another (p. 302)

I had to choose a bat instead of CDs.

★ P ★

pasteurization (pas tər ə zā´ shən) a process to kill germs by heating a liquid to just below the boiling point (p. 267)

periodicals (pir ē od´ ə kəlz) magazines that are printed regularly (p. 212)

physical environment (fiz´ ə kəl en vī´ rən mənt) a region's landforms and climate (p. 143)

Pony Express (pō´ nē ek spres´) a mail route where people would ride horses up to 75 miles a day to deliver mail quickly across the country (p. 252)

population (pop yə lā´ shən) the number of people in an area (p. 49)

port (pôrt) a place where ships can load and unload things (p. 181)

prime meridian (prīm mə rid´ ē ən) a line on a globe that goes from the North Pole to the South Pole (p. 110)

producer (prə dü´ sər) person who makes products (p. 321)

products (prod´ əkts) goods and services (p. 307)

profit (prof´ it) the income a business has left after all its costs are paid (p. 310)

Pronunciation Key

a in hat	ō in open	sh in she
ā in age	ȯ in all	th in thin
â in care	ô in order	ᴛʜ in then
ä in far	oi in oil	zh in measure
e in let	ou in out	ə = a in about
ē in equal	u in cup	ə = e in taken
èr in term	u̇ in put	ə = i in pencil
i in it	ü in rule	ə = o in lemon
ī in ice	ch in child	ə = u in circus
o in hot	ng in long	

Glossary

ravelin (rav´ əl in) a building in front of the main gate of a fort or castle (p. 217)

reaper (rē´ pər) a machine that cuts grain (p. 260)

recreation (rek rē ā´ shən) a way of enjoying yourself (p. 386)

recycle (rē sī´ kəl) to use something again (p. 164)

reference books (ref´ ər əns) books such as almanacs, dictionaries, atlases, and encyclopedias (p. 212)

region (rē´ jən) a large land area that has special features (p. 143)

renewable resource (ri nü´ əbl ri sôrs´) a resource that can be replaced within a short time (p. 319)

representative government (rep ri zen´ tə tiv guv´ ərn mənt) a kind of government in which voters elect people to speak for them (p. 233)

republic (ri pub´ lik) a government in which citizens elect representatives to speak for them (p. 359)

responsibility (ri spon sə bil´ ə tē) a duty, something that must be done (p. 377)

rural community (rur´ əl kə myü´ nə tē) a place in the countryside where people live, work, and have fun together (p. 39)

sally port (sal´ lē pôrt) an opening in the wall of a fort (p. 217)

savings (sā´ vingz) the amount of an income not spent (p. 292)

scarcity (skâr´ sə tē) not enough of something to meet people's wants and needs (p. 329)

sequence (sē´ kwəns) the order of things, such as dates in history (p. 286)

services (sėr´ vis ez) jobs that one person does for another (p. 307)

Southern Hemisphere (suŦH´ ərn hem´ ə sfir) the half of the Earth south of the equator (p. 110)

specialize (spesh´ ə līz) to do one job or make one part of a product (p. 321)

spending (spend´ ing) the amount of income a person uses (p. 292)

sphere (sfir) an object shaped like a ball (p. 110)

state capital (stāt kap´ ə təl) the city in which the state government is located (p.187)

state government (stāt guv´ ərn mənt) the people that carry out and make the laws of a state (p. 187)

suburban community (sə bėr´ bən kə myü´ nə tē) a community located near a large city (p. 43)

supply (sə plī´) the amount of a product for sale at a certain price (p. 308)

symbol (sim´ bəl) something that stands for something else (p. 85)

terreplein (ter´ ə plān) a broad, flat, raised area in a fort (p. 217)

trade (trād) the buying or selling of goods and services (p. 335)

tradition (trə dish´ ən) a special way that a group does something which is part of their culture (p. 105)

Transcontinental Railroad (tran skon tə nen´ tl rāl´ rōd) train tracks that linked the East to the western United States (p. 244)

transportation (tran spər tā´ shən) carrying people or things from place to place (p. 50)

United States Constitution (yü nī´ tid stāts kon stə tü´ shən) the written plan of government for the United States (p. 368)

urban community (ėr´ bən kə myü´ nə tē) a community in a city (p. 49)

vaccine (vak sēn´) a weak or killed form of a disease that is given to people to prevent them from getting a stronger form (p. 268)

Pronunciation Key		
a in hat	ō in open	sh in she
ā in age	ȯ in all	th in thin
â in care	ô in order	ŦH in then
ä in far	oi in oil	zh in measure
e in let	ou in out	ə = a in about
ē in equal	u in cup	ə = e in taken
ėr in term	u̇ in put	ə = i in pencil
i in it	ü in rule	ə = o in lemon
ī in ice	ch in child	ə = u in circus
o in hot	ng in long	

Index

Titles appear in italics. Emboldened page numbers indicate vocabulary definitions. An *m* following a page number indicates a map. The terms *See* and *See also* direct the reader to alternative entries.

Index

of North American communities. *See specific community* of United States Government, 366–368, 370–371, 373, 374–375

History!, 200

Holidays, 105
celebrating culture, 104–109
celebrating the past, 114–117
in St. Augustine, Florida, 203
in United States, 120–123

Homer Price, 309

Homes
of Anasazi Indians, 154
of Iroquois Indians, 206
of Pueblo Indians, 154–155

Honesty, 396–397

Hoover, Herbert, 397

Horner, Dr. Jack, 136

Hudson, Henry, 211

Hughes, Langston, 96–97

Hull House, 83

Human resources, 321

I Love a Parade, 66

If I Built a City, 134

Illinois. *See* Chicago, Illinois

Immigrant, 79, 81, 82–83, 84–89, 90–93
ancestors as, 85
Antin, Mary, 87
education of, 92
from Haiti, 79–81
learning new customs, 79, 81
Leutze, Emanuel Gottlieb, 88
life in a new country, 90–93
places of origin, 84–88
time periods of arrival, 87

Import, 338

Improving communities
group efforts at, 398, 400–401
individual efforts at, 398–399, 402–403

Income, 292–293

Independence, Declaration of, 366–367

India
trade with, 210, 337

Indiana
Fort Wayne, 72, 74*m,* 75
Indianapolis. *See* Indianapolis, Indiana

Indianapolis, Indiana, 170, 186–189, 288
location of, 171*m,* 289*m*
National Institute for Fitness and Sport in, 137
transportation routes to, 187–189

Indians. *See* Native Americans

Industries, 181

Information Age, 262, 263

Informational letter, 184–185

Interdependence, 317, **330,** 323–333, 335–338

Intermediate directions, 98–99

International trade, 338

Internet, 348
email on, 255

Internet searches, 212–213

Inventions, 253, 258–263
in communication, 253–255, 262–263
in farming, 260
light bulb, 259
in medicine, 266–269
in photography, 261
problem solving and, 270–271
in transportation, 244, 246–247

Ireland, St. Patrick's Day in, 109

Iroquois, 209
longhouses of, 208
in Oneida County, New York, 209

Islands
Angel Island, 87
Ellis Island, 86
island communities, 6–7
Kauai Island, Hawaii, 136, 140, 141*m,* 152
Long Island, New York, 4, 42*m,* 43
Monhegan Island, Maine, 7

James I, King of England, 231

James River, 231

Jamestown, Virginia
location of, 207*m,* 230*m*
modern site of, 234–235
Pocahontas and, 231, 236–237
settlement of, 202, 206, 231–233

Japan
Tokyo, 54–55

Jazz festival, 114–115

Jefferson, Thomas, 367

Jefferson City, Missouri, 356
citizen responsibility in, 377
location of, 357*m,* 376*m*

Jenner, Edward, 267

Johannesburg, South Africa, 31

John, King of England, 360, 362–363

Jordan, Michael, 344

Juarez, Mexico, 4, 13

Kansas
Curtis, Charles in, 396–397
state fair, 69, 116
statehood of, 249

Kauai Island, Hawaii, 136, 140, 152
climate of, 152
location of, 141*m*

Kaw Reservation, 396

Keller, Helen, 272–273

Kentucky, 177

Keyword search, 213

King, Martin Luther, Jr., 121, 344

King James I of England, 231

King John of England, 360, 362–363

Kitty Hawk, North Carolina, 247

Kora, 28, 125

Kwanzaa, 107

Lakes, 153

Land
farmland, 39, 44
landforms, **143**–145
ownership of, 228–229
scarcity of, 332–333

Landforms, 143–145

Latimer, Lewis, 259

Latitude, 389

Lawrence, Jacob, 94

Laws
citizenship and, 90, 377
community leaders and, 391, 392–393, 395
community life and, 76–77
Magna Carta and, 360
purpose of, 76–77

Leaders of the community, 390–395, 396–397

L'Enfant, Pierre Charles, 369, 373

Lesotho, 30*m,* 31

Letters
delivery of, 250–252
email, 255
of information, 184–185

Leutze, Emanuel Gottlieb, 88

Levitt, Abraham, 44–46

Levitt, William, 46–47

Levittown, New York, 4, 36
growth of, 44–45
location of, 37*m,* 42*m,* 43

Lewis, Meriwether, 205, 243

Lewis, Michael, 40

Library resources, 212–213

Libya, 30*m,* 31

Lifestyle. *See* Culture

Light bulb, 203, 259

Lincoln, Abraham, 374–375

Lincoln Highway, 246

Line graphs, 158–159

Livestock
African herders, 31
at fairs, **116**

Local government, 382
officials of, 390–393
services of, 355, 384–387, 391

Location, 19

Locator map, 222–223

Locomotives, 244, 246

Index

Index

Television
   Sesame Street program, 24–25
   technology of, 254
Temperature
   climate and, 151
   graphing of, 158–159
Tennis, 93
Terreplein, 216, 217
Texas
   Battle of the Alamo in, 117, 119
   Beaumont, 137, 140, 141*m*, 160*m*, 163
   El Paso, 4, 8–15, 9*m*
   San Antonio, 117, 119
Thanksgiving celebrations, 68
   in Africa, 124–125
   in Plymouth Colony, 122–123, 365
Timbuktu, Mali, 8, 9*m*, 26–29, 32*m*
Time line, using, 248–249
Tokyo, Japan, 54–55
Tomb of the Unknown Soldier, 102, 120
Toms River, New Jersey, 382
   location of, 383*m*
   student community project in, 400–401
Topic, 6
Tornadoes
   drawing conclusions about, 139
   folk tale about, 194–195
Tower of London, 353
Town council, 391, 392
Trade, 334–339, **335**
   between countries, 338, 340*m*–341*m*
   free markets, 339
   then and now, 336–337
Tradition, 105
Trails
   of Pony Express, 252
   of Westward Movement, 243, 245*m*
Trains, 246, 276–277. *See also* Railroads
   elevated trains, 50
   Transcontinental Railroad and, 244
Transcontinental

Railroad, 244, 245*m*
Transportation, 50
   as community service, 385–386
   methods of, 246–247
   trade and, 335
   westward expansion and, 243, 244–245
Travel
   methods of. *See* Transportation
Traverse City, Michigan, 382, 383*m*, 390, 390*m*
Trees
   bats made from, 319, 322–325
   houses built from, 208, 328
   as natural resource, 161, 285, 329–330
Trevithick, Richard, 244
Trios program, 16–17
Tropical rain forest climates, 183
Tropical storms, 183
Tuberculosis, 403
Tubman, Harriet, 190–191
Tundra climate, 183
Tunisia, 30*m*, 31

Underground Railroad, 189–191
Union Rail Station, 188
United Kingdom, 87. *See also* England
United States, 18–25
   communities in, 15–23
   moving to, 78–95
   national celebrations of, 120–123
   regions of, 143–145, 148–149
   voting in, 359
United States Capitol Building, 353, 373
United States Constitution, 368
   Bill of Rights in, 370
   citizenship and, 90
   Magna Carta and, 360
   Roman influence on, 373
United States Government

Bill of Rights, 370
Constitution of, 90, 360, 368
Crockett, David in, 119
Curtis, Charles in, 396–397
Declaration of Independence, 366–367
United States Supreme Court, 371
Urban community, 49
   African population figures, 31
   Chicago, Illinois, 36, 48–53, 48*m*
   Tokyo, Japan, 54–55
Utah, 244
Ute, 173

Vaccine, 268
Vermont, 158–159
Veterans Day, 121
Virginia
   bike ride across, 256–257
   Bridgewater, 4, 36–41
   explorers in, 231, 236–237
   Jamestown, 202, 206, 207*m*, 230–237
   Tomb of the Unknown Soldier in, 102, 120
Voice of America, 257
Volunteers
   Bissell, Emily, 402–403
   citizenship and, 379
   community volunteers, 332–333, 400–401
Voting
   in ancient Greece, 358, 359
   citizenship and, 378
   for community leaders, 394–395
   in a republic, 359

Wagon train mail delivery, 251
Wales, Dr. Joseph, 403
Walker, Madam C. J., 312–313
Wampanoag, 123, 365

Ward, Samuel A., 60
Washington, D.C., 102, 356
   architecture of, 353, 372–373
   location of, 103*m*, 357*m*
   street map of, 369*m*
Washington, George, 368, 369
Washington Crossing the Delaware, 88–89
Washington State. *See* Seattle, Washington
Water
   communities on, 178–181
   explorer routes across, 210, 210*m*
   as natural resource, 161
Water Tower, 5
Watt, James, 244
Weather. *See also* Climate
   drawing conclusions about, 138–139
   extremes in, 183
   tornadoes, 139
   world climate regions, 182–183
Western Hemisphere, 110–111, 111*m*
West region, 143
Westward Movement
   reasons for, 204–205
   routes of, 243, 245
   transportation methods and, 244–247
Wilderness Road, 177
Wilmington, Delaware, 402
Wilmington, North Carolina, 21, 21*m*
Women's baseball league, 331
Wood products, 285, 319, 322–325, 328–330
Woodlands climate, 183
Work, 344. *See also* Business
World climate regions, 182–183
World communities, 26–33
Wright, Orville, 247
Wright, Wilbur, 247
Wyoming, 249

Zambia, 30*m*, 124–125

Credits

TEXT:

Dorling Kindersley (DK) is an international publishing company specialising in the creation of high quality reference content for books, CD-ROM's, online and video. The hallmark of DK content is its unique combination of educational value and strong visual style-this combination allows DK to deliver appealing, accessible and engaging educational content that delights children, parents and teachers around the world. Scott Foresman is delighted to have been able to use selected extracts of DK content within this Social Studies program.
30-31 from *Geography of the World* by Susan Peach. Copyright © by Dorling Kindersley Limited. 112-113 from *Dance* by Andrée Grau. Copyright © 1998 by Dorling Kindersley Limited. 148-149 from *My First Atlas* by Bill Boyle. Copyright © 1999 by Dorling Kindersley Limited.

128 "Celebration" by Alonzi Lopez, from *Whispering Wind* by Terry Allen, copyright © 1972 by The Institute of American Indian Arts. Used by permission of Doubleday, a division of Random House, Inc. 40 from "August" by Michael Lewis. The Estate of Louis Untermeyer for all poems by Louis Untermeyer, as well as those written under the pseudonyms Joseph Lauren and Michael Lewis. Reprinted by permission. 309 from *Homer Price* by Robert McCloskey. Copyright 1943 by Robert McCloskey. Copyright © renewed Robert McCloskey, 1971. Reprinted by permission. 180 "Puget Sound" by Harold W. Felton from *Legends of Paul Bunyon* compiled and edited by Harold W. Felton. Reprinted by permission.

Cover:
(TL) FPG International, (C) Corbis Media

Maps:
MapQuest.com, Inc.

Illustrations:
20, 152, 245, 257 Guy Porfirio 51 Mike Dammer 80 George Hamblin 116 Reggie Holladay 118 Robert Lawson 122, 128, 228 Yoshi Miyake 174 Donna Catanese 176 Ralph Canaday 191 Joe LeMonnier 194, 276 Jay Johnson 206, 224, 242 Neal Armstrong 236 Tom Foty 272 Mark Chickinelli 319, 320 Derek Grinnell 324 Lane DuPont 369, 388 Connie McLennan 402 Linda Holt Ayriss 407 Raoul Vitale EM Leland Klanderman

Photographs:
Every effort has been made to secure permission and provide appropriate credit for photographic material. The publisher deeply regrets any omission and pledges to correct errors called to their attention in subsequent editions. Unless otherwise acknowledged, all photographs are the property of Scott Foresman, a division of Pearson Education.

Frontmatter: H4 (TR) PhotoDisc, (TL) Chuck Kuhn Photography Inc./Image Bank, (TC) Bard Martin/Image Bank, (BL) Stephen Wilkes/Image Bank, (BR) Eyewire, Inc., (BC) PhotoDisc, Inc. H5 (L) Ed Kashi/Corbis, (R) O'Brien Productions/Corbis H6 (Bkgd) Eyewire, Inc., (L) Hisham F. Ibrahim/PhotoDisc, (R) PhotoDisc, Inc. H7 (L) Glen Allison/Stone, (R) Peter Pearson/Stone H8 Earth Imaging/Stone H15 PhotoDisc H17 PhotoDisc **Unit 1:** 1 Tim Thompson/Corbis 2 (L) Jan Butchofsky-Houser/Corbis, (C) Gerald French/Corbis 3 (C) Peter Pearson/Stone 4 (BL) Don Mason/Corbis Stock Market, (T) NASA/Corbis/Corbis, (BR) Richard Bickel/Corbis 5 (TL) Peter Johnson/Corbis, (R) Jose Fuste Raga/Corbis Stock Market 7 Jim Goodwin/Photo Researchers, Inc. 8 (C) © David R. Frazier Photolibrary, (B) Barbara Maurer/Stone, (T) Gerald French/Corbis 11 (T) Franz-Marc Frei/Corbis, (BR) Jan Butchofsky-Houser/Corbis, (B) Gerald French/Corbis 13 Sited by Sensato/Courtesy Hugh Campbell 16 © Garsten Family/Joel Garsten, M.D. 19 (T) ©David R. Frazier Photolibrary, (B) Charles Mauzy/Corbis 20 (T) Courtesy Astoria Chamber of Commerce/Astoria Chamber of Commerce, © David R. Frazier Photolibrary 22 (T) Bill Ross/Corbis 23 (TR) C Squared Studios/PhotoDisc 24 Mark Magner/Sesame Workshop 25 Don Perdue/Sesame Workshop 26 Sandro Vannini/Corbis 27 (TR) Glen Allison/PhotoDisc, (BR) Barbara Maurer/Stone, 28 (BL) Marc Deville/Liaison Agency, (BR) SuperStock, (TL) Powell Cotton Museum/© Dorling Kindersley 30 Anabel and Barnabas Kindersley/© Dorling Kindersley 31 (TL) Pictor, (TR) Jeremy Hartley/Panos Pictures, (BR) Pictor 34 Sandro Vannini/Corbis 36 (B) David Rigg/Stone, (T) Lowell Georgia/Corbis, (C) © 1997 Newsday, Inc. Reprinted with permission. 38 (CR) Tom Prettyman/PhotoEdit 39 (CR) Lowell Georgia/Corbis 40 Tom Bocock, Bridgewater Little League 43 (TR) PhotoDisc, (BL) © 1997 Newsday, Inc. Reprinted with permission., (BR) © 1997 Newsday, Inc. Reprinted with permission. 44 (CL) Levittown Public Library, (BR) PhotoDisc, (CR) © 1997 Newsday, Inc. Reprinted with permission. 45 David Sailors/Corbis Stock Market 46 (BL) Corbis 46, 47 (Bkgd) Levittown Public Library 47 (BR), (BL) Levittown Public Library, (TR) PhotoDisc 48 Reuters/NewMedia, Inc./Corbis 49 (BL) David Rigg/Stone, (BR) © 1986 USPS; All trademarks and copyrights used herein are properties of the United States Postal Service and are used under license to Scott Foresman Inc. All rights reserved 50 (T) Randy Faris/Corbis, (B) AP/Wide World/AP/Wide World 52 (TL) David Ball/Corbis Stock Market, (BL) Adler Planetarium, (Bkgd) Werner J. Bertsch/Bruce Coleman Inc. 53 Art Institute of Chicago 54 (B) SuperStock, (BC) Bruce Heinemann/PhotoDisc 55 (BR) Charles & Josette Lenars/Corbis, (TL) Michael Freeman/Bruce Coleman Inc. **Unit 2:** 65 (C) Louis Goldman/Photo Researchers, Inc. 66 SuperStock 68 (TL) PhotoDisc, (R) PhotoDisc, (BL) M. Gibson/H. Armstrong Roberts 69 (BR) SuperStock, (TR) Michelle Garrett/Corbis 71 (T) Burke/Triolo Productions/FoodPix 72 (TC) SuperStock, (T) Sharon Gerig/Tom Stack & Associates, (BC) SuperStock, (B) Jack Hollingsworth/PhotoDisc 76 (TL) SuperStock 79 (TL) Adalberto Rios Szalo/PhotoDisc, (CR) David Toase/PhotoDisc 82 (B) Bettmann/Corbis, (Bkgd) Bettmann/Corbis 83 Bettmann/Corbis 85 (T) DiMaggio/Kalish/Corbis Stock Market 86 (B) Jim Erickson/Corbis Stock Market, (T) Corbis-Bettmann 87 (BR) Robert Holmes/Corbis, (T) Bettmann/Corbis 88 (TL) PhotoDisc, (B) Bettmann/Corbis 91 (B) Agence France Presse/Corbis, (T) Phil Schermeister/Corbis, (C) Gail Mooney/Corbis 92 (T) Hulton-Deutsch Collection/Corbis, (C) Bettmann/Corbis, (B) AP/Wide World 93 (B) Mitch Hrdlicka/PhotoDisc 94 (B) Corbis, (T) Jacob Lawrence, The Migration of the Negro, no. 3. In every town Negroes were leaving by the hundreds to go North and enter into Northern industry, 1941, casein tempera on hardboard, 12 x 18 in. The Phillips Collection, Washington, D.C. (c) Gwendolyn Knight Lawrence, courtesy of the Jacob and Gwendolyn Lawrence Foundation. 96 (B) Corbis 96, 97 (Bkgd) Corbis-Bettmann 97 p. 97 James Allen/Schomberg Center for Research in Black Culture/Courtesy IOKTS Productions Archive (B) Bettmann/Corbis 98 (C) © Dorling Kindersley 102 (T) Russell Illig/PhotoDisc, (B) George Lepp/Corbis, (C) Philip Gould/Corbis 105 (B), (T) Anabel and Barnabas Kindersley/© Dorling Kindersley, (CR) Ryan McVay/PhotoDisc 106 (R) Amr Nabil, AFP/Corbis, (L) AP/Wide World 107 (R) SuperStock, (L) Charles Gupton/Corbis Stock Market 108 (B) Morton Beebe/Corbis, (T) Spike/PhotoDisc 109 (T) PhotoDisc 112 (L) Pictor, (B) John Hatt/The Hutchison Library 113 (TL) Robert Francis/South American Pictures, (C) Andy Crawford/© Dorling Kindersley, (TR) © Dee Conway, (BL) David W. Hamilton/Image Bank, (BR) David Keith Jones/Images of Africa Photobank 114 PhotoDisc 115 (T) Philip Gould/Corbis, (BR) Ken Franckling/Corbis 116 Siede Preis/PhotoDisc 119 Photo courtesy of the Alamo 121 (B) Bettmann/Corbis, (T) James L. Amos/Corbis 122 PhotoDisc 123 Anabel and Barnabas Kindersley/© Dorling Kindersley 124 (BL), (TL) Anabel and Barnabas Kindersley/© Dorling Kindersley 124 (BR) Corbis 125 (BL) SuperStock, (TL), (R) Anabel and Barnabas Kindersley/© Dorling Kindersley **Unit 3:** 133 Geostock/PhotoDisc 134, 135 (Bkgd) Susan Ley/Animals Animals/Earth Scenes 136 (T) Chris Newbert/Bruce Coleman Inc., (B) Bruce Selyem/Museum of the Rockies, (Bkgd) Galen Rowell/Corbis 137 (TL) Texas Mid-Continental Oil & Gas Association/American Petroleum Institute, (R) PhotoDisc, (BC) PhotoDisc 139 A.T. Willett/Image Bank 140 (T) Dave G. Houser/Corbis, (B) Bettmann/Corbis, (C) Pat O'Hara/Corbis-Bettmann 144 (L) Louis Goldman/Photo Researchers, Inc., (R) Jan Butchofsky-Houser/Corbis, Dave Hopkins/© Dorling Kindersley 145 (L) Courtesy US Army Corps of Engineers, (R) SuperStock 146 John Fleck/Stone 148 (BL), (BR), (C) Dave Hopkins/© Dorling Kindersley, (CL) © Dorling Kindersley 149 (TL), (TR) Dave Hopkins/© Dorling Kindersley, (BR) Dave King/© Dorling Kindersley 150 (BL), (CR) Lawrence Lawry/PhotoDisc 151 (B) Galen Rowell/Corbis 152 (BL) Bruce Coleman Inc./Bruce Coleman Inc., (TL) Pat O'Hara/Corbis-Bettmann 153 (T) Sara Gray/Stone, (B) John Lemker/Animals Animals/Earth Scenes 154 (CL), (CR) SuperStock, (BL) David Frazier/Stone 156 (BL) Horace Bristol/Corbis 156, 157 (Bkgd) Charles & Josette Lenars/Corbis 157 (BR) National Museum of American Art, Washington DC/Art Resource, NY, (BL) Gendreau Collection/Corbis, (TR) John Bigelow Taylor/Art Resource, NY 158, 159 (Bkgd) Joseph Sohm; ChromoSohm, Inc./Corbis 160 Natural History Museum/© Dorling Kindersley 161 (CL) Natural History Museum/© Dorling Kindersley, (C) Wayne Scherr/Photo Researchers, Inc., (TR) Vince Streano/Corbis, (B) Patrick Bennett/Stone 162 (T) Newberry Library, Chicago/SuperStock, (BL) The Huntington Library, Art Collections and Botanical Gardens, San Marino, California/Superstock/SuperStock 163 (R) Bettmann/Corbis, (BL) Ed Eckstein/Corbis 164 (TL) Emma Lee/Life File/PhotoDisc 166 (BL) Jim Winkley/Ecoscene/Corbis-Bettmann 167 (B) Mark E. Gibson/Corbis-Bettmann, (Bkgd) Eye Ubiquitous/Corbis 170 (T) Michael Maslan Historic Photographs/Corbis, (C) PhotoDisc, (B) Cathlyn Melloan/Stone 173 (BR) David W. Hamilton/Image Bank, (BL) Michael Maslan Historic Photographs/Corbis 177 SuperStock 179 (BL) Museum of History and Industry/Corbis, (TR) David & Peter Turnley/Corbis-Bettmann, (BR) Richard Cummins/Corbis-Bettmann 180 (TL) SuperStock, (BR) Lee Foster/Bruce Coleman Inc. 182 (C) DK Cartography/© Dorling Kindersley, (BC) Pat O'Hara/Corbis, (CL) David Muench/Corbis 183 (BR) AFP/Corbis, (BC), (CR) Gallo Images/Corbis, (TL) Wolfgang Kaehler/Corbis, (TC) Gunter Marx Photography/Corbis, (TR) Ruggero Vanni/Corbis, (CL) Jim Zuckerman/Corbis, (BL) Steve Kaufman/Corbis 186 Deborah Van Kirk/Image Bank 187 (B) Cathlyn Melloan/Stone, (TR) Melissa Farlow/National Geographic 188 (T) Bass Photo Co. Collection, 88019/Indiana Historical Society, (B) John Elk III/Bruce Coleman Inc. 190 (BL) Corbis, (C) AP/Wide World **Unit 4:** 199 (Bkgd) M. Timothy O' Keefe/Bruce Coleman Inc. 200 (Bkgd) Nik Wheeler/Corbis 202 (BL) Lee Snider/Corbis, (CR) David Muench/Corbis 203 (L) Schenectady Museum; Hall of Electrical History Foundation/Corbis, (Bkgd) Courtesy St. Augustine, Ponte Vedra & The Beaches Visitors and Conventions Bureau 205 SuperStock 206 (BC) SuperStock, (TC) Nik Wheeler/Corbis 209 (TR) American Museum of Natural History/© Dorling Kindersley 210 (TL) © Dorling Kindersley, (TR), (CL) Clive Streeter/Patrick Mcleavy/© Dorling Kindersley 214 Sisse Brimberg/National Geographic 215 (TR) The Granger Collection, New York 216 N. Carter/North Wind Picture Archives 218 (B) Raymond Gehman/Corbis-Bettmann, (TL) James Blank/Bruce Coleman Inc. 219 Archivo Iconografico, S.A./Corbis 220 (L) Mark L Stephenson/Corbis-Bettmann, (BL)(C) Archivo Iconografico, SA/Corbis-Bettmann 221 (B), (C) Jim Zuckerman/Corbis-Bettmann (TR), (C) Michelle Chaplow/Corbis-Bettmann 222, 223 (B) Guy Motil/Corbis-Bettmann 225 (BR) David Chasey/PhotoDisc, (TL) Bettmann/Corbis, (TR) Stock Montage/SuperStock 226, 227 SuperStock 230 SuperStock 231 (T) Bettmann/Corbis-Bettmann, (B) SuperStock 232 (BL) Stock Montage/SuperStock 235 (TL) Association for the Preservation of Virginia Antiquities, (TR) Association for the Preservation of Virginia Antiquities 237 (B) The Granger Collection, New York, (T) p. 237 Courtesy, National Museum of the American Indian, Smithsonian Institution, Image #N08150 238 SuperStock 240 (T) Bettmann/Corbis, (TC) Leonard de Selva/Corbis-Bettmann, (BC) SuperStock, (B) Corbis-Bettmann 242 North Wind Picture Archives 243 (T) Gary Withey/Bruce Coleman Inc. 244 (T) James L. Amos/Corbis, (B) California State Railroad Museum 246 (T) Bettmann/Corbis, (C) Library of Congress/Corbis-Bettmann, (BL), (BC), (BR) Lake County Museum/Corbis-Bettmann 250 Leonard de Selva/Corbis-Bettmann 251 (BL) Independence National Historical Park Collection, Eastern National Parks and Monument Association, (BR) National Portrait Gallery, London/SuperStock 252 Lee Foster/Bruce Coleman Inc. 253 E.R. Degginger/Bruce Coleman Inc. 254 (T) Science Photo Library/Photo Researchers, Inc. 254 (BL) Schenectady Museum; Hall of Electrical History Foundation/Corbis 254 (TL), (TCL), (CL), (BCL) © 1994 Classic PIO Partners. All rights reserved. Made in the U.S.A. 255 Eric Curry/Corbis-Bettmann 256 (T), © Ben Wymore (TC), © Ben Wymore (B) © Ben Wymore (BC) Lee Snider/Corbis-Bettmann 257 (CR) © Ben Wymore 259 (BR) SuperStock, (TR) Edison National Historic Site/National Park Service/U.S. Department of the Interior, (BL) Schenectady Museum/Corbis-Bettmann 260 (B) Hulton-Deutsch Collection/Corbis, (T) Copyright University of Reading/© Dorling Kindersley 261 (TL) Michael Freeman/Corbis, (TR) SuperStock 264, 265 Smithsonian Institution 267 (T) National Library of Medicine/Science Photo Library/Photo Researchers, Inc., (BL) Alfred Wolf/Explorer/Photo Researchers, Inc., (BR) ©Comstock Inc. 268 (BL) Will & Deni McIntyre/Photo Researchers, Inc., (TL) Bettmann Archive/Corbis-Bettmann (BR) Corbis-Bettmann 270 Owen Franken/Corbis 273 Corbis 274 Morris Bergman, Ed Morgan/Corbis-Bettmann **Unit 5:** 281 SW Productions/PhotoDisc 282 Bob Mitchell/Corbis-Bettmann 284 (TL) PhotoDisc 285 (B) James P. Blair/Corbis, (T) Courtesy of City of Portland 287 J.C. Carton/Bruce Coleman Inc. 288 (T), (B) Patrick Bennett/Corbis, (C) Joseph Sohm; Visions of America/Corbis 290 David Madison/Bruce Coleman Inc. 296, 297 Smithsonian Institution 298, 299 Chick-Fil-A Inc. 301 (T) Bill Losh/FPG International LLC, (B) Fisher/Thatcher/Stone 304, 305 (B)Carin Krasner/Stone 312, 313 From the Walker Collection of A'Lelia Bundles 316 (C) Hisham F. Ibrahim/PhotoDisc, (T) Reuters/STR/Archive Photos, (B) Reuters NewMedia Inc./Corbis 319 Kevin Fleming/Corbis 321 (T) Reuters/STR/Archive Photos, (B) Bettmann/Corbis 322 (CL) Baseball Hall of Fame Library, Cooperstown, NY, (CR) Reuters NewMedia Inc./Corbis, (T) Courtesy University of Louisville 323 Louisville SLugger Museum 326 (R) Corbis, (Bkgd) Hulton-Deutsch Collection/Corbis 327 Hulton/Archive Photos 328 PhotoDisc 329 SuperStock 330 (T) Steve Solum/Bruce Coleman Inc. 331 (BL) Minnesota Historical Society/Corbis, (BR) Wally McNamee/Corbis 332 (B) Corbis, (T) PhotoDisc 335 (T) Don Brewster/Bruce Coleman Inc. 336 Reuters NewMedia Inc./Corbis 337 (BL) The Cummer Museum of Art and Gardens, Jacksonville/SuperStock, (BR) Corbis 338 SuperStock 340 George Hall/Corbis 341 (TR) D. Boone/Corbis, (TL) Michael S. Yamashita/Corbis, (B) Jody Dole/Image Bank 344 (BC) Bettmann/Corbis, (TL) Corbis, (TC) Jean-Antoine Houdon/Corbis-Bettmann, (TR) Neal Preston/Corbis, (B) Museo Capitolino, Rome, Italy/ET Archive, London/SuperStock 345 (Bkgd) SuperStock, (BR) Anne Frank Fonds- Basel/Anne Frank House, Amsterdam/Archive Photos **Unit 6:** 352 (T) Robert Holmes/Corbis-Bettmann, (B) PhotoDisc 353 (R) PhotoDisc, (L) Eyewire, Inc. 355 Ron Rovtar/FPG International LLC 356 (T) SuperStock, (C) Sam Kittner/National Geographic, (B) Torres; Bruno/Corbis-Bettmann 358 British Museum/© Dorling Kindersley 359 (B) Stephen Conlin/© Dorling Kindersley, (T) Vega/FPG International LLC 360 (T) Corbis-Bettmann, (B) SuperStock 362 Corbis-Bettmann 365 SuperStock 366 SuperStock 367 Tim Wright/Corbis-Bettmann 368 (B) Peter Stackpole/TimePix, (T), (C) Jean-Antoine Houdon/Corbis-Bettmann 370 (BL), (R) Corbis-Bettmann, (TL) Bridgeman Art Library International Ltd. 372 PhotoDisc 373 (B) Arthur Tilley/FPG International LLC, (T) PhotoDisc 374, 375 Smithsonian Institution 379 Bob Rowan/Corbis-Bettmann 380 British Museum/© Dorling Kindersley 382 (C) James L. Amos/Corbis-Bettmann, (B) Philip Gould/Corbis-Bettmann 386 (BL), (CL), (BCL), (TC), (B) SuperStock, (CL), (TR) Eyewire, Inc., (TL) Michael Nelson/FPG International LLC 390 (BL) Michael Malyszko/FPG International LLC, (T) Eyewire, Inc. 391 (TL) Bob Thomas/Stone, (BCR) Eyewire, Inc., (TC) Robert Holmes/Corbis-Bettmann, (TR) AP/Wide World, (BCL), (BR), (BL), (BC), (C) SuperStock 392 (L) Eyewire, Inc., (C) Bob Thomas/Stone, (R) Ryanstock/FPG International LLC 393 (TR) Antonio Mo/PhotoDisc, (TC) Michael Krasowitz/FPG International LLC, (B) PhotoDisc, (TL) SuperStock 394 (C) David Roth/Stone, (T) Eyewire, Inc., (B) Andy Sacks/Stone 396 (L) Harris & Ewing/Corbis-Bettmann, (R) Corbis-Bettmann 397 Frent; David J./Corbis-Bettmann 400 (B, TL) Laurie V. Schnitzer/Courtesy Silver Bay Elementary School 404 PhotoDisc 406 Gianni Dagli Orti/Corbis **End Matter:** R2, R3 Earth Imaging/Stone R26 Corbis-Bettmann R30 Corbis-Bettmann R32 Bettmann/Corbis End Sheets: PhotoDisc, Inc.